D1188284

Lou's on First

Tom —
You're on First
With Me

Lou's on First

*A Biography
of Lou Costello*

By Chris Costello
with Raymond Strait

Cooper Square Press

The excerpt from *The Abbot & Costello Book by Jim Mulholland* (Popular Library; © 1975 by Film Fan Monthly) appears with the kind permission of the author.

First Cooper Square Press edition 2000

This Cooper Square Press paperback edition of *Lou's on First* is an unabridged republication of the edition first published in New York in 1981. It is reprinted by arrangement with the authors.

Copyright © 1981 by Chris Costello and Raymond Strait

Designed by Dennis J. Grastorf

All rights reserved.
No part of this book may be reproduced in any form or by any electronic or mechanical means, including information storage and retrieval systems, without written permission from the publisher, except by a reviewer who may quote passages in a review.

Published by Cooper Square Press
An Imprint of the Rowman & Littlefield Publishing Group
150 Fifth Avenue, Suite 911
New York, New York 10011

Distributed by National Book Network

British Library Cataloguing in Publication Data Available

Library of Congress Cataloging-in-Publication Data

Costello, Chris.
    Lou's on First : a biography of Lou Costello / by Chris Costello with Raymond Strait.—
    1st Cooper Square Press ed.
       p. cm.
    Originally published: New York : St.Martin's Press, c1981.
    ISBN 0-8154-1083-2 (alk. paper)
     1. Costello, Lou. 2. Comedians— United States— Biography. Motion picture actors and actresses— United States— Biography. I. Strait, Raymond. II. Title.

PN2287.C635 C6 2000
791.43'028'092— dc21
[B]

                        00-034644

⊖™ The paper used in this publication meets the minimum requirements of American National Standard for Information Sciences— Permanence of Paper for Printed Library Materials, ANSI/NISO Z39.48–1992.
Manufactured in the United States of America.

To my mother, Anne Battler Costello, who finally gets her share of the spotlight. I hope she approves, and understands how much I still love her.

CHRIS COSTELLO

AND

For my mother, Geraldine Oma Strait, whose last wish in this world was that I get a steady job and settle down. I hope she accepts my compromise.

RAYMOND STRAIT

Acknowledgments

THE AUTHORS wish to acknowledge the invaluable assistance of the following people and thank them for their contributions to this project in order for it to be as accurate as humanly possible in the final draft: Elena Verdugo, Charlie Marion, Ann Corio, Charles Barton, Dorothy (DiMaggio) Arnold, Ralph Handley, Ophelia MacFashion, Ophelia Watson, Marty & Pat Costello, Michael Monteleon, Frank Worth, Everett H. Broussard, Mike Mazurki, Lois Van, Howard Koch, Marie Kirk, Carole Costello, Patricia Costello Humphreys, Susan Costello, Beverly Washburn, Michael Ansara, Bob Hope, Arthur Lubin, Abe Haberman, Nat Perrin, Danny Thomas, Ralph Edwards (for use of material from *This Is Your Life—Lou Costello*), Walter Slezak, Patricia Medina, Elizabeth Taylor, Milt Bronson, Dr. Vic Kovner, Sr., Joe & Ernie Besser, David Rose, Henny Youngman, Hillary Brooke, Virginia O'Brien, Robert Easton, Lucille Ball, Steve Allen, De De Polo McKean, Tom Ewell, Abe Greene, Ken Berry, Joby Baker, Allan Jones, Louis Nye, Tom Poston, Cary Grant, Jonathan Harris, Leonard Stern, Martin Ragaway, Harry Crane, Joe Kenny, Betty Abbott, Robert Arthur, George Raft, Sidney Miller, True Boardman, Harry Von Zell, Charles Townsend, Elvia Allman, Joan Fulton Shawlee, Lew Rachmil, Betty Hutton, May Mann, Paul Zelanka, Mac Brainard, Mort Rittenberg, Richard Deacon, Nick Condos & Martha Raye, Kate Smith, Howard Christie, Connie Haines, Stanley Roberts, Jean Porter, Mary Failla, Alex Gottlieb, Leo Weberman, Bernie Sheldon, James Bacon, Walter Battler, Ruth Grose, Arthur Manella, Kathryn Grayson, Gale & Virginia

Gordon, Maxene Andrews, Mrs. Bobby (Maxine) Barber, Irving Mills, Stan Irwin, Sid Kuller, Max Fink, Sam Weisbord, Margaret Hamilton, Leonard Spigelgass, Charles Van Enger, Allen Gilbert, Carol Bruce, Melvin Joseph Bassett, Joe Elias, Josie Elias, Mildred Jamais, Milton Krasner, Gene de Paul, Tilla de Thomas, George Folsey, Stanley Cortez, Julia Boutee, Charles Lamont, Olive Abbott, George Maldonado, Vivian Starks, Stan Oliver, Wayne Powers, Paul Blane, Dr. Terry Robinson and John Casserino.

A VERY SPECIAL THANK YOU
Wade Crookham, Jim Mulholland (for unlimited use of his book *The Abbott & Costello Book* which was so helpful chronologically), The National Broadcasting Corporation (and especially Eileen Flores) in Los Angeles and New York, The Motion Picture Academy Library, Dan Silverman of the Universal Studio Publicity Department, the Universal Studio Research & Legal Departments, Jeff and Greg Lenburg, Peggy Torres (who so graciously conducted interviews in Paterson, New Jersey), The Motion Picture Country Home, Chic-a-boom Memorabilia Store (Los Angeles), Ralph Edwards Productions, Steve Allen (for use of his scripts in which Abbott & Costello appeared), The Writers Guild of America West, The Directors Guild of America, The Producers Guild of America, The Lou Costello Jr., Recreation Center, Wayne Powers, Jim Pearsall (for suggesting such an apropos title for the book), Stan Oliver (for use of documents from his personal collection) and last—but certainly first—all the relatives and in-laws of the Costello and Battler families who produced Lou and Anne and helped make this book possible.

plus . . .

My deepest love and affection and appreciation go to my sisters Carole and Paddy for their uncanny remembrances of detail which insured this being a family book.

CHRIS

Contents

Foreword

M Y FIRST PERSONAL CONTACT with Lou Costello was in October, 1956, when Abbott & Costello presented a gold recording of their classic "Who's on First?" routine to the Baseball Hall of Fame (Cooperstown, New York) before a national audience on the *Steve Allen Show* over NBC-TV. A year later, about the time Lou Costello split with Bud Abbott, he appeared on my show and did routines with our regular gang of comics—Louis Nye, Don Knotts and Tom Poston.

Each of our shows was presented live—with very little rehearsal—and it was not surprising that Lou Costello fit that format perfectly. His years in vaudeville and burlesque had taught him the ad-lib skills live TV requires. I had seen Abbott & Costello on film in the forties, when the team was in its heyday and I was a young man in radio. But it wasn't until the late fifties, after having been personally involved in television with its array of talented guests, that I was more fully able to appreciate Lou Costello's remarkable brand of comedy.

The Abbott & Costello team portrayed a relationship between a smart guy and a dumb guy, a type of comedy duo of which there were many in vaudeville. Abbott played the role of a very knowledgeable and authoritative character who was very quick and was always bossing around an apparently uncontrollable character (Lou Costello). Most of the comedy of such a relationship comes from the fact that the so-called dumb character wins out anyway.

Significant about Abbott & Costello humor, in today's social context, is that I don't remember a single line in their films or stage appearances ever being off-color—even though they came out of burlesque. They proved that you don't have to be dirty to be funny.

Only a very talented team like Abbott & Costello could have survived the transition from burlesque and vaudeville to radio to films to television to night clubs, over a period of twenty-two years.

No list of great comedy teams would be complete without the names of Abbott & Costello. They left a legacy and, fortunately, we can still see their films on television today—and I'm certain they've won a new generation of fans.

The story of Lou Costello's rise to one of Hollywood's biggest names and moneymakers is an interesting one in itself, but this book searches deeply into Lou Costello the man, a kind man known for his many humanitarian deeds and a man who along life's way encountered some personal tragedies. Lou Costello was a family man, so this is the story of a family too, and in it we find love, laughter, relationships, and pathos.

STEVE ALLEN

Lou's on First

CHAPTER I

The Formative Years

A s a kid my father seldom got more than a base hit when he played sand-lot baseball. Full-grown, he was only five feet five. But he had speed. Consequently, whenever he got a hit, one of the opposing players always cautioned the pitcher to keep an eye open because "Lou's on first." I don't know if that was the origin of the famous skit that he and Bud Abbott introduced as a team, but it might have been.

The Costello family name was originally Cristillo and Dad's father, Sebastian Cristillo, came from Caserta, a town in Italy, north of Rome. His father, Anthony Sebastian Cristillo, was the local chief of police. "Chris," as my grandfather was known, was born in 1880, the youngest of four children. He had two brothers, Phillip and Joseph, and a sister who joined a cloistered order of nuns, the Sisters of Sorrow, with whom she remained for the rest of her life.

My grandfather studied for the priesthood with the ambition of becoming a missionary, but his parents wanted him to become a parish priest. He would have dropped out earlier than he did, except for the pressure they put on him. When they died, he left the seminary and eventually, Italy. Phillip had already emigrated to America and had settled in Paterson, New Jersey, where he worked as a weaver. In time he was able to send for Joseph, who worked in a dye house and, in turn, brought over the youngest brother.

It was 1898, and Chris had hardly unpacked from the trip across the Atlantic when he met the lovely girl who lived next door to the family he moved in with. Helen Rege, as my grandfather remembered her, was a beautiful rose. "I took one look at her," he recalled, "and knew she was a genuine Irish sort of girl. She had jet black hair and the bluest eyes I've ever seen." Helen was fourteen, Chris barely eighteen. In 1902, four years later, they were married in Saint Anthony's Catholic Church in Paterson. It was a blending of the Italian and Irish Catholics and their home became an orthodox bastion of Catholicism.

They moved into 14 Madison Street, in Paterson, close to where Chris worked with Phillip, and all three of their children were born there. Their firstborn, Anthony (later known as Pat) arrived in 1903. Dad, Louis Francis Cristillo, was born on March 6, 1906. Marie Katherine, their only daughter, was not to come along until 1912, six years later.

Helen Rege was the eldest of six children whose mother, Mary Tuohy, died quite young, shortly after Helen had married Chris. Being the oldest, Helen became like a second mother to the children, even though her father later remarried. So the Rege house was always filled with family.

Shortly after Marie, the youngest, was born, the family moved to a larger house on Market Street. Across from them, side by side, were a fire station and an orphanage—there was never a dearth of playmates. From the very beginning, my father was both an athlete and a ham. He made friends with the kids at the orphanage, and whenever the orphan school played other schools or orphanages, he always managed to play for them.

A very funny, albeit almost tragic, incident occurred when Marie was quite small. It was Christmastime and Lolly (as a child Helen couldn't pronounce her name, so she called herself Lolly and it stuck) was getting the children ready to go visit her father, who lived in College Point on Long Island. Marie was standing on a chair in the kitchen, looking into the large mirror over the sink as her mother combed her long hair. The child was impatient, but her mother didn't care. Every curl on her head was going to be in place before they left.

Dad was in the living room playing. Pat was practicing his violin in the bedroom. Dad had to pass the bedroom enroute to the kitchen, where he kept going, getting a glass of water, returning and repeating the whole process all over again. Lolly was busy with Marie and didn't notice what was going on. Pat noticed, because my father's trips to and from the kitchen became more frequent and he was traveling faster each time. Finally Pat put down the violin and followed his younger brother back to the living room to find the entire room in flames.

Lolly's brother Pete was chief of the fire station across the street, and the firemen were summoned immediately. When things finally settled down, Dad was asked to explain. He had been showing a friend his new Magic Lantern (the equivalent of today's movie projector), which required a candle to operate. He lit the candle, was too close to the Christmas tree, and—poof—it went up fast. Along with it went Lolly's new piano, which Chris had bought her for Christmas. The furniture was seared and would have to be recovered. It was a terrible loss, and in those days there was no insurance for it. Dad's friend was standing off to one side, crying his eyes out. Lolly turned to him and asked, "What's the matter? Are you burned?"

"No," he said, crying even harder.

"Then go on home now. Can't you see we're all upset?"

"But I can't go home. My new cap got all burned up and my mother is going to kill me."

Lolly threw up her hands in frustration. "He's crying because he lost his cap. I lost my *piano!*"

My father got his backside warmed for that by my grandfather. To further complicate matters, he and Uncle Pat had recently taken up the "F" word (they couldn't have been more than four and seven). They took pens and wrote it all over the upholstery in the living room. They got it for that, too. It wasn't so much the act—my grandfather understood that boys will be boys. The point was, he was embarrassed to call in an upholsterer to redo the damage and see what had been written there.

Although he was loved by everybody, Dad had the reputation of being "a bad boy." It was an inside joke that started when he was in fifth grade—also the origination of his famous expression, "I'm a baaaad boy." He loved to clown around—even in school—and broke up the classroom. Sometimes even Miss Whitehead, the fifth-grade teacher, had to stifle a snicker. Nevertheless, one day she had him stay after school and write, "I am a bad boy," 150 times. Thus, the beginning of one of his most famous show business lines.

Dad always wanted to be in show business. From the time he was four years old, he play-acted with his friends or alone in front of a mirror. Nobody knows where he got it; there were no actors on either side of the family. His mother and father indulged his fantasy, certain it would all go away in time.

As boys, he and Pat were given a quarter a day to go to school with. A nickel for bus fare each way and fifteen cents for lunch. A new movie house, *The U.S. Theatre,* was built in Paterson, and the day it opened Dad and Uncle Pat played hookie to see the silent Western that was featured. After the movie ended and the lights came up, Chris leaned over from the seat behind them and said, "I hope you both enjoyed the movie. I'll see you when I get home." The spanking Dad got did not deter him for one minute. He spent every penny he could spare on films (when he wasn't sneaking in). He absolutely idolized Charlie Chaplin, and it was Chaplin, indirectly, who influenced my father to change his course in life. Instead of a dramatic actor, he wanted to become a comic. Dad went through several stages with musical instruments. First it was the piano, because his mother hoped he would play. Then he wanted drums. Chris went out and bought him a good set. The drums were soon found up in the attic, with a large hole in the bass drum. He loved singing and dancing, was a great ballroom dancer, and had a smooth, melodic singing voice that was always right on pitch. But those were all side interests.

Dad was not an inconsiderate child. As a youngster he looked out for his sister and any other kid who was younger than himself. When Marie went out on roller skates, Dad was right behind her. If his friends complained about his "always bringing along your sister," he would reply, "It's her first time on skates. I don't want her to get hurt."

When he went to Boy Scout rallies, he always brought home a bag full of candy for Marie. Marie remembers that from the very earliest times he had a deep and sincere love of Christmas. "I often thought that I'd be eighty-five years old before someone had the nerve to tell him there wasn't really a Santa Claus," she recalls. "If a child didn't believe in Santa, it would absolutely kill him. I believe Lou went to his death believing there really is a Santa Claus."

It's a wonder Dad survived childhood. He was a daredevil, afraid of nothing. Before the move to Market Street, they lived on the third floor at Madison Street, where the stairways had

4

old-fashioned, polished-smooth wooden bannisters. Aunt Marie says she doesn't think my father ever walked down those stairs as a child. He would go zipping down the bannister, all three flights, while my grandmother gasped, "My God, he'll break his back or his head." But he was too agile. Yet, in order to be funny, he would purposely trip or fall just walking through the house, which was something else his mother had to get used to.

He loved doing things for his mother, and the dearest possession she ever had was the small, black onyx ring he gave her as a little boy. Dad was devoted to his mother, not only as a child, but even after he was married and had his own family.

When he was twelve years old, sitting on the front porch with his mother in the porch swing, he said, "Mom, one day I'm going to be a movie star and make you proud of me. You just wait and see. You'll be the most famous mom in the world."

Shortly thereafter he entered the Charlie Chaplin Halloween contest, which was held in the Paterson Armory. Nobody in the family remembers where Dad got the costume, but he was very much a Chaplin look-alike. At the end of the show, all the contestants had to join in a grand march so the judges could select the winner. Dad was the only one during the march who kept doing pratfalls and tripping on his cane. It brought attention to him—and so did my grandmother, who, within earshot of the judges, kept pointing her finger at Dad and saying, "Now that's a good one." He won first prize, and when he removed his mask, everybody was flabbergasted to see that it was Dad. My grandmother always swore she didn't know who it was until he'd revealed himself.

Dad was an outstanding baseball and basketball player, and it was sports that kept him in school. At Central High School in Paterson, in order to play either game, one had to be attending school on a regular basis. My father made sure he put in enough time to stay on the team.

The Armory Five, named after the old armory they played in, was the basketball team my father starred on as a teenager. In spite of his diminutive size, he had great agility and was an expert foul shooter. At one point he won the Foul Shot Championship of Paterson. The Armory Five played in what was known as the Sandy Hill section of Paterson, and included guys with names like something out of Damon Runyon: Costello, J.

5

Harold, Nicholas Straub, William Probert, Joseph "Red" Duncan, George Probert, and a coach named Jim Kelly. The manager was George Storms. There were a couple of other players—a guy named McCue and another named Breslin. Then there was Slackie Knolls. Joe Hepworth, Dad, and Slackie gained entrance into the big professional games by sweeping the floor of the armory. It was from this early interest that the Armory Five emerged.

Dad was never what you would call a loner. A childhood friend, Mary Failla, remembers that there would often be as many as twelve in a group that went to basketball games, movies and dances. Without my grandparents' knowledge, Dad often joined those friends at the Orpheum Theater to watch the girls dance without any clothes on. Ironically, he would someday come back in burlesque and play at that same theater.

Even in basketball he managed to do a bit of acting. When he couldn't get into the pro games by cleaning up, he would sometimes fast-talk the pro players and carry their bags so it would look like he was part of the team, just to get in to see the game.

In baseball he was an outstanding shortstop and about the size of Albie Pearson, who once played outfield for the Los Angeles Angels—little and feisty and accurate as a spitting cobra. As a member of the Paterson High School baseball team in 1921, he helped defeat all the leading high schools in northern New Jersey. Dad was a sparkplug on the team, and always thought big time and talked constantly of going to the majors someday.

Since there was only one high school in Paterson, and no league in existence, the boys went out and booked their own games. They competed against Ridgewood, Jersey City, Hackensack, Dover, and Englewood, compiling a win-loss record of sixteen and four. Ray Goode, in charge of public relations at the Paterson YMCA, praised Dad's team as "one of the best defensive clubs in this area. They had a crackerjack infield that was the best in the state. As far as the outfielders were concerned, they were all big and strong and could hit the horsehide a country mile."

Boxing was another of Dad's interests as a teenager, and he became acquainted with Johnny Lane, who was a good fighter. Good for a local boy, anyway, who went on to fight professionally. Dad was impressed. Once again, without the consent or

6

knowledge of his family, he decided to try something new. Under the name of Lou King, he became a boxer. His friend Abe Greene became his manager; however, Dad's career in the ring did not last long.

It was quite by accident that Lou King was unmasked. My grandmother's brother Mike loved the fights, so one night he had tickets and took my grandfather along with him to Ringwood, New Jersey, where Dad was fighting. He said, "Chris, you got to see this new fighter Lou King. I hear he's coming on strong." My grandfather, who was not a sports enthusiast, mumbled something, but went along anyway. It was Dad's eleventh fight.

The following morning at the kitchen table, when Dad joined the family for breakfast sporting a bright new black eye, my grandfather looked across at him and said, "Good morning, Lou King." It was my grandmother's first knowledge of what Dad had been doing—and the last time he fought in the ring.

All of my father's heroics were not in the athletic arena. A blue law that was very strictly enforced dictated that on Sundays all commercial activities cease. The clergy were fully behind that enforcement because it left the church as the only game in town. Most citizens went to church in the mornings, and many spent the afternoon at one of the nearby beaches available to them during the hot weather months.

On an unusually hot day in July one year, Dad's family and the Sheldons took off for Asbury Park, which had a full mile of boardwalk along an immaculate beach. It was a festive event. The Sheldons' son Bernie, a close buddy of Dad's, my father, and Uncle Pat were off to their own fun and games while the adults laid out the picnic. My grandmother brought along every conceivable Italian dish. Mrs. Sheldon matched her, recipe for recipe. Mr. Sheldon and Grandpop liked to sit on the beach drinking homemade red wine and playing cards until it was time to eat. Uncle Pat brought along his violin.

Dad and Bernie were wrestling in the sand and Uncle Pat was fiddling up a storm when the boys heard a scream for help. They stopped and looked out over the water. One of them spotted the girl and yelled, "There she is!" Dad and Bernie ran into the water and swam out to the troubled youngster. They reached her just as she was about to go under and pulled her ashore. She was much too young to be swimming out so far (nine years old, they later learned). Bernie thought she was dead. Dad turned her on her stomach and began artificial respiration. Bernie was yelling, "Lou ... Lou! She's dead! You can't help her." Dad kept it up.

A crowd gathered around them when a man emerged from the sea of faces, crying, "My daughter! My daughter!" He fell on his knees beside Dad. "Is she going to be all right? Is she alive?"

Dad responded, "I'm doing what I can for her." He was the only person there who thought she could be brought back to life. One kind soul said, "You've done all you can. It's no use, kid." Dad refused to give up. He turned the girl on her back and started mouth to mouth resuscitation. After what seemed an interminable amount of time, the youngster's body began to quiver—a sign of life. By the time Dad brought her back to consciousness, lifeguards and medical help had arrived.

The girl's father, with tears streaming down his cheeks, kept pleading with Dad to tell him what he owed him for saving his daughter. "Anything you say."

"For what?" my father said. "It could have been my own sister." He quickly disappeared then, embarrassed by the furor.

It was a restless time in my father's life. By then he'd had a variety of jobs, none of which gave him much to build a future on. Going to Hollywood and becoming a star were still the two things most important to him. Too young for World War I, my father stayed home with the family, graduated from high school, and was working in a hat store when Uncle Pat came home, after the war, from the U.S. Navy.

It was the beginning of the Roaring Twenties and the Jazz Age, and Uncle Pat's dedication to music started to pay off. He had somewhat abandoned the violin and was now blowing a hot sax and playing one-night stands on the road. The way it happened is that he had gone to New York to purchase a new horn when he met Wayne Scott, a musician with a band. One thing led to another, and Scott offered him a job with his band—at $85 a week, which was a hell of a good salary in those days following World War I.

Uncle Pat said, "I'll have to call you tonight and let you know."

Back in Paterson he discussed the job offer with Grandpop, whose instant, explosive response was "Absolutely not!"

8

"But why, Pop?" he asked.

"Because I don't want you carousing around New York playing music all night long."

"Pop," he said, "there's a train leaving New York at two A.M. I'll be on that train every night and come straight home." It took several hours of wrangling and pleading before my grandfather finally conceded that Uncle Pat could "give it a try," but if he failed to live up to Grandpop's conditions, then the deal would be cancelled. Of course, he lived up to all his promises and went on to eventually have his own group, Pat Cristillo & His Gondoliers. Actually, for a while he had an earlier band called the Silk City Night Owls, but the Gondoliers was the best and better known of the two.

My father was green with envy. Uncle Pat was in show business, and all his life that's all Dad had ever wanted to do. It didn't seem fair when his parents insisted that he stay in school and get a good education so he could "find a good job, get married, and raise a decent family."

Dad did as he was told, but under the trim, athletic body (he was never roly-poly as a youth) the seeds of rebellion had already germinated, and it would not be long before they would burst forth. It had to happen.

CHAPTER II

Hollywood Failure

Dad's itch to be in show business was developing into a case of theatrical hives. Even on the day he graduated from high school, the funny-man inside him had to be recognized. He raced up on the stage to pick up his diploma—and promptly did a pratfall. The high-school auditorium audience roared with laughter. Dad beamed and bowed. Mr. Wilson, the principal, could only utter, "Oh, Lord!"

Having viewed Charlie Chaplin's *Shoulder Arms* two dozen times, Dad's first prop—the unlit cigar jammed into his jaw—was the result. Using the cigar as a gimmick to age his baby-face teens, he made the rounds of local booking agents, but with little success. Vaudeville was the current day mecca for comics, but still there was no room for the little man with a cigar.

In 1927 he could no longer keep the dream to himself. At the dinner table one night, where all family problems and ventures were first discussed, he broached the subject to his father. "Pop," he blurted, "I want to go to Hollywood."

My grandfather nodded his understanding and replied, "That's nice, but we have no money for a vacation."

Dad exchanged glances with his brother. The two of them had discussed Dad's ambitions many times and had rehearsed my father on handling his proposal with his father.

"Not a vacation, Pop. I want to be an actor—become a movie star."

Grandpop looked around the table at the members of his family and, gesturing with his fork, said, "Did you hear that? He wants to be a movie star." Turning back to Dad, he said, "You don't look like no Rudolph Valentino to me." Several of the family nervously tittered. My grandfather was not a man who took the careers of his children lightly. He had made plans. There was tradition to be considered. Grandma said nothing, but she knew about my father's desires for a career. He'd talked of little else for months, when he could get her alone in conversation.

"But Dad," he said, "I don't have to be a Valentino to be a movie star. I *know* I can do it."

Before his father could say anything else, Pat spoke up. "Pop, the same thing you tried to do to me, you're now trying with Lou. We respect your wishes, Pop, but we have our own lives to live."

"The answer is no," he said.

Uncle Pat didn't give in that easily. "I still think you ought to let him try. If he doesn't get his chance, his spirit will be broken. Then, if he ends up a bum, he'll blame you and Mom for it!"

Grandpop looked at his wife, and she nodded ever so slightly. He turned again, his eyes going first to Dad, then to Uncle Pat, and then back to Dad.

"We are in hard times. How you gonna live? You'll starve to death in California."

It was Uncle Pat's turn again. "No, Pop. That won't happen. I'll send Lou money out of my salary with the band. Just until he gets started good." He winked at Dad.

Caring for his children as he did, he finally succumbed to the pleadings. "All right. You win. But you be sure and write your mother every day so she doesn't worry so much about you. Okay?" Dad jumped up, ran around the table to my grandfather and gave him a big bear hug.

When it was time to leave, Grandpop, who knew an officer at the bank, borrowed $200. "Here," he said, "take this. Take the bus. Hitchhiking is dangerous." My grandmother packed food for Dad to take along on the trip, and Uncle Pat and his friend, Mike Archer, drove him into Newark to the bus station. He asked them not to wait around because he didn't like saying good-bye. Actually, when they were out of sight, he got on the main drag out of town, stuck out his thumb and was on his way to Hollywood, figuring the $200 would be better spent on food and shelter along the way.

There were times during the trip west that he rode the bus, believing it was a good investment to ride a few hundred miles on the bus and sleep, instead of spending the night in a hotel and not picking up any mileage. At other times he would take up with another hitchhiker going the same direction and spend some miles with him, but essentially he did it alone, always with that one goal in mind—go to Hollywood and become a star.

Dad's arrival in Hollywood was anything but spectacular, although several research sources swear that he rented a limousine outside Los Angeles and rode into Hollywood in style. If he did, that style changed rapidly. The nearest he got to being a movie star was working as a laborer on the Metro-Goldwyn-Mayer (MGM) lot, where a friend, Eddie Devine, operated a parking lot and let Dad sleep in cars at night until he could afford to rent a small apartment. Uncle Pat sent money to him each month to help out, and Dad finally did find his apartment. It was small but neat—his first home away from home. He took great pride in having his own place, but it was some time before he could afford to have the gas or lights turned on. He had no bed linens, so he slept between mattresses to keep warm during the chilly California nights. In order to save money to have his utilities turned on, for an entire month he ate nothing but bread and jam.

Working in the labor gang, he was around stars and spent a lot of time on the sets where major films were being shot. One day it seemed as if luck might have smiled on him. Somebody failed to show up to do a stunt in a silent film called *Trails of '98* (1928), starring Dolores Del Rio and Harry Carey. The set was lit up and ready for shooting. The stars were waiting. Dad was alert, and very bold. He went up to the assistant director and said, "I'll do it."

The assistant looked at him skeptically. "I don't know. We need someone to jump off a balcony."

"No problem," Dad said.

The assistant took him to the director. "This guy says he can jump." The director didn't question Dad's credentials. He was in a hurry and worried about budget and costs. His crew and cast were standing by.

My father did the jump in one take, and the director asked him to leave his name. "We may need you again." As a matter of fact, Dad did another stunt scene in the film, which involved a barroom brawl. He carried it off like a pro.

Dad couldn't wait to let the family back in New Jersey know that he was really in pictures at last. He sent a wire to his brother, telling him to look for the picture when it opened in New York.

Uncle Pat remembers it well. "It was a big epic picture, and I watched the papers for several months before it was finally advertised. Then it was everywhere. The studio did a big publicity campaign, one of their last for a silent picture. Talkies were just a year or so away."

The film opened at a theater on Broadway in New York. Uncle Pat took the entire band to see Dad's debut. "We got to the theater, sat down, and waited. The film started and we hardly blinked as the action unfolded on the screen. We watched half the movie and still no Lou. I was beginning to feel embarrassed. What if they had cut him out of the picture? The boys in the band would have had a field day at my expense. Intermission came."

Dad came on during the second half. "It was a scene in which he walked into a bar, there was a fight, and he was in the middle of the fray, taking falls and doing some fancy stuntwork. Then the scene changed, and Lou and another guy were outside the bar, getting into a dog sled. The next time he appeared, his leg was bandaged as a result of the barroom fight and he was on crutches. He wore a beard in the picture, and we were all amused because he was so young looking and had this tremendous beard."

But he was *in* films. Later on he did some stunts in a Joan Crawford picture, but nothing came of it. Essentially he was still working on the labor gang, not on the screen.

After a year in Hollywood, it became obvious even to my father that he wasn't going to be the next big star of the screen. Discouraged but not defeated, he kept plugging away. Talkies were the coming thing and even experienced actors were having difficulty securing work. Some just couldn't cut it and more and more the studios turned to the Broadway stage for their actors. Eileen Pringle, a seasoned actress, gave Dad some good advice: "Lou, if you really want to be a part of this business, I suggest you go back to New York and learn your trade. Pay your dues, kid, and they'll discover you. You won't have to ask them. They'll want your talent."

Dad took her advice. He set out to hitchhike back to Paterson. He got as far as St. Joseph, Missouri, where he ran out of money. He had enough left for one last meal. Finding a very inexpensive restaurant, he went in, sat down, and ordered breakfast, which was a very healthy repast in 1930 when prices were next to nothing for food. As he wolfed down a large serving of ham and eggs, he pondered his next move. Should he phone Uncle Pat (collect) for money to come home or try to find some kind of job in town. Fate intervened. After finishing breakfast, he paid his bill and started to leave. In the window by the door was a handwritten sign that read: "Dutch comic wanted. Inquire at the Lyceum Theater." Turning back to the cashier, he asked, "Where is the Lyceum Theater?"

A middle-aged woman with a pained expression who had heard it all from bums to beef barons looked at him rather owlishly and finally answered: "It be a snake you'd done been bit, sonny. Just turn around and follow your nose."

Although he didn't understand, he walked out onto the sidewalk. There, in plain view, directly across the street, was the Lyceum Theater—a burlesque house. He really knew nothing about burlesque or the stage. But he did know how to put up a front. He applied for the job and convinced the manager that he was indeed a Dutch comic, which meant that you had a Dutch accent and could do comedy. My father used to say that a hungry man can perform tasks he never knew he was capable of. Having just eaten, he wasn't hungry, but he was facing the night with no place to sleep. Maybe the manager was desperately in need of a comic for that night, but the fact is, Dad not only got the job, he worked at the Lyceum for over a year. And during that time, he shed all his comic crutches—the puttied nose, the funny hats, the traditional baggy pants. His natural ability, combined with an acute sense of timing, were his stock in trade and served him well. He started out at $16 a week; a year later, when he asked for a raise, the manager shook his head.

"Lou," he said, "I can't afford any more than what you're getting. Times are hard."

Dad didn't buy that. "I've helped bring in business and the

show is playing to good audiences. I deserve a raise. It's been over a year now since I started and I'm still being paid the same."

The manager said, "I know you deserve it, but it's impossible right now. At least you have job security. That's more than a lot of guys can say these days."

With a year of actual stage work behind him, Dad felt he could do better in New York. He gave notice to the Lyceum and left for New York, now using the name "Costello", which Uncle Pat had adopted some time back. Here's how he came into the name. Uncle Pat was working in New York at the same time when Lillian Russell's daughter Dorothy was performing in a vaudeville act at Loew's Theater. When my uncle's band quit for the night, they would all go over to catch the last show, then grab a bite to eat. Dorothy often joined them and for some reason never could remember my uncle's name. He kept repeating it—"Anthony, like in Saint Anthony"—but to no avail. One particular evening, however, she very cleverly asked, "Where are you from?"

"Paterson, New Jersey," he responded.

"That's it!" she said. "I'm going to call you Pat, like in Saint Pat." Everybody laughed, but the name stuck.

"Costello" happened in a Jewish delicatessen on Forty-seventh Street in Manhattan, where Uncle Pat was being introduced. His name bounced around between Cristillo and Costello, and finally Uncle Pat said, "What the hell. If you can't beat them, join up." So he adopted Costello, which it's been ever since. Dad said, "If it's good enough for Pat, it's good enough for me." Consequently, when he arrived in New York City from St. Joseph, it was as Lou Costello—and that's the way it stayed.

When Dad called and told the family he was coming home, Uncle Pat and his band, the Gondoliers, were playing at the Abbey Inn in Union City, New Jersey. It was Dad's idea that the whole family meet at the Abbey when he got into town. Everybody was very excited. My Aunt Marie bought a black velvet suit with red piping and a big red bow for the occasion. Aunt Marie was a natural beauty with extra-long eyelashes that needed no enhancing. She wore very little makeup. Dad's first

15

comment after seeing his sister for the first time in two years was, "Will you just look at those eyelashes?" It was a great family reunion. Italian families love them.

Nonetheless, a family reunion was not a job, and Dad did not set burlesque on fire. He made the rounds and worked for quite a while at whatever he could find. His break finally came, as it had in St. Joseph, through happenstance. He had learned from the year of walking the boards in Missouri, and now he had put together his own act. Nothing heavy, just a few songs and jokes to get jobs in the local bars and cafés around Paterson. Lew Fields, of the vaudeville team Weber and Fields, had a brother Nat, who was a producer. The summer following Dad's arrival back home, Nat Fields brought the show *Take a Chance* to Paterson, where he saw my father perform in a local bar. He was so impressed he hired my father on the spot as a comic in a show playing at the Orpheum Theater in New York.

The Orpheum was a very important theater for vaudeville and part of the Orpheum Circuit. It was a big step up for Dad who, in spite of his determination to become a big star, was often so shy around theater people that some of them considered him a snob. Once the ice was broken and he got to know the cast, he became everybody's friend. Generous to a fault all his life, he was a patsy for anybody with a hard-luck story. When family and agents advised him to be more careful with his money, he'd just shrug and say, "I know what it's like to be broke. They'll pay me back when they make it, and even if they don't it doesn't matter."

Although my grandparents were ecstatic that Dad had come home, Grandpop had to stifle an urge to tell him to go out and find steady employment. My grandmother, a very dominant matriarchal woman, shushed him. "Don't worry about Lou. He'll find himself one of these days and surprise us all. He's got lots of talent. You'll see, and so will the world."

So far, the world wasn't that keenly aware of Lou Costello. When he finished the show in New York, he found other work—but always in the theater. The die had been cast and he wasn't about to give up show business.

This was during the time motion pictures and vaudeville merged. Many movie houses ran two-reeler films (usually a first-rate picture along with a B-rated one). At the end of the second film, the screen would come up and several vaudeville acts would come out on the stage and perform for the audience. Dad worked one of these theaters, the Capitol Theater in Passaic, New Jersey, following his New York stint. He was booked there for two weeks. Al Williams, an old pal of both Dad and Uncle Pat, thought it would be fun for the two comics to do some skits together. Although there had been a straight man in the New York show, Dad preferred working alone. But he went along with Al, and the two of them hit it off pretty well. One day Uncle Pat had gone to see them at a matinée performance. Afterward he suggested the three of them grab a bite before the next show. Al declined and told the other two to go on without him. "I really don't feel so hot. See you guys when you get back." When they returned a couple of hours later, they found Al slumped over the dressing table, dead of a heart attack.

It was a disastrous end to Dad's first coupling with a partner. He saw it as an omen to work as a single and forget partners. (My father often saw events as omens of things to come, but he didn't always follow his own intuition.)

Big changes in his life and career were just around the corner, but unlike President Hoover's "prosperity," they were of a permanent nature.

CHAPTER III

The Comic Takes a Bride

ONE OF THE MOST SURPRISING FACETS of my father's character in burlesque had to do with his sense of morality. At times vaudeville could, and did, get raunchy, especially when comics from burlesque made the transition to vaudeville theaters. But Dad never had any problems in this respect. People were amazed that none of his burlesque routines were off-color, while his contemporaries were often downright smutty. That sense of morality carried over into his partnership with Bud Abbott. There never was an Abbott & Costello routine that couldn't be done in a minister's parlor. Dad always felt that he didn't have to be dirty to be funny. The public apparently agreed with him, as did other comics, such as Phil Silvers, Bobby Clark, and Steve Allen, who have often publicly expressed their amazement about it.

This quality in my father attracted women to him, especially young ladies in burlesque who were accustomed to being taken for granted by the men they worked with. Dad treated them all with respect. He understood that burlesque was show business and that women worked at that business. He respected them and they respected him.

While dad was working in various shows in New York, Ann Corio's *This Was Burlesque* drew capacity audiences at the Republic Theater on Broadway. Dancing as a "pony" (the shortest girl on the end), in the chorus in Ann's show, was a beautiful young girl named Anne Battler (his future wife and my mother). She had joined the chorus line during her first year in New York after moving there from Providence, Rhode Island, where she had studied and taught dancing while still living at home with her parents.

Anne had been dancing in the Corio production about a year when Dad was hired as a "dancing juvenile." Ann Corio remembers those early days:

"I met Lou before he was taken seriously by anybody as a comic. As a dancing juvenile, he was the lowest paid performer on the burlesque roster. He would fill in a spot for a few minutes during costume changes. (I think he did some sort of tap dance.) I remember he loved to do little unimportant crossover sketches, but the 'Top Bananas' (star comics) did not want dancing juveniles doing anything funny. Lou, however, was a natural comic. He wasn't a juvenile for very long, and in spite of the comic stars he became a favorite of audiences."

Anne Battler never seemed to have any genuine interest in pursuing a career. She appeared more or less to be making use of her time while waiting for something important to happen in her life. Totally unimpressed with comics, the last thing in the world she wanted was to go out with one of them.

One of three daughters born to William and Isabelle Battler, Anne came from a close-knit family. Born in Glasgow, Scotland, she came to the United States with her father in 1920 at the age of eight. Her mother and two sisters stayed behind. Mr. Battler wanted to come to America first to see if it was a decent place in which to bring up his family. He selected his middle daughter to go with him. Six months after their arrival in Pawtucket, Rhode Island, he contracted pneumonia and was to take a long time to recuperate. When his wife heard the news, she packed up everything, sold most of the furniture, and brought the rest of the family to America on the first available ship.

Interestingly (long before they knew anything of Hollywood and name changes) all three girls changed their names. In chronological age order, Isabelle became Irene; Hannah became Anne; Mary opted for Mayme.

Aunt Mayme recalls that my mother was a very lively youngster with an exceptionally healthy appetite:

"She would eat anything and everything. As a matter of fact, up until she married Lou, Anne tended to be on the plump side. Only her dancing kept her from getting fat."

The Battler daughters were close as children and remained equally so as adults. Each was involved in her own pursuits, however, and my mother took dancing classes. To earn extra money she also taught dancing to children. Irene was also an excellent dancer. She and mother won many medals for their exhibitions of Scotch dancing.

A highly proficient tap dancer by 1930 when she was about eighteen years old, Mother decided to attempt a career in show business, starting out in Providence, where she shared an apartment with some girlfriends.

After a year or so, she moved to New York and landed the job with Ann Corio. It was there that she met my father. Both she and Dad became very good friends with Ann while working in her show. Ann tells of their budding romance:

"Lou and I were so close that people mistook him for my brother. The first I knew of any romantic interest he had in her was when he came to me one day and asked, 'Who is that cute dancer on the end?' And cute, pert, and tiny she was. He wanted me to introduce them, but Anne wasn't interested. 'What would I want with a burlesque comic?' she told me. 'I can starve to death on my own.' "

Dad never gave up. He continued to pester Ann Corio to intercede for him. Finally she persuaded Mother to go out and have something to eat with him between shows. While she was waiting for him in the wings, he made a quick turn onstage and knocked over a clothes tree, which fell into the wings and hit her on the head. From that point on, Lou and Anne were inseparable.

On January 30, 1934, they were married. Theirs had not been a long drawn-out courtship. The Battlers adored my father from the very first day Mom brought him to meet them. Pop Cristillo had the same feelings about Mom and always treated her like another daughter. My grandmother Cristillo was more reserved. I don't think she ever thought there was any woman who was quite right for her Louis, but if this was the one he chose to be his wife, then she would accept it. It's also doubtful my grandmother enjoyed being the "second" woman in Dad's life.

Nevertheless, the two families came together and became "family." Dad was doing a show in Boston when they were married. The wedding took place in a small Colonial church and

Dad forgot the ring. My grandmother Battler slipped off her own wedding band and handed it to him. So my mother was married with her mother's ring. It was a very emotional ceremony. A reception followed at my mother's parents' home in South Attelborough, Massachusetts.

Their first home as husband and wife was a basement apartment with slanted floors in Manhattan. Grandpop Cristillo came over from Paterson on Friday nights and gave my mother cooking lessons. My grandmother was no ace in the kitchen, but my grandfather was an expert. Mother, eager to learn Italian cooking to please her new husband, was a willing student and readily adapted to my grandfather's kitchen style.

Dad, always a prize-fight fan, took Mother and Ann Corio to the fights one night. Ann has vivid recollections of the event:

"I'd never been to a prize fight and Lou got good seats at ringside. He excused himself for a few minutes and returned with some newspapers, which he passed out to Anne and myself. I said, 'What is this for?' He said, 'To cover your lap.' I thought he was kidding. Then he said, 'You don't want to get splattered with blood, do you?' The first round was all I could take of the fight. I couldn't stand seeing someone get beat up. I started to cry. I sensed that Anne wasn't enjoying it either. Much to Lou's annoyance, he had to take us home. We went someplace to eat and he kidded us sportingly about it, but didn't really let it bother him too much. Lou was not the kind of man to hold anger. He got over being upset quickly."

Shortly after their wedding, my mother and father were still working together in a show. One night, while driving home from the theater, they had a terrible accident. It was very late and both were tired. Dad was driving and apparently had dozed off at the wheel. The car went thirty-five feet over an embankment and came to a halt. They crawled out and, not realizing either was seriously injured, took a bus to Paterson and then walked several blocks from the bus stop to Grandpop Cristillo's. An ambulance was called. It was only after an examination at the hospital they discovered Mother had a broken neck.

Mother's condition brought out the maternal instincts in my grandmother Cristillo. Mom was in a full body cast for months after the accident. During her convalescence after the cast was removed, Dad's mother took Mom to church faithfully every Thursday night for the Saint Jude novena. Grandma Cristillo was a great believer in prayer, and it was not unusual for her to walk to the Jewish temple to pray instead of traveling the longer distance to the parish church. She used to say, "So it's Jewish. God hears me just as well at Temple." The accident was the end of Mom's career as a dancer—and I don't think she ever missed it. Her life was taken up completely as a wife and would be later on as a mother. Still, I know that for a very long time my father carried with him a heavy sense of guilt for Mother's injuries.

From then on Dad completely threw himself into his work, and the sadness in his heart was transformed—in the classic manner of a clown—to zany antics to make people laugh. He continued to polish and hone his craft and was very much in demand on the burlesque circuit, although he preferred playing in New York to be close to his family. Not once during this period did he ever lose sight of his ultimate goal: becoming a movie star. If others forgot, he reminded them. My grandfather shrugged his shoulders. "You've got a future in burlesque," he said. "Why are you worrying about movies? Hollywood is thousands of miles away. Be happy with what you've got. Remember, you've got a baby on the way. You're a family man now, so keep your feet on the ground."

Dad did have his feet on the ground, but that didn't stop him from having a dream and being ambitious to fulfill it. Mom was pregnant with their first child. It was a long hot summer of 1936 for her while she carried my sister Paddy (born Patricia Ann). Paddy was born September 28, 1936, at Homeopathic Hospital in Providence, Rhode Island, even though Mom and Dad lived in New Jersey. With Dad away from home, she felt more comfortable being with her own family. Dad picked Patricia as a name simply because he liked the sound of it.

Mom took to motherhood as if it were God's sole intent for her on this earth. She was totally fulfilled, feeling they were now a real family. Dad shared her joy and was a doting father as long as he lived.

While Mom was pregnant with Paddy, Dad was working with a straight man by the name of Joe Lyons at the Eltinge Theater in New York on West Forty-second Street. Appearing on the same bill was the comedy team of Harry Evanson and Bud Abbott. Bud's widow, Betty, remembers how the new team of Abbott & Costello came into being:

"Bud was in the business all his life. He was born on October 2, 1895, in Asbury Park, New Jersey, to Rae and Harry Abbott, Sr. His mother was a bareback rider with the Barnum & Bailey Circus. His father worked as an advance man for the troupe. While Bud was a baby, his parents left the circus and moved to Coney Island, where Mr. Abbott helped to organize the Columbia Wheel—the first burlesque circuit.

"In 1911, when Bud was sixteen, his father secured a job for him as assistant treasurer of the Casino Burlesque Theater in Brooklyn. His duties involved being paymaster to the top stars (and often listening to their complaints, which he passed on to the management).

"I was born Jenny Mae Pratt, but when I got into show business I changed it to Betty Smith. Bud and I met while I was dancing in the show at the Casino Burlesque Theater. In 1918 we got married in Alexandria, Virginia. (We had been together for fifty-five years when he died on April 24, 1974.)

"Bud used to stand in the wings and watch the acts and expressed to me his desire to work on the stage. I suggested if he wanted it so badly, why not do it? So, we teamed up. Bud played straight man and I was the comic. It soon became obvious to me as we toured the circuit that all the comics wanted to work with Bud, and I knew my days were numbered as his partner. We became known as Bud & Betty Abbott, but more and more it was becoming Bud and somebody else. If a comic's straight man got sick or split, they always begged Bud to fill in. I didn't mind. They just changed the marquee around and I got a rest. Consequently, Bud had a chance to work with some of the finest comedians of the day, one being Harry Evanson. Which brings us to the Eltinge Theater in New York in 1936, where Bud and Lou, who had met each other working the circuit, got to know one another better."

Backstage between shows Bud would do skits with Dad that he had done with Harry Steppe—a very clever Jewish comedian who was the creator of the famous "Lemon Bit," which was to be so successful for Bud and Dad as a team. Having worked up these routines, there were times when Dad filled in for Bud's comic, and before long people began to comment about how good they were together.

23

It happened that Dad and Joe Lyons had a two-week engagement out of town, and while he was gone, Bud wrote him and said, "When you're through with your engagement, come and see me." It was at this point that Bud stopped working with Harry Evanson and was without a partner. Dad wrote back: "Don't do anything, Bud, till I get there."

Thus, the team of Abbott & Costello was formed when Dad returned from his out-of-towner. Shortly afterward they began working the circuit as Abbott & Costello, spending the first year of their partnership (and the last year of burlesque) with that show. (On May 3, 1937, Mayor LaGuardia of New York shut down all the burlesque houses because he felt they were creating a bad image for his city.)

At this point Bud was the number one straight man in burlesque. The average salary for a comic was less than $100 a week. In those days it was the straight man who was the star of burlesque, not the comic. Traditionally, he received top billing and earnings were split sixty-forty in his favor, more often than not. Bud and Betty had been signed by Harold Minsky to appear in *Life Begins at Minsky's* at the Republic Theater on Times Square at $250 a week. When Bud and Dad went to work for Minsky, it was as equal partners too. They went on the road with the Minsky show and were phenomenally successful. Harold Minsky, who really wasn't a Minsky (his widowed mother married Abe Minsky) always claimed to have personally discovered and trained the team of Abbott & Costello. The facts refute that claim.

The team was being booked by an agency in New York and had signed a long-term contract with Emmett Callahan, who operated a string of burlesque houses. The boys were working at the Apollo Theater on Forty-second Street in New York. "The Lemon Bit," "Crazy House" and "Who's on First" were refined and perfected during this period of time. The boys' rapport and timing merged with their talent and it became obvious to eagle-eyed old-timers that Abbott & Costello was a team that would outlast burlesque.

Callahan allowed the pair to do some engagements outside their contract. It was during one of those engagements in Philadelphia that Bud and Dad met a man who would change the course of their lives and careers—the young agent Eddie Sherman, who was convinced that burlesque was finished. After the show he went backstage and made them an offer: "How would you like to be booked into one of the most popular night spots in America?"

Bud was a dyed-in-the-wool follower of the burlesque circuit and didn't believe all the rumors of burlesque's demise. "Maybe in New York," he said, "but there are a lot of other places where it is still a big thing. I'd rather stay with something I'm sure of."

Dad felt different about the future. He knew that he would never attain his ambition of becoming a movie star doing routines in front of a bevy of unclothed ladies. "What can you do for us?" was his sensible question.

"I can get you into the Steel Pier in Atlantic City. That's what I can do for Abbott & Costello."

"Doing what?" Bud asked, his voice firm with doubt.

"Performing in a minstrel show. It's a start in the right direction."

"A minstrel show?" Bud retorted. "We don't do blackface."

"Shut up, Bud," Dad said. "Let's hear him out."

"All the important people in show business keep their eyes on the Steel Pier."

Eddie was right about that. The big bands were starting to fill in the gaps and would soon become the major billing in night clubs throughout the country. A change was taking place in show business. Vaudeville was declining, and my father was acutely aware of what was happening.

What Eddie Sherman didn't tell the boys was that he was compelled to bring an act into the Steel Pier for a particular date and didn't have anybody to book. Dad saw it as a chance to be seen by important people and reluctantly agreed to take the short end of the split. He wanted it that much.

"Okay, okay," Bud said, "I'll do it—just this once. But I know it is not our type of show."

"Trust me," Eddie said, "and you won't be sorry."

There was the matter of their contract with Emmett Callahan plus their present agents, Letty and Smith. "Let me take care of the agents," Eddie said. "You handle Callahan."

Ann Corio was in the box office at the Apollo Theater when Dad and Bud went to Callahan and explained their dilemma:

"Callahan was a gentleman who never held anybody back. Besides, he didn't know when he might have to turn in another direction himself, especially if the closing down of burlesque houses caught on nationwide. The country was in the middle of conservative times (despite the great liberal programs of President Franklin Roosevelt to fight the Depression). Callahan gave them his blessing and released them from their contract."

Eddie managed to wrangle their agency contract from Letty and Smith and the act was booked into the Steel Pier for a ten-week engagement. They had given up a steady $250 for $150 a week. What future they had, depended on the ability of their enthusiastic new agent to get them bookings. If Bud was skeptical, my father was exactly the opposite. He believed that the two of them were the best act in burlesque and there was no reason why they couldn't be the best in night clubs—and eventually in movies.

My mother never gave my father advice about his work unless he asked, which he rarely did. When he related to her the signs of the future, she merely said, "Whatever makes you happy, Lou, makes me happy."

CHAPTER IV

Abbott & Costello

ALTHOUGH A NUMBER OF PEOPLE have taken credit for the more famous Abbott & Costello routines, it was John Grant, a comedy writer my father had known in burlesque before he ever met Abbott, who refined the routines and continued to write for them after the two were a team. Dad not only believed Grant to be the best writer in the business, but he was forever loyal to people who befriended him or to those he felt indebted to in his career. Grant later went to Hollywood and became the chief gag writer on most of the Abbott & Costello films.

With much reluctance on Bud Abbott's part and genuine enthusiasm from my father, they were introduced (several numbers down the program) in the minstrel show at the Steel Pier in Atlantic City. The audience was hardly in awe of this new team of comics who didn't even have star billing, so the applause was lukewarm. Their opening bit was their race track routine, which became popularly known as the "Mudder":

BUD: Didn't I see you at the race track yesterday?
LOU: Yeah, I was there. I like to bet on the nags.
BUD: (grabs him) Don't talk like that about horses!
    Do you realize that I have one of the greatest mudders in the country?
LOU: What has your mother got to do with horses?
BUD: My mudder *is* a horse.
LOU: What? I will admit there's a resemblance.

BUD: Now stop that!

LOU: Is your mudder really a horse?

BUD: Of course. My mudder won the first race at Hialeah yesterday.

LOU: You oughta be ashamed of yourself, putting your mudder in a horse race.

BUD: What are you talking about? My mudder used to pull a milk wagon.

LOU: What some people won't do for a living!

BUD: I take very good care of my mudder. If she don't feel like running, I scratch my mudder.

LOU: Now ain't that cozy! I suppose if you get an itch, your mudder scratches you.

BUD: You don't follow me.

LOU: Not when you're related to a bunch of horses, I don't. I won't even *speak* to you.

BUD: Will you make sense? I said I've got a fine horse and he's a mudder.

LOU: *(does a take)* He's a mudder! How can *he* be a mudder?

BUD: Because *he* makes a better mudder than a *she*. Now I can't waste my time with you. I've got to go to the track and feed my mudder.

LOU: And what do you give the old lady for breakfast—oats?

BUD: Don't be old-fashioned. Modern mudders don't eat oats. They eat their fodder.

LOU: What did you say?

BUD: I said I feed my mudder his fodder.

LOU: What have you got—a bunch of cannibals?

Their so-so welcome from the audience became a thundering roar of applause at the end of their routine. It was the same at every show, with the opening applause increasing as word got around just how great the team was. They could do dozens of shows without repeating any routine simply because they had all those years of vaudeville to borrow from. Routines were dusted off, updated, and played to gales of laughter from audiences who came to Atlantic City to have fun. Dad absolutely refused to use material that had not been successful in vaudeville. His theory was that a good joke is a good joke—and when updated to fit the times was an even better one. He stayed with that premise throughout his career. All new material had to have some basis in vaudeville (or at least he had to be convinced that it did).

Following their engagement at the Steel Pier, Eddie had no trouble booking the act—but not at star salaries. The money was much less than they had brought in during their Minsky days and Bud was quick to point out that fact. "You know, Lou, we could have made a big mistake switching over. Maybe we better go back to what we know works."

They were now playing spots like Willow Grove Park in Philadelphia, the State Theater in Baltimore, and the Carman Theater in Philadelphia. They were in no manner national figures and were paid peanuts for their engagements: $20 a day in some areas, $125 a week in Philadelphia—which seemed to lend some credence to Abbott's complaints. He convinced Dad to have a meeting with Eddie Sherman and put their grievances before him. If he couldn't produce, then maybe they ought to either get back into vaudeville or find somebody who could book them for bigger money.

Eddie argued that they were in a totally different field of entertainment now. "You guys weren't doing that well in vaudeville," he said.

"Better than we are now," Bud replied.

"Yeah, I know," Eddie said, "but vaudeville's dead. Your kind of talent will grow. You've got the chance to become big stars. Don't blow it for a few bucks now and nothing more later. Besides, they want you back in Philly—and at a better salary."

The boys went along with Eddie on the condition that things had to get better or they'd have to find a new manager. Things did get better. In Philadelphia at Fay's Theater they were paid $175 a week; in Baltimore at the Hippodrome it was $300. They became headliners at Loew's State in New York. Dad and Bud now sensed their real potential and told Eddie they wanted to do something besides theaters.

My father said, "Eddie, we're unique. There is nobody in legit theater anything like us or as good. I think we should be doing radio and movies. Look what Laurel and Hardy have done with pictures—they're an institution."

"And you will be too," Eddie promised. "Trust me."

Eddie was not that big. He could handle the management of

his mushrooming duo, but he'd need more clout in the booking area. He went to see an executive at the William Morris Agency—probably the biggest in the country—and presented his problem. Convinced that he might have something, some of the top brass decided to see the act while the boys were playing SRO (standing room only) at Loew's. They were impressed and made a deal with Eddie Sherman to become agents for the team.

Abe Lastfogel, the farsighted president of William Morris, assigned one of his young agents, Sam Weisbord, to handle Abbott & Costello. Weisbord was youthful, but filled with zeal for his job. Once the contracts were signed and the team was officially in the William Morris stable, he went to work planning and plotting the team's future. He agreed with Dad that radio would give them a big boost—not just local radio, but big-time network radio.

This was during a time when sponsors controlled the radio waves. Vaudevillians were coming into radio en masse. Fred Allen, Eddie Cantor, Jack Benny, Bob Hope, Bergen & McCarthy, Fibber McGee & Molly. The red and blue networks of the National Broadcasting System (NBC) dominated the medium, but the Columbia Broadcasting System (CBS) was striving through its young president, William Paley, to corner a share of the sponsor money. Rudy Vallee dominated the Thursday night time slot at nine P.M. on NBC for some time. CBS, attempting to steal some of Rudy Vallee's thunder put the *Kate Smith Hour* on opposite him. To that time, however, Paley had not been able to overcome the popularity of Vallee. Ted Collins produced the Kate Smith show and controlled her career since she relied on his judgment emphatically.

Henny Youngman, the comedian known for his one-liners, was a regular on Miss Smith's show and under contract. Henny received an offer from Paramount Pictures in California and Ted Collins, not wanting to thwart an opportunity for Youngman, agreed to let him out of his contract if he could find a replacement that would be suitable to Collins and Kate Smith.

Milt Bronson, a longtime friend of Abbott & Costello recalls the circumstances that brought them to Kate Smith's show:

Henny had seen Bud and Lou and urged Ted Collins to go to Loew's State and see the team work. Ted went, but was not impressed with their routine "Who's on First." Since the *Kate Smith Hour* was radio, Ted was afraid Bud and Lou were too visual and would die on the airwaves because people wouldn't understand what they were talking about.

Picking up on a golden opportunity for Bud and Dad, Weisbord joined in the pressure on Ted Collins. Youngman wanted out of his contract to make motion pictures; Collins needed someone to replace him; and Weisbord felt that Abbott & Costello was the precise act to take Youngman's place.

Weisbord convinced Collins to listen to the guys again—this time in a less formal atmosphere—in the producer's office. Collins was still not impressed, in spite of their glowing reviews and press clippings. They'd been a knockout, Weisbord boasted, at Billy Rose's Case Manana nightclub in Manhattan as well as Loew's State Theater.

"I can't put a burlesque act on radio—and certainly not with Kate Smith," Collins declared. "We're a family program and there's no room for off-color humor."

"Look," Weisbord explained, "this is not just a burlesque act." He waved the reviews in front of Collins. "Every one of these rave notices makes a point that the boys have a clean act."

It took a lot of selling before Collins agreed to give the boys a chance. He agreed as much on Weisbord's youthful persistence as for the act's talent. He reasoned finally that perhaps there wasn't anything to lose if he had them on the show just one time. It might work and probably wouldn't hurt the ratings (which were below those of Vallee anyway) because most folks tuned in to hear Kate Smith sing, not her guests. They would receive $350 for the single performance, but most importantly, it would allow them the opportunity to be heard nationally for the first time on prime-time radio.

Dad and Bud were very nervous the night of the show. They were accustomed to live audiences and as Collins had suggested, their material was visual as well as audio. Bud still had apprehensions about leaving burlesque, although with the money getting bigger with each engagement, his ambivalence was beginning to subside. My father worried more that he'd forget lines. It was just pre-show jitters. Dad never messed up a line in his life (although his tendency to ad-lib often confused others).

The show went on. Ted Collins introduced Abbott & Costello, Henny Youngman's replacement "for tonight." The applause light in the studio went on and the studio audience applauded on cue—although not with any great enthusiasm. They did not do "Who's on First" during their initial appearance. Perhaps that is the reason they were only fairly well received instead of getting the bombardment of plaudits they got later on when they did the routine on the show.

Collins was impressed enough to ask the team to return. His only condition was that one of the boys would have to do something about his voice. The radio audience, according to mail and phone calls, had difficulty distinguishing the two. It was then that Dad raised his voice to a higher pitch (for which he gained additional fame because of the little-boy-with-a-changing-voice quality that endeared him even more to the audience).

Sam Weisbord believes that he first saw Abbott & Costello at the Brooklyn Strand and later at Loew's State. He recalls his first and subsequent encounters with them as their agent:

"I had seen their show and I thought they were great. Since I was the favorite agent of the *Kate Smith Hour*, it was logical that I would try to book them on the show once they were William Morris clients. Both Ted and Kate Smith liked me and you might say that I booked the show with talent for them.

"Once the boys were on the show, Ted Collins couldn't seem to get enough of them. They went on for ninety-nine weeks as regulars. I remember there were times the live audience in the studio would be going crazy for them—so much so, they'd run overtime and Ted would walk out on the stage and jab Lou (not hard) in the ribs trying to let him know they'd have to get off so Kate could go on. There's no doubt they were very popular with the audience and I think once they were made regulars, their salary was upped to $750 a week—which wasn't at all commensurate with what an act of their caliber should've been getting—but they were going up the ladder."

By the time they left Kate Smith, they were earning $1,250 a week. They became so popular, they even filled in for Kate when she was on vacation. In spite of pre-performance jitters, they took to radio just as they had to burlesque and the stage. Weisbord says, "They worked radio as if it were second nature to them. Thanks to Abbott & Costello, the *Kate Smith Hour* replaced Rudy Vallee as the number one show in the Thursday night slot."

Kate Smith took an immediate liking to my father and Bud and gave them hints about how they should look, dress, and present themselves off the air. "You're going to be recognized now and people will judge you on how you present yourself." She loaned them both money (without any expectation of repayment) to buy the clothes she felt would be an asset to their rising fame. She financed a Packard automobile for Dad.

Dad had been the owner of that new car only a few hours when he and Uncle Pat left home to do the show in New York that night. They weren't moving along fast enough for a cab driver who kept bumping them from behind, continuing to taunt Dad. Dad turned to Uncle Pat and said, "Pat, if that sonofabitch does that just one more time, I'm gonna get outta this car and punch him!"

Sure enough, as Dad brought the car to a stop, the cab driver tapped the bumper once again, this time a little bit harder. Dad got out, walked back to the driver of the cab, and gave him a hard left hook to the jaw. The cabbie slumped over the steering wheel, out cold—the horn giving off a steady sound. Then Dad walked across the street to where a policeman was talking with some kids on the corner. He tapped the cop on the shoulder and said, "Hey, officer, there's a cab driver slumped over the steering wheel in the middle of the street. Maybe you better check to see if he's okay." As the policeman went to investigate, Dad got back in the Packard and he and Uncle Pat very innocently drove on to the theater to do the Kate Smith show.

He parked his car at the theater and went inside after instructing one of the doormen to keep an eye on it. No sooner was he inside the theater than *crash!* When told that someone had smashed into his car, Dad very philosophically said, "Just goes to show you: never mess around with a cabbie!"

I've known my father to be a very loving and generous man all his life, but one time stands out in particular. My grandfather was an insurance agent on a debit route, which meant going from door to door to collect premiums on overdue policies (payment by mail was not yet the popular mode). From stories Grandpop told at the dinner table, Dad knew there were a lot of hungry families on his insurance route. One night after supper, Dad said, "Pop, I want you to make a list of twenty-five of the poorest families on your route. When you get the list together, I'd like you to go to the grocery store down the street where you deal and have them make up twenty-five baskets with turkeys and all the trimmings. I want to make sure those people have a good Thanksgiving dinner."

That was done and the baskets were loaded into the car. Dad got someone to drive, and Mom and my aunt Marie delivered a basket of groceries to each family. Aunt Marie recalls the day:

"Well, there were these little half-clothed kids with bare feet . . . and the mother cried, the kids cried, and Anne and I cried. It went on that way all day. When we got home that night, Anne said, 'Can you believe this day?' Believe it or not, we felt like a million dollars that night—and your father was too shy to even talk about it."

Dad was now rubbing elbows with the rich and famous in show business and the celebrity world, and he loved it. He made friends with other entertainers, friends that lasted his lifetime. While playing the Steel Pier in Atlantic City, the Condos Brothers played several engagements there and Dad became friendly with them. Nick Condos often joined in with Dad and Bud in poker games between shows, playing for peanuts. In the years to come, they would get together again—and play for very high stakes.

The Joe DiMaggios became friends with Dad. Joe's first wife, Dorothy, and my mother became close during the time Dad was doing the *Kate Smith Hour*. When Dad would be out of town or Joe on the road with the Yankees, Mom and Dorothy often got together for dinner or went shopping to fill in the hours without their husbands. A friend of Joe's usually chaperoned them and they had some fabulous times. One night Joe's friend Vic escorted Mom and Dorothy to dinner at the Hollywood Restaurant in Manhattan. Vic requested a table for three. The maître d' seated them at a table in the back of the restaurant. Vic had gone for cigarettes and when he saw where they were seated, he began making frantic gestures to get the attention of the maître d'. When he did, he said, "You can't sit Mrs. Lou Costello and Mrs. Joe DiMaggio in the back of the room."

The embarrassed man quickly returned to the table, apologizing profusely to Mom and Dorothy. "Oh! Oh! I am so terribly sorry, ladies. I have mistakenly given you the wrong table." He then led them to the bandstand area and practically had them sitting in the band. Mom, always a witty lady, nudged Dorothy and said, "I don't know what Vic said, but with two more words we would have been playing saxophones."

Mom and Dad were still living in Paterson at the time, and Dad commuted back and forth to New York every day. One day my parents had some sort of spat. Now Mom was always a very meticulous and smart dresser but confided to Dorothy that she bought most of her clothing at Lerner's—$2.95 dresses—still had to watch the household budget. Meanwhile, my father was wearing expensive gabardines that were hand-stitched. On this particular day, Mom went to Dorothy and said she wanted to go up to Great Barrington, New York, to visit her aunt. So Dorothy packed my mother and the baby into her car and drove them there. Mom decided to stay a few days to teach Dad a lesson.

When Dorothy got back to New York and saw Dad, she tried to explain to him how difficult it was for Mom to make ends meet while he spent money on clothing like Mr. Astor. "Look, Lou," she said, "go see Anne and talk to her. Listen to her side." Dad wanted Mom to come home, so he went after her—and he must have taken Dorothy's advice because it became less of a chore for Mom to handle the household budget—and Dad gave up the expensive suits.

Although Dad and Bud were an immediate success on the Kate Smith show, their early shows were quite short compared to what they would be later on. It was during the early shows that the team kept trying to use "Who's on First" and repeatedly Ted Collins vetoed it. "It's too visual," seemed to be his stock answer. Dad insisted it would be the best bit they could do on radio. "For Christ's sake," he grumbled to Bud, "baseball's the national pastime. What's wrong with Collins?"

"I know that, and you know that," Bud replied, "but he runs the show—we don't."

Not satisfied, my father schemed with Bud to find a way to

get the baseball bit on the air. They started rehearsals on Monday as usual and Dad reported to Ted Collins that they didn't have a routine worked up yet. He used the same ploy right up to the day before the show was aired. Bud was worried. Dad wasn't. Collins came to them and asked, "Well, what are you going to do this week?"

"Maybe we better skip this week," Dad said, pretending to be totally unprepared. That was a joke. They had literally hundreds of routines, but Dad had made up his mind. They *would* do the baseball skit.

"Oh, no you don't," Collins responded. "You still have that silly baseball thing— What do you call it?"

"You mean the 'Who's on First' piece?" Dad said.

"Yeah, that's the one. Use it."

"You sure, Mr. Collins? Last time we did it, you didn't think it was so funny." Dad wanted to be sure the entire thing was Ted Collins' idea.

"I think it's funny now. It's in the show."

Every single night Abbott & Costello did a show, Sam Weisbord was there with them. He believed in them and he was there the night they did "Who's on First" and saw history made in show business. The audience went absolutely bananas. The network switchboards lit up. Sam knew, as did Kate Smith, Ted Collins, and the world—Abbott & Costello had made a big step toward superstardom.

Here's the way they did the baseball routine that night:

BUD: You know, strange as it may seem, they give baseball players peculiar names nowadays. On the St. Louis team Who's on first, What's on second, I Don't Know is on third.

LOU: That's what I want to find out. I want you to tell me the names of the fellows on the St. Louis team.

BUD: I'm telling you. Who's on first, What's on second, I Don't Know is on third.

LOU: You know the fellows' names?

BUD: Yes.

LOU: Well, then, who's playin' first?

BUD: Yes.

LOU: I mean the fellow's name on first base.

BUD: Who.

LOU: The fellow's name on first base for St. Louis.
BUD: Who.
LOU: The guy on first base.
BUD: Who is on first base.
LOU: Well, what are you askin' me for?
BUD: I'm not asking you. I'm telling you. Who is on first.
LOU: I'm askin' you, who is on first?
BUD: That's the man's name.
LOU: That's whose name?
BUD: Yes.
LOU: Well, go ahead 'and tell me.
BUD: Who?
LOU: The guy on first.
BUD: Who.
LOU: The first baseman.
BUD: Who is on first.
LOU: *(trying to be calm)* Have you got a first baseman on first?
BUD: Certainly.
LOU: Well, all I'm tryin' to find out is what's the guy's name on first base.
BUD: Oh, no, no. What is on *second* base.
LOU: I'm not askin' you who's on second.
BUD: Who's on first.
LOU: That's what I'm tryin' to find out.
BUD: Well, don't change the players around.
LOU: *(exasperation creeping into his voice)* I'm not changin' anybody.
BUD: Now take it easy.
LOU: What's the guy's name on first base?
BUD: What's the guy's name on *second* base.
LOU: I'm not askin' you who's on second.
BUD: Who's on first.
LOU: I don't know.
BUD: He's on third. We're not talking about him.
LOU: *(almost begging)* How could I get on third base?
BUD: You mentioned his name.
LOU: If I mentioned the third baseman's name, who did I say is playing third?
BUD: *(back to basics)* No, Who's playing first.
LOU: Stay offa first, will ya?

37

BUD: Please, now what is it you'd like to know?
LOU: What is the fellow's name on third base?
BUD: What is the fellow's name on *second* base.
LOU: I'm not askin' ya who's on second.
BUD: Who's on first.
LOU: I don't know.
BUD & LOU: *(together)* Third base!
LOU: *(tries again)* You got an outfield?
BUD: Certainly.
LOU: St. Louis got a good outfield?
BUD: Oh, absolutely.
LOU: The left fielder's name.
BUD: Why.
LOU: I don't know. I just thought I'd ask.
BUD: Well, I just thought I'd tell you.
LOU: Then tell me who's playing left field.
BUD: Who's playing first.
LOU: Stay outa the infield!
BUD: Don't mention any names there.
LOU: *(firmly)* I wanta know what's the fellow's name in left field.
BUD: What is on second.
LOU: I'm not askin' you who's on second.
BUD: Who is on first.
LOU: I don't know!
BUD & LOU: *(together)* Third base! *(Lou makes funny sounds)*
BUD: Now take it easy, man.
LOU: And the left fielder's name?
BUD: Why?
LOU: Because.
BUD: Oh, he's center field.
LOU: Wait a minute. You got a pitcher on the team?
BUD: Wouldn't this be a fine team without a pitcher?
LOU: I dunno. Tell me the pitcher's name.
BUD: Tomorrow.
LOU: You don't want to tell me today?
BUD: I'm telling you, man.
LOU: Then go ahead.
BUD: Tomorrow.
LOU: What time?

BUD: What time what?

LOU: What time tomorrow are you gonna tell me who's pitching?

BUD: Now listen, who is not pitching. Who is on—

LOU: *(excited)* I'll break your arm if you say who is on first.

BUD: Then why come up here and ask?

LOU: I want to know what's the pitcher's name!

BUD: What's on second.

LOU: *(sighs)* I don't know.

BUD & LOU: *(together)* Third base!

LOU: You gotta catcher?

BUD: Yes.

LOU: The catcher's name.

BUD: Today.

LOU: Today. And Tomorrow's pitching.

BUD: Now you've got it.

LOU: That's all. St. Louis got a couple of days on their team. That's all.

BUD: Well, I can't help that. What do you want me to do?

LOU: Gotta catcher?

BUD: Yes.

LOU: I'm a good catcher, too, you know.

BUD: I know that.

LOU: I would like to play for St. Louis.

BUD: Well, I might arrange that.

LOU: I would like to catch. Now Tomorrow's pitching on the team and I'm catching.

BUD: Yes.

LOU: Tomorrow throws the ball and the guy up bunts the ball.

BUD: Yes.

LOU: So when he bunts the ball, me, bein' a good catcher, I want to throw the guy out at first base. So I pick up the ball and I throw it to who?

BUD: Now that's the first thing you've said right!

LOU: *I don't even know what I'm talkin' about!*

BUD: Well, that's all you have to do.

LOU: I throw it to first base.

BUD: Yes.

LOU: Now who's got it?

BUD: Naturally.

LOU: Naturally.
BUD: Naturally.
LOU: I throw the ball to naturally.
BUD: You throw it to Who.
LOU: Naturally.
BUD: Naturally, well, say it that way.
LOU: That's what I'm saying!
BUD: Now don't get excited, don't get excited.
LOU: I throw the ball to first base.
BUD: Then Who gets it.
LOU: He'd better get it.
BUD: That's it. All right now, don't get excited. Take it easy.
LOU: *(beside himself)* Now I throw the ball to first base, whoever it is grabs the ball, so the guy runs to second.
BUD: Uh-huh.
LOU: Who picks up the ball and throws it to What. What throws it to I Don't Know. I Don't Know throws it back to Tomorrow. A triple play!
BUD: Yeah, could be.
LOU: Another guy goes up and it's a long fly ball to center. Why? I don't know. And I don't care.
BUD: What was that?
LOU: I said, I don't care.
BUD: Oh, that's our shortstop.

CHAPTER V

Westward Ho!

BUD ABBOTT FELT they needed a scriptwriter for their radio show. My father didn't think it was necessary. Eddie Sherman agreed with Bud, and Dad went along with it on one condition: John Grant, his old friend from vaudeville, would be put on salary by the Kate Smith production office—actually Ted Collins. It was a good pairing of old friends. Grant knew how to adapt their sure-fire vaudeville routines to radio. Consequently, their popularity (and the increased ratings for Kate Smith) continued to rise.

There was one bad side effect to Grant's hilarious skits: they were so good; the audiences laughed and howled for such a long time; the act inevitably ran over time. At one point one of Kate Smith's numbers had to be cut, and Ted Collins again resorted to going out onstage, poking Dad in the ribs, and whispering, "You gotta get off so we can get Kate on!" That brought on even more hilarious laughter from the audience.

Although Collins loved the act, his first loyalty was to Kate Smith and *nobody* (not even Abbott & Costello whose antics increased the show's ratings) was allowed to cut into Kate's time. Sam Weisbord usually found a way to smooth the waters, but Collins was ambivalent. On the one hand, he had a smash act every week; on the other, a star who demanded her own space.

Although Bud was conservative when it came to breaking into Hollywood, it was my father who understood the business of show business almost instinctively. "There is a time to rise and a time to star," he would say, "and there is also a time to move on to bigger things." He knew the public wanted change and what the public wanted, entertainers would have to provide—or they would soon be shoved out of the way by energetic newcomers.

Eddie Sherman shared that view, as did Sam Weisbord. Consequently, Abbott & Costello were booked for a Broadway show (their first and only). The Shubert Brothers with Olsen and Johnson were producing the new show, *Streets of Paris.* Bobby Clark (a star in burlesque, vaudeville, Broadway musicals and film shorts) was the star of this new show. Clark was the comic's comic and it was unheard of that anybody upstaged him or beat him in the field of comedy. That was before his encounter with Abbott & Costello. Clark was known to be brusque and even arrogant with the supporting players in his shows. At rehearsals he initially dismissed the value of Abbott & Costello. That, of course, was before he saw them work. He *was* impressed afterward and made a note that they would bear some watching. And well he should have. Their old-time burlesque routines (with which Clark was thoroughly familiar, having originated some of them) were brought up to date by the progressive expertise of John Grant and some other writers, and they were right on target.

Abbott & Costello were the big hit of the revue. Dad never did anything the same way twice, and he never failed to hit home.

New York critics are the toughest in the world. They succumbed completely to the fresh charisma of Abbott & Costello's presentations. Ed Sullivan, one of the toughest of the lot, critiqued: ". . . the timing of Abbott and Costello is in reality a very studied perfection of talk, movement, and timing. . . . the timing of his [Costello] action . . . a second earlier or a second later would have cut the audiences howls in half."

The show opened at the Broadhurst Theater on June 19, 1939. Just one month earlier the new Glenn Miller band had set the popular music world on its ear at the famous Glen Island Casino. The Depression was ending. Europe was girding for war. Hitler's Nazi hordes had already overrun the Sudetenland of Czechoslovakia, and America nervously hoped that its only involvement in the growing hostilities would be to become the arsenal for other countries involved in the fray.

Dad and Bud were the most successful new team on Broadway. The *New York Daily Mirror* suggested that Harry Kaufman and the Shuberts had already booked the team to appear in a second show for them—a report that was totally speculative and which was never validated.

One week after the opening, Mom returned to Rhode Island for the birth of their second child, Carole Lou, on December 23, 1939. Mom had a terrible time with the birth because the baby was twisted around in the womb. After that, Mom decided to deliver her next children by Caesarean section.

Carole Lou was named after my father, and because it was almost Christmas Eve he also picked Carole for her. Altogether, it was really a very Merry Christmas for the Costello family. Hollywood was making noises that sounded like *maybe* Abbott & Costello might have a chance in pictures when the Broadway show closed.

The show was performed for the last time in February of 1940. When it came down to the hard facts of movie offers, most studios hemmed and hawed that Abbott & Costello were "radio comics"—too verbal for motion pictures. Just the opposite of what had been said by Ted Collins when they made the transition from burlesque and vaudeville to radio.

My father was undaunted. "Look," he told Eddie Sherman, "I think they want us. They just want us for nothing. I want to do movies and always have, but not under the same conditions I would've done them when I was out on the Coast starving to death on the MGM labor gang. You keep plugging. Something will happen."

Meanwhile, Mike Todd (the great impresario who later made *Around the World in 80 Days* and married Elizabeth Taylor) had purchased the rights to *Streets of Paris*. He re-signed Dad and Abbott and starred them with Gypsy Rose Lee at the New York World's Fair. Abbott & Costello was no longer a nickel-and-dime act. Between the closing of the revue on Broadway and their opening at the World's Fair, the team was getting $3,500 a week in motion picture theater bookings. They played the famous Roxy in Manhattan three times that year. They were simultaneously doing four shows a day at the World's Fair, a weekly radio show (which included daily rehearsals) and a midnight show in a night club off Times Square.

Fortunately, comic bits were never a problem. John Grant had a magic typewriter that turned old routines into contemporary gems. The money machine was working overtime and Dad, as he would all his life, spent it like he was printing the money himself.

Dad and Bud never had been great buddies offstage, nor were their families ever close. Away from their work, they were more like neighbors, each with his own backyard and his own set of friends. While they worked, however, between shows there was always a poker game going on in their dressing room. Agents and managers were surprised they appeared so cool on opening nights, but they were not. The gambling merely took the edge off the evening. I think quite truthfully they were always on edge—often with each other—and the card playing kept them from having to deal with what was ahead or each other.

Hollywood was inevitable—certainly for my father who had never given up his lifelong dream. The first offer did not come from Universal, which the team was later to save from near-bankruptcy. Ironically, the first one was from MGM, where Dad had worked on the labor gang so many years before. MGM had always been the most luminous studio in the Hollywood firmament. Stars dripped from their talent roster like diamonds from a DuPont matron. Louis B. Mayer, head of MGM, offered Abbott & Costello less than $20,000 to do a couple of spots in their big musical extravaganzas.

My father didn't want to be an also-ran. Abbott thought he was crazy when he turned it down. "I want to be a star, not an 'also featuring' credit behind Judy Garland or Clark Gable."

While the Abbott & Costello career was being negotiated, my mother and father still lived in Paterson, above my grandparents. Family was family and this played an important part in my parents' lives—especially for my mother, who now had two young daughters to take care of. It was during the winter of 1939-40, when Dad and Bud were burning up the boards in New York that my oldest sister Paddy decided to run away from home. She was all of two or three years old.

It was, as my mother recalled, the coldest day of the year. Snow was swirling down in torrents swept by heavy winds off the North Atlantic Ocean—it was bitterly cold. Mother picked up the phone and called Aunt Marie downstairs. "Marie, Paddy has decided that she's leaving home. So if you see her down there on the porch tell your mother not to get excited."

Aunt Marie was sitting in the dining room with my grandmother. In a minute or so they heard the front door open. They turned and looked toward the hallway and sure enough Paddy, dressed in snow hat, ear muffs, boots, and woolen clothes went outside and closed the door behind her. She stayed out on the front porch for a few minutes, then came back into the house shivering from the cold outside. Saying absolutely nothing to my aunt and grandmother, she climbed back up the stairs. When Mom saw her she asked, "Why Paddy, I thought you were leaving home. What happened?"

Paddy, in a very tiny and subdued voice, peeped, "I think I'll go tomorrow." That became one of my father's favorite stories about his children.

Dad stayed in touch with the DiMaggios, and often took them along when he and Mom went to the fights. They would pile into Dad's car and find all the little out-of-the-way fight cards in northern New Jersey. Dorothy remembers one such night with a grimace:

"We'd been watching several matches and it made me cringe to see those young kids getting beat up. Anne, Lou, and Joe were all screaming for blood and I, very upset, grabbed the towel on the side of the ring and tossed it into the ring screaming, 'Stop the fight! Stop the fight!'

"One of the fighters was carried out to his dressing room, a bloody mess. I turned to Lou and said, 'Please, Lou, go help that poor kid. Please!' We followed Lou up the back stairs to the dressing rooms, where Lou found the young boy. He was overwhelmed that Lou Costello and Joe DiMaggio had come back to see him. Lou talked with the boy and found out that he was helping support his parents. I don't remember exactly how much cash Lou had on him, but it was several hundred dollars. He took the money out of his wallet and handed it to the kid. 'Take this,' he said, 'it'll help you until you can find something easier to make a buck.' That was one of many times I saw Lou try to help a kid."

The pressure of work made my father anxious, and I suspect the same could be said of Bud Abbott. They were like a marriage and even in marriage partners need time away from each other. In order to do this Mom and Dad bought a little house in Miami, Florida. As often as possible, they would all fly down, relax a little bit, and then fly back to New York refreshed. My mother looked forward to those times together with my Dad as much as he looked forward to getting away from New York and work. He took Mom's father down a couple of times—his first time on a plane. It was during one of those visits that my grandfather Battler suffered a heart attack and died. Betty Hutton's mother made the sad trip back to Providence with Mom and Dad when they returned with Grandpa's body.

While MGM was reconsidering their offer and trying to decide whether to up the ante, Matty Fox (an executive from Universal Studios with offices in Manhattan) heard about the MGM bid. He checked with the William Morris office and was told the deal was still pending. Fox immediately contacted Eddie Sherman and requested a meeting. Both Eddie and Sam Weisbord met with Fox and he made a counterproposal. Although Bud and Lou would not be the stars in a picture he had in mind, they would be paid $35,000 (about twice the MGM offer) and their routines would be featurd. Bud was anxious to do it. So was my father, even though he felt their parts should be larger and include dialogue as well as their skits. The Fox offer was accepted, however, and contracts signed.

Everybody in the Cristillo family was agog with excitement. Working in New York was one thing, but becoming a movie star—wow!

When Dad moved to Hollywood to do his first picture, he brought Mom and my sisters with him. They took a house on Crescent Drive in Beverly Hills and had my grandmother Cristillo come for a visit. The first film Abbott & Costello did for Universal was not a feature—it was a short to help popularize President Roosevelt's new daylight saving plan and was appropriately titled *Daylight Saving*. It also served as a screen test for the team.

Their first full-length film was *One Night in the Tropics*. The cast of the film, starring Allan Jones, included Robert Cummings, Nancy Kelly, William Frawley, and Abbott & Costello as two bumbling detectives. Although John Grant received no writing credits, he was responsible for the five routines that were left in the final cut of the picture.

Leonard Spigelgass was assigned to produce. He explains how he came to take the job even though he didn't want it:

> "I needed the job and the money. The Depression wasn't over and work was scarce—even for us producers. I had always felt the original (based on a property called *Love Insurance*) would've been a good film for Carole Lombard and Clark Gable. It's the story of a girl who is very rich and who is beset by fortune hunters. Her father hires a 'love detective' to make certain that the men around her are appropriate catches. The detective ends up falling in love with her himself. It was a perfectly good, legitimate comedy. We also had a Jerome Kern score which, by the way, is the only score Kern ever wrote that wasn't a hit. *Remind Me*, from the film, later became a semi-hit, but on the whole neither the film nor the score did very well."

When Jerome Kern learned that Abbott & Costello would be appearing in the film (he wrote the score for *One Night in the Tropics*), he flew into a rage. Although he had never met either of the entertainers, he made it plain he did not approve. Unfortunately for him, he did not have final approval of the cast—Universal Studios retained that.

Spigelgass stayed up late many nights with screenwriters Gertrude Purcell and Charles Grayson, trying to develop a scene in the film for the comic duo. The studio (which was run by bureaucratic committee) didn't really care that much about Abbott & Costello. The team had been signed to do a picture, so it was up to somebody to insert them and get it out of the way. The picture was plagued with problems.

Allan Jones was the star and had story approval as well as approval of the director. Three days before the picture was scheduled to start shooting, Spigelgass came to him and said, "Would you mind, Allan, if I put two comedians into this film? They've just been signed by the studio and we'd like to introduce them in this picture."

"Fine," Jones responded, "but I've read the script. Where will you put them?"

"We could write in a scene that takes place in a casino," Spigelgass replied. "It won't interfere with the plot or you."

Jones said that would be all right with him. No problem.

47

When Dad and Bud arrived on the set for the first day of shooting, both men were charming and easy to work with. Allan Jones remembers that Dad, in particular, was very warm and likable and that they got along great throughout the filming. "Lou was a lot of fun on that picture."

Nonetheless, both of them were scared to death when their first bit was actually filmed. Dad went to Mr. Spigelgass and said, "What are we supposed to do, Leonard? We don't know how to work without an audience." That seemed to be my father's primary concern throughout the picture—no audience.

In an effort to calm Dad down, Spigelgass said, "I too can't work without an audience—the moviegoers who sit in the theaters to watch the films I produce." He grinned. "But you and Bud do have an audience—the crew that will be making the picture with you."

Spigelgass was right. When Dad and Bud went into their routines, the crew couldn't help but laugh, which created an additional problem on the set. The director would yell "Cut!" until everyone on the set would quiet down. Often it would start up all over again as soon as the director yelled "Action!"

Here are some of the routines Abbott & Costello performed in their first full-length film:

"Smoking"

BUD: Stop smoking in here, Costello.
LOU: Who's smokin'?
BUD: You are!
LOU: What makes you think I'm smokin'?
BUD: You have a cigar in your mouth.
LOU: I've got my shoes on, but I'm not walkin'.

They also did their "Money-exchanging" routine, which gave Dad his first screen slap from Abbott. The routine, "Jonah and the Whale," which was very frustrating for Dad because Abbott continues to interrupt him, was used later in *In the Navy*.

In this skit Dad attempts to tell a joke that he claims he's written by himself, based on the bibical story of Jonah and his experience with the whale. Bud asks, "What kind of a whale?"

"How do I know what kind of a whale?" Dad yells. "Do you

think I hang around with 'em? What do you think I do—belong to a whale gang?"

It continues, leaving Dad totally frustrated as Bud reveals the punch line.

There is another bit, which was one of the funniest flimflam skits ever written. In the film it involves a scene in which Bud fires Dad for bungling his job. Dad demands to be paid off:

LOU: I was supposed to get a dollar a day. That's three hundred and sixty-five dollars. (Bud then proceeds to cheat Dad out of his salary with a hilarious series of deductions.)

BUD: Okay. Let's see. There's twenty-four hours to a day and you only worked eight hours a day. Then, you only worked one-third of each day. Now, one-third of three hundred and sixty-five is approximately, one hundred and twenty dollars. (Dad, by now, is just demanding his money. Bud continues his deductions.)

BUD: Then, of course there's weekends, vacations, lunch hours, and holidays.

Dad is finally left with a single dollar bill, which a passing waiter snatches from his hand.

LOU: Can I have my job back?

BUD: Well, I guess so.

LOU: But not for the same money.

They also did the "Mustard" routine, which was probably their most popular skit next to "Who's on First." Dad buys a hot dog, but does not want any mustard with it. He tells Bud that mustard makes him sick. Bud is insulted. He becomes indignant, explaining to Dad that thousands of people work in factories just to manufacture mustard and Dad's selfishness will not only result in mass unemployment, but will also send children to orphanages. Dad, unable to comprehend this, says:

LOU: Are you trying to tell me that those thousands of people are making one little jar of mustard just for me? Well, you can tell 'em not to make any more, 'cause I'm not gonna eat it!

49

Both Bud and Dad were blessed with a wonderful director by the name of Eddie Sutherland. Sutherland had been on the stage himself at one time and had worked for Max Sennett. He soothed the team on the set—especially Dad—when he felt they needed it. Spigelgass believes that's what made Dad more sure of himself in front of the camera. Also, knowing that Dad could not just start and stop a joke as the director made his commands, Sutherland never once stopped the cameras rolling when the boys were on. Dad had once asked him, "When are you going to stop shooting this? I don't know what to do next. I can't just pick up in the middle."

Somehow the picture got made. In those days, if a picture ran ninety minutes it would've been impossible to add anything more. Every exhibitor had to do a certain number of minutes in order to pace himself and assure his audiences of a certain amount of shows a day. There was plenty of additional footage on Abbott & Costello, thanks to Eddie Sutherland's method of shooting a film.

After the picture was completed, Sutherland phoned Jones and said, "Well, we shot seven routines of Abbott & Costello and had to cut the story all to hell. Do you have any editing approval?"

Jones regretted that he didn't. "When you think you have yourself protected, something always comes up you didn't think about." (Years later, Allan Jones was in South America and happened to see a theater marquee that read: "Abbott & Costello in *One Night in the Tropics*." He said, "I looked for a moment and thought: Where the hell am I?")

The picture was premiered in Huntington Park, California, an industrial suburb of Los Angeles that was favored by the movie studios because it seemed to represent the average moviegoer. Dad and Mom attended the premiere, as did Bud and Betty Abbott. Dad was frozen with fear, while Bud seemed to take it more in his stride (in keeping with his image as a straight man). Dad needn't have worried. The audience reaction told the story. It was almost impossible to hear the dialogue because the audience laughed and howled throughout their routines, catching punch lines here and there.

The *New York Times* film critic Bosley Crowther made it

abundantly clear that although the picture was a bomb, Abbott & Costello were a hit:

> Abbott and Costello stand out as logistical wizards amid the helter-skelter confusion of the story. . . . When Costello is rooked of a year's salary by a series of logical deductions for holidays and lunch hours, or when he and Abbott become involved in cosmic issues over the question of eating a hot dog with or without mustard, *One Night in the Tropics* becomes a riotous excursion.

Everybody agreed that Abbott & Costello were the find of the year—except some of the executives at Universal who looked only at their financial statements and not at the talent of Abbott & Costello. Some of them actually felt that Abbott & Costello were not an asset, simply because an otherwise bad picture didn't make money. But not all of them.

On the way home that night Dad discussed the picture with Mom—rather, he picked it apart. "You know, honey, that picture is all wrong."

"What do you mean, Lou?" she asked. "Didn't you hear that audience? You were great."

"That's what I mean. The picture should've been scripted as an Abbott & Costello film. We should've been the stars. In order to showcase us Universal screwed up Allan's movie. That bothers me because he's a nice guy."

CHAPTER VI

Buck Privates

THE BIGGEST MONEYMAKER Abbott & Costello ever had in pictures was *Buck Privates*, a film that almost wasn't shot. There was a private war going on within the studio hierarchy, and Universal's "committee" couldn't even agree how to operate the studio, much less whom to star in pictures. Universal was in serious financial straits and it was a situation of one body with too many heads. Fortunately, the saner heads prevailed.

A member of the committee with some foresight memo'd Matty Fox in New York that Abbott & Costello might very well make money if properly presented in a picture built around them—something my father had already advocated. Fox summoned Eddie Sherman and the duo to the East Coast for a meeting.

Dad didn't fool around. He could smell a deal a thousand miles away. Fox welcomed them into his inner office and before they even got comfortably seated, Dad said, "Mr. Fox, we'll have to get right to the point because I've got to go to another meeting at the Paramount offices. They've offered us a pretty big deal and I don't want to blow it. I'm sure you can understand that."

Abbott and Eddie Sherman looked askance and then both gave my father puzzled looks. The exchange was not wasted on Matty Fox, and he respected my father for thinking big, because that's the way he operated. "What kind of pictures are they offering you?" he asked.

Dad, ever the ham when he had an audience, said, "As a matter of fact, we can choose our own kind of scripts."

"That so," Fox replied. "Just what kind of scripts do you have in mind— Or have you given it any thought?" He was playing Dad's game and both men were enjoying the repartée. Abbott and Eddie Sherman kept quiet.

"I think we ought to make a soldier picture."

"That's interesting. How did you come to that conclusion?"

"Because guys are being drafted and there's going to be a war. Do you want to see our drill routine?" Before Fox could respond, Dad said, "Come on, Bud. Let's show him." When they finished the bit, Fox was obviously impressed. Both Dad and Fox knew they had just gambled—and everybody had won. Fox agreed to a long-term contract. And, Dad and Bud would have a say in what pictures they would make—not total say-so, but a voice. And to prove it, he immediately agreed to the soldier picture.

The scene then returned to California, where high-level meetings were held to iron out the conditions of the contract. Universal offered $50,000 a picture, four pictures a year. Eddie Sherman said that would be fine, providing Abbott & Costello also got ten percent of the profits. There was no way Universal could agree to such terms. They took a break so each side could consider alternatives.

This time Dad thought Eddie Sherman was wrong. "They're not going to give us any percentage. If they do, every star in Hollywood will hold off till they get it. Let's go back in and ask for a bigger bundle per picture."

Eddie disagreed. "I'll bet they'll go for it—especially when I make my new offer." His new offer was either $60,000 per picture or $50,000 plus the ten percent. Rule by committee never sees things clearly. Universal quickly agreed to the latter deal, figuring Abbott & Costello wouldn't gross that much and they'd be saving $10,000 a picture, $40,000 a year for seven years. That was over a quarter of a million dollars. Their nearsightedness enriched Abbott & Costello by $1 million the first year. Eddie Sherman had gauged his opponents as accurately as a backwoodsman with a bead on a jack rabbit in the middle of the road.

Meanwhile, following *One Night in the Tropics*, Abbott & Costello filled in as the summer replacement for the popular *Fred Allen Show* and made several guest appearances on the equally popular *Edgar Bergen & Charlie McCarthy* program. Consequently, they were getting the exposure that would lend itself to a box-office smash—if they could only find the right vehicle for their screen talents.

Even when Dad was doing a radio show, his warmth came through to the people he worked with. Harry Von Zell, the well-known announcer for the *Fred Allen Show*, found Dad to be the sparkplug of the act:

> "I always remember Lou being very unpredictable whenever he and Bud worked on a routine, which kept Abbott on his toes.
>
> "I'm sure Lou never stood offstage, waiting to go on, trying to figure out what he was going to say. When it came time for him to go out there with Bud, he'd just go out and whatever happened, happened. Some of those theaters, including the balconies, seated as many as 3,000 people. Lou had a special sense of knowing when the audience wasn't in step with us. I've seen him jump off the stage and walk through the audience, doing things like trying on ladies' hats. By the time he got back onstage, they were howling with him. It didn't matter if he was funny—*he made them laugh.* And if Bud had delivered a particularly harsh line to him, he'd immediately win the audience over to his side with a comeback such as, 'You shouldn't talk to a nice little fat man like that.' The audience loved him."

Alex Gottlieb was selected by Milton Feld, one of several executive producers at Universal Studios, to produce *Buck Privates*. Alex had met Feld in New York several years before through Feld's sister, having done her a favor. Feld never forgot the favor—or Alex Gottlieb. Alex had been writing grade-B films at Universal (pictures with a budget of $250,000 tops and that hopefully made money). One day Feld called Alex into his office and asked him if he'd like to produce a film for Universal. He explained the Abbott & Costello team and said, "They've been signed to a long-term contract and we've been instructed to keep them busy. Ever seen them?"

"God, yes," Alex replied. "In New York, when they were doing *Streets of Paris.* I laughed my fool head off."

Feld explained further. "I want to make a series of B pictures with them and we need a writer-producer to work on their pictures."

"Why did you pick me?" Alex asked.

"Because you're now the twenty-seventh writer I've spoken to today and every one of 'em before you turned down the job!"

Alex frowned.

"They don't want to get thrown in with cheap burlesque comics who'd probably go nowhere anyway."

"Milton," Gottlieb said excitedly, "they're all wrong—and the studio's wrong too! I saw those two guys perform and the way they affected the crowds. Those people never stopped laughing. Milton, if I take this job, I promise you—within a year's time Universal will have the number one box-office team in the motion picture business."

"Look Alex," Feld said, "all we want at Universal is a series of grade-B pictures to round out our program. Nothing more, nothing less."

Alex Gottlieb was not deterred. "I'll make Universal rich and I'll make stars of Abbott & Costello. You can make book on it!"

Alex took it one step further—to Nate Blumberg's office, the executive head of Universal. "Within a year I'll make Abbott & Costello stars."

Blumberg thought he was as crazy as Feld did. "Alex, all I want is a little more product. No miracles."

"You watch."

Blumberg threw up his hands. "Alex, do anything you want with them. Just make those pictures, okay?"

Alex left Blumberg's office with one parting statement. "You know something else, Nate—you won't have to spend a lot of money on their films to get people to laugh."

One afternoon Alex was sitting in his office working out the story for *Buck Privates* when his secretary walked in and said, "A man named Lou Costello would like to see you."

"Wheel him in."

Dad, short and fat, came bouncing in and pulled a dirty gag on the secretary who first blushed and then cracked up. He then proceeded to Alex's desk and said, "Are you going to be my producer?"

Informed that he was, Dad began a litany of his own background. Suddenly waxing serious, Dad said, "Alex, I have only one ambition in life and if you'll help me fulfill it, anything you want me to do as far as work goes, I'll do."

"What is it, Lou?"

Dad, like a little boy about to share a secret dream, said, quite seriously, "I wanna be a star."

Alex smiled and asked, "What about Bud Abbott? What does Bud want?"

Dad smiled, and not missing a beat, he said, "He wants to drink!"

Alex laughed. "Well, that's a good combination, Lou. Let's see what we can do."

"I gotta let you in on something, Alex. Bud has epilepsy, and I'm usually the first person to notice a seizure coming on. So if you ever see me grab him and argue with him, and maybe punch him in the gut, I'm really doing it to bring him out of the attack, okay?"

Alex nodded. "I understand, Lou, and thanks for letting me know."

"Just one more thing, Alex—please make me a star!"

Gottlieb got up and walked Dad to the door. "That's the easy part, Lou."

Gottlieb and my father became the best of friends from that day on and he produced eleven of their pictures—not only at Universal but also at Hal Roach and Warner Brothers Studios.

Arthur Lubin was hired to direct *Buck Privates*, and he went on to direct four more of their films. Both Bud and Dad liked working with the same people. Dad said that if you have a team that always works together, it saves a lot of time because everybody knows everybody else.

Although Alex Gottlieb was *offered* the position of producer, Lubin was not. He was *told* that he'd direct the film and he was dubious about the new assignment:

"I was honest. I said, 'I'm sorry, but I just don't feel I'm the right director for this project. I know nothing of dancing.' They all looked at me in the executive office with puzzled expressions. One of the men said, 'Dancing? What do you mean?' I replied, 'There's a troupe at the Figueroa Theater called the Abbott Dancers. Isn't that what we're talking about?' Everybody laughed. Then they explained who Abbott & Costello were."

In addition to Abbott & Costello, the following actors rounded out the cast: Lee Bowman, Alan Curtis, Jane Frazee,

Nat Pendleton, and songwriter Don Raye. The Andrews Sisters, who were even more popular than Abbott & Costello at that time, were under contract to Universal and had made one picture, *Argentine Nights*. The studio was so certain that film would flop, they dropped the girls' contract. Maxene, one of the Andrews Sisters, has some fond—and some not so fond—remembrances of those days at Universal Studios:

"When *Argentine Nights* was shown in Argentina, the Castillo regime took it as such an affront, they banned the picture. Because of the publicity, the film caught on again with audiences in this country. That's when Universal came after us to renew the lapsed option. Foolishly, we allowed them to do it.

"At that point Universal executives were still not sure if Abbott & Costello could carry a picture alone—or whether the Andrews Sisters could either. Universal came to the collective decision that a hot singing group and a fantastic comedy duo just might bring it off. That's how we got signed to do *Buck Privates* with Bud and Lou.

"Universal was a terrible studio at that time. The executives running the studio would do anything they could to keep you from making demands. Lou caught on to this early. If there was anything he wanted, he knew he'd have to fight for it—and he did. God bless him for that. He didn't do it to be difficult or hot headed, and he didn't fight only for himself—he fought for everybody involved in the Abbott & Costello film. Lou never fought over anything in front of other people either. If he had a beef with the studio, he brought in Eddie Sherman and they'd go to the front office together. That's where he made his demands."

Once the Andrews Sisters were signed to do the picture, songwriters Don Raye and Hughie Prince set out to write the songs, one of which was the fabulous "Boogie Woogie Bugle Boy," a perennial hit. According to Maxene Andrews, Universal didn't appreciate the potential of that song:

"When Don and Hughie wrote 'Boogie Woogie Bugle Boy' for us, we had to learn the dance routines at night! We were busy shooting during the daytime, and we were not allowed to learn dancing on Universal's time. We begged the executives to bring in Nick Castle from Twentieth Century-Fox to choreograph that song for the film. Universal didn't want a choreographer. So, in spite of the studio, we all made *Buck Privates* big."

There were men in the front office at Universal who were skeptical about the Andrews Sisters. "The Andrews Sisters can't sing boogie woogie," they said. "Boogie's too tough for them." History proved how wrong they were about that.

"Apple Blossom Time," another song from *Buck Privates*, became so popular, the Andrews Sisters made it their theme song. (When a song is used in a film, it's customary for the studio to pay the publisher a fee for the right to use it. The publisher of "Apple Blossom Time" asked $200. Universal refused to pay it because they didn't want the song in the film. In the end the studio relented and the song stayed in, but the Andrews Sisters paid the $200 themselves.)

It was Arthur Lubin who went to bat for the Andrews Sisters and insisted that Milton Feld keep "Apple Blossom Time" in the film:

> "Milton just couldn't see how it would fit into an Army picture, but I convinced him of the boy/girl significance. Even so, Universal was hesitant to spend any kind of money on the Abbott & Costello films. However, since the studio was nearing the red, they soon realized that if Bud and Lou could continue making movies like *Buck Privates*, they could in fact save the studio."

Despite the film's potential importance to the studio, "Apple Blossom Time" was cheated of the dramatic staging it deserved as a major production number. Universal refused to customize the costumes or improve the set—a fake apple tree with crepe paper blossoms pinned to its branches. This cheapness was typical during Abbott & Costello's tenure at Universal, and the Andrews Sisters' as well.

It wasn't long before my father found a way to compensate himself for the stinginess Universal dealt him and his friends. It started with *Buck Privates* and continued throughout his career at Universal. If he wanted a piece of furniture or some article from the set, he'd go to the front office and tell them he'd like to have it when the film was finished.

The initial answer of the studio bosses was, of course, emphatically "No!"

My father, his cigar (unlit) jammed into the corner of his mouth, head down like a bull, wouldn't accept their refusal: "I certainly hope nobody gets careless and drops a cigarette down in the cushions—or a cigar. It would be a shame to see it burn up." They soon learned it was better to relent than take the chance that he could possibly be serious. No one outside the executive offices at Universal ever held that against Dad. They all knew how cheap the studio was and Dad became the champion of the underdog. Since his death, the legend has grown out of all reasonable proportion—but he did bring home a lot of studio artifacts over the years.

From the first day on the set, Dad went out of his way to make friends with the crew. Between takes, when Bud would go off alone to his dressing room, Dad would hang around with the guys in the crew, always joking and helping everybody relax. Milton Krasner, who was the cameraman on that film (and later, on *Pardon My Sarong*), remembers my father and Bud:

"I used to watch them play poker between takes. The stakes were often very high. If they were really into a game and didn't want to stop, they'd pay the assistant director not to call them back on the set until they'd finished the hand."

Leonard Spigelgass, the producer of Abbott & Costello's first feature-length film, *One Night in the Tropics*, also gives some clue as to how Abbott & Costello differed in their approach to moviemaking:

"Bud was a very quiet, rather introverted man who, even in those early days, seemed to drink quite heavily. He was always a little bit distant.

"Lou, on the other hand, was a warm, lovable, and dear man, who always displayed a vulnerability. Nevertheless, he was also very show biz. For his size he was extremely sure-footed and I often marveled at the way he brought off a scene that would've tripped up a slender man. But Lou had a special kind of agility in his movements that carried everything out to the letter. If he thought he could do something better, he'd improvise—certainly a trait of the real trouper. I also felt closer to Lou in my feelings. There was more of a love for him.

"Whereas Bud was quiet and much to himself, Lou was outgoing and always had something going to bring on a laugh. He had two special qualities that made his humor stand out. One was his innocence and the other was in his character. I never saw Lou display any form of ego, which is very rare in Hollywood."

On the first day of shooting of *Buck Privates*, Joe Kenny, the first assistant director, left for the studio during a torrential downpour (typical of California's winters). Enroute he was involved in an accident that totally destroyed his car and landed him in the hospital with a broken back and neck. He was laid up for weeks in a body cast, unable to move, and every day after the set shut down, the crew took turns visiting him. Joe remembers one time in particular, the afternoon my father went to see him:

"He came in with a box of fruit and cigarettes—and some booze. I was totally surprised, because I'd only met Lou one time on the set of *One Night in the Tropics*. He put all of the stuff on a table and then turned around and said, 'Come on! Get your ass out of bed.' That was very funny, because I couldn't even turn over in bed. But he gave me a great lift that day and I count it as one of the wonderful things that's happened to me. He was that kind of guy—he cared about others."

During the filming of *Buck Privates*, there were no problems between Bud and Dad nor were there any difficulties experienced by the director with either of them. Once John Grant had incorporated their routines into the script, they got right into the business of making films. Arthur Lubin was delighted with the way they worked:

"There was nothing I could tell Lou when it came to his routines. He knew exactly every move to make, right down to the split-second timing. My biggest problem was when Lou became very spontaneous and would begin to ad-lib a great deal. It was sometimes difficult to keep him within camera range (probably because of his early burlesque days).

"Both men took direction well. I cannot ever remember Lou having a temper tantrum on the set because he couldn't shoot a scene correctly on the first take. Because Lou never did a scene the same way twice, I shot all of their scenes with two or three cameras simultaneously so as not to lose Lou's reactions. This was actually a time and money saver, because they were always well-rehearsed when they walked on a set." (The three-camera procedure became a standard process on all future Abbott & Costello films.)

Buck Privates was shot on the back lot of Universal in twenty days and cost approximately $180,000 to produce. It was quietly previewed at the Alexander Theater in Inglewood, California, in February 1941, just five months after the Draft Bill was passed. Alex Gottlieb attended the preview:

> "Because it wasn't a major Hollywood film, I wasn't sure we could get an ample audience. Bud and Lou were still virtually unknowns to the moviegoers of America. But when the film started, the audience began to laugh and they never stopped! The 'Drill' routine is still one of the funniest bits ever put on film.
>
> "Afterward, Milton Feld ran up to me in the lobby and practically screamed, 'You sonofabitch! You were right! The're going to be the biggest stars this studio has ever had!' When I finally caught my breath, I said to Milton, 'Costello will be a big star. Abbott will be what he needs to work with.' That was never meant to be a malicious statement. I think facts bear me out."

The team worked beautifully together. During the shooting of the "Drill" routine, they started their dialogue and suddenly Dad turned to Bud and threw him a line that was not in the bit. "What time is it?" he asked. Without missing a beat, Bud, being a fabulous straight man, snapped back: "None of your business." The line was left in the picture. Alex Gottlieb was so impressed with the comedy that, when the picture was recut, he took all the film from the various takes and spliced them together to make the scene longer and enhance its value in the film. Later, when he explained to my father what he had done, Dad was amazed.

"You can do *that?*" he said.

Gottlieb firmly believed it was the "Drill" routine that made Lou Costello a star.

The critics hailed my father as the funniest man since Chaplin. The *New York Times* review reported the film as "One hour and a half of uproarious monkeyshines. Army humor isn't apt to be subtle and neither are Abbott and Costello. Their antics have as much innuendo as a thousand-pound bomb but nearly as much explosive force."

Buck Privates (1941) established Abbott & Costello in motion pictures. The picture eventually grossed over $4 million and bailed out Universal. More importantly to my father, he was finally a movie star.

CHAPTER VII

Movie Stars

Success must be followed up immediately with a new product. Alex Gottlieb compiled a list of all the pictures that had ever been made by comedy teams: Wheeler & Woolsey, Laurel & Hardy, and the Marx Brothers. All of these teams were passé or breaking up, so the time was ripe.

The day after the preview of *Buck Privates*, Arthur Lubin was given a $5,000 bonus by the studio and told to develop a new project for Abbott & Costello. Four weeks later he had them back on the sound stages making *Oh, Charlie*, later retitled *Hold That Ghost*. The film starred, in addition to Bud and Dad, comedienne Joan Davis. When the film was about halfway through production, the returns started coming in from *Buck Privates*. The figures surprised even the most optimistic Abbott & Costello flag waver, so the studio temporarily shelved *Hold That Ghost*. In many cities *Buck Privates* was grossing second only to *Gone with the Wind*.

It suddenly seemed logical to Universal that the comedy duo make a Navy picture along the same lines as *Buck Privates*. *Hello Sailor*, the working title, was later changed to *In the Navy*. Dick Powell, who had been dropped from his Warner Brothers contract, was signed for the romantic lead (providing he get star billing along with Abbott & Costello). The Andrews Sisters were taken aboard and once again their songs balanced Abbott & Costello's comedy. John Grant supplied the stock gags.

An exact replica of a ship's deck was built on the stage at Universal and shooting began. From the first day of shooting, it was nothing but fun. Dad was able to be himself, and every outrageous bone in his body got into the act. There were three cameras shooting simultaneously and, as usual, it was difficult to shoot because everybody on the set kept breaking up. But it was finally completed.

A copy of the film was immediately sent off to the Department of the Navy in Washington, D.C., for approval. The Navy brass refused to approve the picture because of the ending, which involved some very un-Navy-like maneuvering of a ship within the fleet. It was the scene where Dad became captain of the ship through a subterfuge in order to impress the Andrews Sisters with his importance in the Navy. As captain of the flag-ship—a battleship no less—Dad appeared to maneuver the craft in a manner that had the whole fleet crisscrossing back and forth in order to avoid the battleship that was running amok. The admirals felt it made the Navy look like idiots. The "real" scenes were shot in a large tank on the Universal lot and toy miniatures became the fleet.

Universal had a crisis. It was important to release the picture as quickly as possible to cash in on the popularity of *Buck Privates*. Cliff Work, as assistant to Nate Blumberg, who was top man on the Universal committee, went to Alex Gottlieb with the problem. Gottlieb screened the picture a couple of times looking for an answer, then called Cliff Work, who was elated with his idea. He added a personal aside: "Will you give me half the quarter million if I save this film for you?" There was no answer.

Gottlieb suggested that they reshoot for a day and reroute the scene so that the maneuvering sequence could be retained. The inserted scene had Dad accidentally drinking a sleeping potion and then *dreaming* that he became captain of the ship. When the copy was sent to the Navy, this time they approved.

In the Navy was made, premiered, and released in 1941. Few modern films have its kind of track record. The profits were immediate and huge—initially outgrossing their first hit, *Buck Privates*, and Universal was able to ask more money from the film exhibitors (theater owners).

With great success both Dad and Bud moved their relatives to the Coast to be near them. Dad bought his parents a beautiful home on Coldwater Canyon, complete with curved walk and white picket fence and gate. The carpenters at Universal made up a handsome white shingle sign listing the address and it still stands outside the home today. The same type of sign was made for our home on Longridge Avenue in Sherman Oaks, with a carved-wood "L.C." on each of the gates. "L.C." became Dad's brand and later, when he purchased the second ranch in Canoga Park, he named it the "L.C. Ranch."

Moving to California was a difficult decision for my grand-parents, who had deep roots in Paterson. But Dad insisted; he wanted to maintain that family unity. Eventually the Cristillos moved en masse to California. It wasn't long afterward that Joe and Dorothy DiMaggio moved to the West (right after the 1941 World Series), which was a real plus for Mom, because she missed the closeness of the relationship they shared in New York.

My father was always doing something for his family and I'm reminded of an incident that happened on Mother's Day, just before the move to California. My grandmother Cristillo had been invited to the Elmwood Country Club in Paterson for lunch, and shortly after she'd left the house with a lady friend, my grandfather came racing to Aunt Marie's bedroom and pounded on the door. "Hey, chicken," he yelled, "wake up. I wanna show you something your crazy brother did."

Aunt Marie parted the parlor curtains to look outside. There, in the driveway, covered in cellophane and a big red ribbon that said "Happy Mother's Day" was a brand-new Cadillac. My grandfather carefully removed the wrapping, put the ribbon and bow in the back seat and drove with Aunt Marie in the new car to the country club, where he had my grandmother paged. My grandmother came out to the door and, with a worried ex-pression on her faced, asked, "Is something wrong with Lou?"

Grandpop said, "No, Lolly, but I want you to close your eyes and come with me." He led her to the front of the club and then, dropping the keys into her hand, said, "Lolly, look what your son did for Mother's Day." She opened her eyes, dropped the keys, gasped, and promptly fainted.

My father loved nothing more than surprising and shocking people with unexpected gifts. Over the years we all became will-ing victims of his whimsy. It was Dad's way of sharing his income with people he cared about.

Both he and Bud developed an inner circle of friends which,

behind their backs, became known at the studio as their "entourages." Murray Teff (sometimes known as "Charlie" Teff) became Bud Abbott's right-hand man. Dad had Milt Bronson and Bobby Barber. Off camera Dad and Bobby did a lot of clowning around and pulling pranks like throwing pies. Professionally Bobby did his job and was dedicated to my father as was Milt Bronson. Bobby, however, knew how to keep my father in good spirits and they dearly loved each other. They would often set up a joke on the unsuspecting visitors to the set. For instance, Dad would suddenly whisper to Bobby, "Give me a little trip." Dad would do his pratfall and it would take a few seconds for the visitor to know it was all a joke. Bobby loved to do his imitation of a clown who had just been kicked out of Saudi Arabia. He would stand up on a chair and say, "Peoples of the world . . ." At the same time he would go into a whole routine while peeling a banana. By the time he had finished the skit, people would be coming up to him wanting to help him "get back home to Saudi Arabia." My father usually doubled up in laughter watching Bobby put people on. It was one way in which he found comic relief from his own problems.

My father and Bud Abbott shared an addiction to gambling and were extremely competitive in material acquisitions. This led to some fiery arguments that broadened the differences they had by nature of their divergent backgrounds.

Deanna Durbin, who—until Abbott & Costello—had been Universal's biggest star, was given a dressing room on wheels. My father, not to be outdone by anyone else on the lot, went to the front office and asked for "a trailer dressing room," bigger than the one Deanna Durbin had. Dad was told that his dressing room was quite adequate. He listened, then replied: "Not only do I want a trailer dressing room larger than the one Miss Durbin has, but Bud wants one too." The executives still hedged, so Dad made one more pitch. "Let's put it this way. If you want Abbott & Costello to be cooperative and want the picture to roll without any hitches, those two trailers will be ready for us on Monday."

Monday morning the two trailers were in place. From then on, their daily poker games alternated back and forth between my father's and Bud's trailers. One day my father would win; the next day Bud would win the money back. It was only when they brought in outsiders—people they didn't know—that they sustained heavy losses. Both men were sure they could beat anybody at cards. The truth is, they had trouble beating each other. But they loved gambling.

Friction between the two of them was becoming more noticeable even by their director. Yet they kept it off the set. Loud arguments could be heard inside the trailers, but whenever the assistant director called them to be on the set, they'd emerge very professionally—and one would be hard pressed to find any differences between them. They were, as one crewman on their pictures explained it, "like bread and butter. Lou was the bread and Bud was his butter." Dad was a notorious ad-libber and often would get completely away from the script. When he did, Bud would bring him right back in and nobody knew the difference, except those familiar with the original script. Usually his innovations were better than the original scripting, because he could play the scene more comfortably in his own words.

My father was not a heavy drinker—Bud was. This may well have been one of the reasons they did not socialize together more often. Where Dad was a very outgoing man, Bud was withdrawn, a loner. Possibly it was his epilepsy that made him self-conscious, and drinking may have helped him feel more secure. Arthur Lubin remembers a conversation he had with Bud, in which he related his fears:

"Bud told me once that, having epilepsy, he'd often be too frightened to sleep at night and found that by drinking, it gave him the consolation he needed. He said, 'Sometimes I wake up in the middle of the night screaming.' "

As forgiving as my father could be, he had the memory of an elephant. Before he and Bud had signed with the William Morris Agency Bud had insisted, as was the straight man's option in burlesque, that he get the larger share of the sixty-forty split of their salary. It was always a sore spot with my father, intensified, I'm sure, by the hangers-on who constantly told him *he* was the act and Abbott was merely his foil. Although the Morris office had changed that split to fifty-fifty, Dad felt he'd been short-changed and it was time to rectify that. There was nothing Bud could do about it, short of breaking up the team—and my father would've done just that. There were times when he could be—

and was—stubborn to a grievous fault. He insisted that the percentages be changed, Bud finally relented, and for the rest of their careers as a team, my father received sixty percent, and Bud forty percent, of the salary paid them. Dad also wanted the team renamed Costello & Abbott. Universal told him they had purchased Abbott & Costello and *they* would break up the team before they'd accept anything else. Dad backed off, but from then on there was a permanent chill between my father and Bud whenever they weren't actually working. If either gave a party the other usually stayed away. The exception was when both had to attend for business reasons. Sam Weisbord was painfully caught up in those renegotiations and feels, even today, that the money wasn't worth the chasm it created between the two men. As to their relationship with Universal Studios, he sees that differently from most others:

"There wasn't that much of a problem. Universal was thrilled with the box-office receipts from their pictures. Even though MGM had a larger stable of stars and Universal was known for turning out low-budget films, the studio appreciated what Abbott & Costello were worth to them. Bud and Lou were like two burlesque clowns on the Universal lot—having a ball! Lou really ran the roost, however, not Bud."

Without a doubt their manager Eddie Sherman was really the third member of Abbott & Costello. It was he who expanded their career into more than one area and got them top dollar. Not once did Eddie ever interfere with my father's innovations on the set or try to interject his thoughts into any of the Abbott & Costello scripts. He concerned himself only with the business of managing the act. Had he done otherwise, my father would've let him know in plain terms that he was out of order.

Everett H. Broussard, film editor on the majority of the Abbott & Costello pictures at Universal, recalls a classic example of my father's attitude about outside interference with his work:

"One thing about Lou Costello that impressed me was the way he ignored precision. For instance, one time he had a cigar in his left hand during a take and then in the next take, the cigar appeared in his right hand. The script supervisor said, 'Lou, the cigar's in the wrong hand.' Lou answered, 'So what? If you're gonna watch the cigar, then I'm not funny.' He was right, but it had to be his idea."

He didn't like anybody else to take such liberties—not even Bud Abbott."

Although there was a producer and director assigned to each of the Abbott & Costello films, my father actually controlled the shooting schedules. Dad could be in the middle of a scene with the cameras rolling, but if he saw a clock that said four P.M., he'd yell, "Cut!" That mystified some people, but not those who had worked with him. They knew his habits. He had a pattern and he had a stock answer for anybody who questioned him about it: "I cease to be funny at four o'clock," he'd say. "I'm tired and I'm gonna go home."

Although Bud had it written into his contract that he didn't have to work past that hour, he'd sometimes say, "Come on, Lou, let's do one more take." Dad would reply, "You go ahead and do another take. I'm going home." He might then turn to the director and say, "Give him a close-up, will ya?"

Although Dad was adamant about quitting time, he respected the professionals who put the film together. He'd look at the dailies every day, but he rarely ventured into the cutting room and usually accepted the decision of the editors.

It was part of his routine to sit around in the mornings before shooting started, mingling and talking with the crew and the director. He knew them all personally, knew their problems, and could always be counted on to come through for them. He loved feeling needed.

Our Longridge home was more than just a house. It was the family seat. Everyone on both sides of our family seemed to gravitate there. My father brought my mother's family out to California along with his own, so the San Fernando Valley was well endowed with former residents of Paterson, New Jersey. Dad continued to bring home anything that wasn't tied down on the set once shooting on a scene was finished. It got to be a joke that our home was furnished in "early Universal."

That house *was* a major investment in more ways than one. When Mom and Dad purchased the place, it was a one-story modest home one block south of Ventura Boulevard, the main San Fernando Valley thoroughfare. Dad kept adding and adding on until it was a beautiful two-story, twenty-four room mansion. Still, there never seemed to be enough room for everybody.

I remember Mom saying there was always someone at the front door and someone seated at the bar. It wasn't exactly a private place.

The house itself was incredible once completed, situated on more than an acre of land. The San Fernando Valley was underdeveloped when my parents purchased that house. Dad wanted to build and he wanted to build big, grandiose-type things.

Off the garage area there was a projection room with twelve reclining chairs. The movie screen was covered by a velvet curtain. Dad hired an artist to hand paint magnificent peacocks on the curtain, which glowed almost phosphorescently when the ultraviolet lights shined on it. There was a large pool table in the middle of the projection room, separating the chairs from the screen. Dad's film vault was just off the garage, where he kept his personal library of film. On the ground floor, next to the projection room, was my father's office. The master bedroom was also downstairs and was an incredible room. It had, attached in a separate area, a sauna and steam room. Dad's dressing room was a large room with a skylight dome overhead. It was a room that was semicircular in shape. There was a hidden doorway in his dressing room that my sisters knew about and loved charging back and forth through as kids. Mother had her own dressing room off the bath. The entire master bedroom was done in mirrors and cream-colored satin. The furnishings were all custom-made.

We had a small library-den toward the north part of the house, next to the formal dining room. The windows faced Longridge Avenue. In that room Dad had shelves mounted on the wall that displayed miniature wooden carvings of characters that he portrayed in his films. He also kept his plaques and awards in the library.

Upstairs we had a sitting room, two playrooms (one was off Paddy's bedroom on the south end of the house), three bedrooms and three baths. The kitchen was accessible by way of a small back stairway that led downstairs. There was also a master stairway that ended in the foyer of the house. Additional maids' rooms with bath and sitting area were adjacent to the kitchen.

The front entrance opened up to the formal living room, which joined the formal dining area, where there was a small door that led to the pantry area and into the kitchen.

Walking out into the backyard there was what looked like another guest house, but it was actually a storage area. In one section we had a hand-built stage where, as children, Paddy and Carole put on plays. It was later removed and a guest room erected in its place. There was a pool and another small guest house to the left. To the right was a lanai with a sundeck on top. We had a large fish pond with real fish and a bridge over it, a wishing well, a small tunnel that Dad's eight-passenger train traveled through, two dollhouses, a basketball-tennis court, Carole's bird aviary and a small garden with a stone statue of Cupid shooting an arrow. It was like living in a small private park.

If there was no real privacy in our completed mansion, there was even less when Dad took us all out to dinner or to some affair. At times it may have irritated the rest of us, but he was never offended or put out by fans. People came over to our table for an autograph and he would always go into his schtick for their benefit. In that respect he was super, never pushing them away. He would tell us, "*They* are the reasons why I am here today."

We lived a very luxurious life.

Nevertheless, the studio got its full measure from my father. Within one year, 1941, Abbott & Costello completed a total of four pictures. (Some of them were shot in fifteen or twenty days.) *Keep 'Em Flying* followed the release of *Hold That Ghost*, which had been made before *Buck Privates*.

Carol Bruce, a young actress working in only her second film, was featured in *Keep 'Em Flying* as the romantic interest of singing star Dick Foran. She recalls that it was my father who helped her overcome her awe of working with Abbott & Costello:

"I remember my excitement at them, particularly Lou. Right away I sensed that most people gravitated toward him rather than Bud, who always went off by himself when not working. The first day on the set I was absolutely terrified. It showed. Lou kept saying, 'Brucy, relax. Just relax. It ain't gonna hurt. It's easy.' He always had a big smile for me and encouragement. He was a father image for me. I would've done that picture for nothing, because it was really fun working with Lou. He was a crazy, insane, marvelous nut and I loved him. I saw his temperament flare occasionally, but it was never detrimental. Lou seemed to know what was right and what was wrong. He had a sense of the power that was his at Universal and he used it to his advantage—as well as for the other actors and the crew.

Carol remembers a very funny incident with Dick Foran while working on *Keep 'Em Flying:*

"Dick was a tall, very macho man. I'd heard about Hollywood wolves and when he asked me to come to his dressing room one day, I thought—well, here it comes. But I went there out of curiosity and he asked me in and closed the door. I was expecting the worst. He smiled and looked at me warmly, then said, 'Would you like to play jacks?' I thought he was kidding. He wasn't. It was something to see—this tall, handsome, macho man sitting on the floor playing jacks.

"I recorded two songs for the picture: 'You Don't Know What Love Is' and 'I'll Remember April.' Lou didn't think they fit and had them cut out of the picture. I felt a lot of rejection and trauma when I viewed the picture the first time and found them missing. I was young and it took a long time before I realized that Lou knew what was best for the film. It was Abbott & Costello who'd get credit for the success or failure of the picture—not Carol Bruce."

Martha Raye's song "Pig Foot Pete" stayed in the picture and it eventually became a big-hit single for Ella Mae Morse. That was no consolation for Carol and Dad tried to make up for it one day by taking Carol on a shopping spree. They were in Chicago at the time, on a nationwide tour to promote the picture. Carol remembers it as children's day in a toy factory:

"I'd see an outfit and Lou would say, 'Go ahead and try it on, Brucy. Universal's paying for all of this.' I was reluctant, but Lou insisted. He'd pick up a garment and say, 'You like this? We'll take half a dozen.' My eyes were bugging out of my head. The team was making millions for Universal, so I guess he felt he was entitled to some fringe benefits."

Dad and Bud had so much going on, they could hardly keep up with what was happening in their lives. Irving Mills, owner of the third largest booking agency in show business, came up with the idea for *Laugh, Laugh, Laugh*, a recording of Abbott &

Costello doing their most famous gags. Mills remembers the recording session at RCA's studios and refers to it as a comedy of tardiness:

"We were to start recording at eight o'clock sharp—until I received a call from Eddie Sherman telling me they'd be late. Bud and Lou had been asked to add their foot and hand prints to the collection in concrete at Graumann's Chinese Theater. Those two were the type of guys who'd agree to do something or appear somewhere and forget to tell Eddie. That's what happened.

"I met the three of them about seven and we drove to the Chinese Theater. There were thousands of people lining the sidewalks and traffic was backed up for blocks. There was even a big brass band to welcome them. It was useless for us to get to the theater by car, so we parked at the Roosevelt Hotel down the street and went to the bar. Eddie went across to the theater and told the guy in charge where we were and to please call when they were ready.

"A runner eventually came and said they were ready. Eddie, Lou, and Bud went over, leaving me at the bar. A short while later they came back. 'They're not ready,' Lou explained. 'The guys pouring the cement are new at the job.' We had some more drinks. Meanwhile I was getting very nervous, because I knew RCA was holding the studio for us. So I phoned them and explained.

"The runner came back again and Eddie and the guys went back to the theater. I heard the cheers and the big brass band hailing their arrival. By now it was after eight, so I made another call to RCA. Meanwhile the three of them returned to the bar, once again put on hold. Bud and Lou ordered steaks, which took another forty minutes. When the food was finally served, the runner showed up and I was left to look at their dinners. Finally they were immortalized in concrete and we left for the studio.

"It was *very* late. We had hired a group of professional *laughers* for the record and they were all half asleep. The musicians were in poor shape too and we had a hard time getting everybody revved up for the session, but we finally cut it. The record didn't sell—it lacked the Abbott & Costello spirit—but it's probably a collector's item now. Yet, the recording session, and all that led up to it, was right out of the Abbott & Costello routine book."

Dad was making big money now. In addition to films, there were endorsements and business investments that added to his annual income—a lot of which he used to outdo Bud Abbott. If Bud bought a house, ours had to be bigger. When Bud put in a swimming pool, Dad built a bigger one. By the time he finished adding on to the Longridge home in Sherman Oaks, we had twenty-four rooms. The main house had a bar that stretched the full length of the den—no one in show business had topped that. He constructed a theater and accumulated a library of films that exceeded five hundred.

When Bud bought a restaurant on Ventura Boulevard that specialized in Italian food, Dad bought a nightclub—the Band Box—in Hollywood, where he produced extravagantly fabulous floor shows. Whenever Bud bragged that he was making so much money he had to stay up all night counting the profits, Dad said, "That's nothing. We don't even count the money anymore—we weigh it!" Dad bought an eighty-foot subchaser from the Navy and converted it to a luxury yacht for weekend cruises. It became a part of his "fleet," which included five automobiles—his favorite being a very long, red limousine. My father was a kid at heart and these things were his toys.

Bud and Lou had continued to do radio shows ever since their debut with Kate Smith, namely: the *Fred Allen Show*, the *Edgar Bergen & Charlie McCarthy Show*, and other guest appearances. Inevitably they would have their own show—and they did. The *Abbott & Costello Show* was broadcast for the first time on Thursday night, October 8, 1941, at seven P.M., from the NBC studios at Sunset and Vine in Hollywood. It was a half-hour show sponsored by Camel cigarettes (and was to run in the top fifteen shows for six years). Ken Niles was the announcer and the Leith Stevens Orchestra conducted (later replaced by the Freddie Rich Orchestra). Connie Haines, formerly singer with the Tommy Dorsey Band, appeared on the show for four years.

The *Abbott & Costello Show* was an immediate hit. Here are a couple of the routines that kept the show on top for so long:

They'd open the show with Dad's famous:

"Heyyyyyyyy Abbot-t-t-t-t!" and then immediately go into one of their routines. For instance, when Dad wants to buy a house but doesn't have enough cash, Bud offers to help him:

BUD: I'll get you a loan in the bank.
LOU: Who wants to be alone with you in a bank?

BUD: I'm trying to tell you, that you can get a lien against the house.
LOU: Lean against the house? What's the matter with the joint? Is it gonna fall down?
BUD: Talk sense, Costello. To get in the house, you must go through escrow.
LOU: Why can't I go through Glendale?

Another routine involves Dad explaining to Bud that he spent the night sleeping on a bench in the park:

BUD: It's a wonder you didn't freeze to death.
LOU: I had my radio with me. That keeps me warm.
BUD: How can a radio keep you warm?
LOU: I tune in Gabriel Heatter!
BUD: Costello, I'll have you know that last night I had a date with Betty Hutton.
LOU: You make a lovely couple—Hutton and nuttin'!
BUD: In our new picture *I'm* taking care of the love interest.
LOU: Oh yeah? What do you know about makin' love, Abbott?
BUD: Why, yesterday at the studio, Hedy Lamarr and Lana Turner had a hair-pulling match over me.
LOU: Yeah, but it was *your* hair they were pullin'!

Once a year the *Abbott & Costello Show* was moved to New York to be aired from there for several weeks, and while they were on the road Dad took special care to be protective of Connie, the show's singer. Mildred Jamais, Connie's mother, always appreciated his concern. "Lou sensed that my daughter was a very shy girl who could be easily hurt. I've always been grateful he took such good care of her."

When the show went off the air at the end of the season, Connie would often go on tour with Bud and Lou, traveling across the country, coast to coast, by train.

"It was during those trips that I witnessed the gambling side of Bud and Lou. I watched them lose as much as thirty-five thousand dollars in a game as we moved across country by rail. The money passed back and forth between them until some third party got involved and won it all. To a young kid like me thirty-five thousand dollars was like a million.

"Every night on the train Lou would get us all together and we'd put on shows in the club car. We had our musicians with us, so they'd supply music. Bud and Lou did their comedy routines and I sang. The passengers loved it. They almost couldn't believe they were seeing Abbott & Costello in person—and for free!"

No matter where he went, Dad would always plug his hometown on the air and send a big hello to all his friends in Paterson. Abe J. Greene recalled the first time he heard Dad mention his name on his radio show:

"He remembered everybody. And he was always doing something for somebody in Paterson. He was generous, at times, to a fault. Every year he'd come back to Paterson for the Old Timers' Midget Baseball and Basketball Game and, without fail, he'd always leave a cash gift for the teams."

Dad premiered several Abbott & Costello films in Paterson, where they were screened at the Fabian Theater, to raise money for the local charities. Among them was St. Anthony's Catholic Church, my grandparents' family parish. In one instance Dad and Bud raised $14,000 to pay off the church mortgage. That was followed up with thousands more, to help build a new church. My father commented on St. Anthony's in a *New York Times* interview: "Funny thing, it was the parish priest at St. Anthony's who tried to keep me from running off to Hollywood when I was a kid. Now I'm helping them build a new church because I disobeyed him."

My father tried to run everything, tried to make everybody happy. His entire philosophy about life was like that of a little boy who sees the world as a lavish birthday party with more than enough ice cream and cake for everybody. It would soon be time for the rose-colored glasses to come off. It was the eve of Pearl Harbor and my father would play a big part in the war effort.

CHAPTER VIII

The Home Front

Dad had already been performing at military bases as a part of the USO Hollywood contingent, when he and Bud were asked to perform at an Army base just outside San Francisco with Judy Garland's former husband, composer and orchestra conductor David Rose. Right in the middle of a routine, the commanding officer stopped the performance to make this announcement—the Japanese had bombed Pearl Harbor. The show was cut short and the troupe put aboard a plane for the return trip to Los Angeles. As they made their approach to the Burbank Airport in the San Fernando Valley, the runway was completely blacked out. It was a shock to everyone. Just yesterday America had been supportive of the war effort—but not in it. Now we were very much involved and rumors ran rampant on the West Coast of an imminent Japanese attack and invasion of California.

In spite of the war (and for many reasons because of it), the film industry went about the business of making motion pictures. More now than ever before, the public needed entertainment—needed comedy—to balance the awful specter of a world war.

My father and Bud were still at it—gambling at poker in their dressing rooms. At those times money had no real meaning to either of them. It was just paper to play with and have fun with. During the filming of their next picture, *Ride 'Em Cowboy,* they stashed thousands of dollars in cash in those trailers. George Raft, the movie tough guy, had known Dad and Bud in New York and their acquaintance was renewed in Hollywood. He remembers some of their games:

"If you're playing poker as a pastime, fine, but those two played as though money was going out of style. I was on a plane with them once, coming from New York to the Coast—when they had sleepers on planes. They never got any sleep—stayed up all night, often at two thousand dollars on the turn of a card. I've always felt that Lou wanted to beat the world. That was his weakness."

Dad gambled not only on the set, but he had his own box at the race track, where he'd be thrilled as much by the extravagance of passing out ten-dollar bills to the racing fans in the general admission section as he was by betting on the horses.

Even though Dad had more work than he could handle and spent a lot of his free time at the track or playing cards, he was a concerned and caring father when it came to us kids. When the Japanese were threatening to bomb the coast of California early in the war, Dad moved my mother and my two older sisters to Palm Springs, about a hundred miles inland from Los Angeles, sincerely believing that the Japanese wouldn't find them in the desert community.

Dad was always conservative with his children—actually, quite strict. Paddy, my oldest sister, paved the way for the rest of us kids, taking the brunt of my grandmother Cristillo's unsolicited advice. My sister was a rebel and it was inevitable that she and Dad would have their run-ins. My father ran a tight ship, with only one captain—himself! Consequently, Paddy was more my mother's daughter than my father's.

"I can't really explain why. Maybe it was just a lack of communication. My father wasn't an easy person for me to talk to. Being the oldest child, I was rebellious even in my high chair. Dad couldn't handle that. He came from a very authoritarian Italian household where kids didn't express personal choices. I did. I was something money couldn't take care of and he thought money could take care of anything. He also found it hard to show affection—certainly with me."

My father might be described best as being serious funny. Usually a quiet man at home, it took an audience of one or two to turn him into Lou Costello the comic. If one of us kids got sick, he couldn't stand it. When Paddy was about four or five years old, she was put to bed with some childhood disease. Almost every night until she was better he'd come into her room and do things like walk into the wall, trip over his feet—anything to get both his mind and hers off the illness. Naturally she thought he was funny and the more she'd laugh the more he'd continue the routine.

No matter what time of the night it was, if one of us kids cried out or made an unusual noise, my father was the first one out of bed to check on us. Paddy tells of one such incident with a great deal of fondness.

"We had a governess once, named Cookie, and one time in the middle of the night I heard noises coming from our playroom. Frightened, I ran downstairs to my father, who was watching late-night TV and told him there were snakes in our playroom. Dad and Sven (our butler) immediately dismantled the vacuum cleaner and sneaked up the stairs with appliance parts in their hands, ready to kill dragons—or snakes. Dad went into our bedroom and awakened Carole. 'Carole, Carole!' he said. 'Are there snakes in the playroom?' Carole, who was half asleep, answered 'Yes, Daddy, there's snakes in there,' and then rolled over back to sleep. Dad followed the noise to the bathroom, where he found Cookie suffering from too much champagne she'd had earlier that night at a party."

As you know, Carole was born partially paralyzed and was troubled by physical problems as a child. Shortly after the family moved to California, she developed a thyroid problem and was treated with X-ray (which, we would later learn, was not the best treatment in her case). My mother took care of her religiously, nursing around the clock if necessary. Later on, when Carole would get into some mischief, Mom would say to her, "How can you do these naughty things? I carried you under my heart for nine months, and massaged your little body so you would be able to walk today. Now be a good girl, Carole."

Sonja Heine owned an ice skating school in Westwood, California, and before I was born, Mom took Paddy and Carole there regularly for lessons. One time Mom had dyed their leotards kelly green and it was funny how they slipped on the ice and got their outfits wet, which caused them to run like crazy. By the time my sisters got home, their legs were streaked a ghastly color. Carole cried and cried, and swore she'd never skate again—but she did. It was all part of growing up the way we Costellos did.

Away from home, Dad worked very hard. Life at the studio was business, not family. One of the songs intended originally for *Keep 'Em Flying,* "I'll Remember April," written by Don Kaye and Gene de Paul, and sung by Dick Foran, was cut out of that picture and showed up in *Ride 'Em Cowboy.* Alex Gottlieb phoned Don and Gene and invited them to the sneak preview of the *Cowboy* film—without explaining the switch he'd made. Gene de Paul describes his and Don Kaye's reactions:

One of the scenes involved a midnight horseback ride, and it opened with a beautiful long shot of the horses on a winding trail. Dick Foran and Anne Gwynne were riding at the back of the pack. (Remember, this takes place at midnight.) Dick proposes to Anne that they go off on their own. She gets his point and they turn off and ride to a secluded spot. They dismount and Anne sits down on a log very conveniently placed there by the prop department. Dick, without taking off his cowboy hat, puts his boot on the log and begins to sing. The opening words of 'I'll Remember April' are: 'This lovely day will lengthen into evening.' Don and I nearly fell out of our chairs. It's midnight and here he is singing about this lovely day. We went to Alex Gottlieb and asked him if he was trying to crucify us. His response was: 'Well, we thought it was so beautiful we had to use it in this scene.' "

Don and Gene, following the preview of the film, took the soundtrack of their song to "Hank the Night Watchman," a Los Angeles disc jockey, and persuaded him to play it as a "mystery tune" on his show. Before the record had stopped spinning, the switchboard lit up. Don and Gene wanted to distribute it right away, but Universal wouldn't allow it—not until after the picture was released. In the end it became a major hit and a standard. This is just another example of the silliness that went on in the executive offices of Universal Pictures while my father was under contract there. Ella Fitzgerald was among the cast of stars who performed in *Ride 'Em Cowboy.* She sang "A Tisket A Tasket," the tune that made her famous, and "Cow Cow Boogie," which was later recorded by Freddie Slack and his orchestra for Capital Records and made a star of his singer, Ella Mae Morse.

After *Ride 'Em Cowboy* my father was showing signs of fatigue—so was Abbott. But neither complained, even though Universal was driving them like a team of mules. At one point

Milton Berle joked about it: "Things are a little slow in Hollywood. Abbott & Costello haven't made a picture all day."

It was a period in which, despite their tremendous popularity, they seemed to be bored, particularly my father. Where once he might've said, "I can do the scene better," he now seemed not to care. He was slowing up and no one seemed to know why. He'd always been a human dynamo and would brush off my mother's concern by saying, "Making movies is hard work. I'll take a month or two off pretty soon. I'll be okay."

My father wanted Grandpop Cristillo to manage his money. He trusted his father's judgment, but the hangers-on and leeches all too often had Dad's ear and it soon became apparent to Grandpop that it was better to let someone else take over that obligation. Dad lost a lot of money through the action of slick Hollywood con men with get-rich-quick schemes. He believed everybody was an okay guy until after he found out different—at his own expense.

Mom occasionally would have down spells. As outgoing as she was, she became easily depressed when things went wrong. My grandfather Cristillo was very close to Mom. He could sense the slightest change in her moods and would put his arm around her when he'd see she wasn't up to par. Referring to her true name, he would say, "Now, Hannah, it's gonna be okay." If Dad had any trouble, she felt it just as strongly as he did. But where Mom might brood over a thing, Dad did something about it.

Dad ran into problems with the California Board of Equalization, for instance, in connection with his nightclub. There was some obscure statute forbidding performers from owning and operating a nightclub in California. He blew up when notified he'd have to get rid of the club. Mom became depressed. After he simmered down, he did the sensible thing. The club was put in Aunt Marie's name (Bud had the same problem with his place, Windsor House. His sister Olive took over.) So, on paper at least, Aunt Marie owned the Band Box.

Contrary to plans, Dad never did have much time off between pictures. He did, however, insist on a Christmas vacation—and got it. That might seem like a small accomplishment since almost everbody gets off at Christmas, but that wasn't necessarily true with Abbott & Costello, or with Universal Studios. But my father was like a stone wall when it came to Christmas. It was *his* time of year.

Christmas shopping was probably the only adventure on which my father would blow more money than he did gambling. He bought for everybody—even people he hadn't met. Christmas parties—every year—at the Costello home were the talk of Hollywood. Everybody stopped by for a few drinks—and a gift. A lot of petty jealousies sprang up. Sitting around the pool or at the bar, strangers mixed with superstars and many of their conversations concerned one question: "Well, what did he give you?" Dad would spend days in the jewelry and department stores—sometimes with my mother, sometimes alone—selecting gifts: dozens of cashmere sweaters in all colors and sizes; gold watches by the gross; and even furs. It was little wonder so many people flocked to our house on Christmas.

Also, there were our decorations. The house looked like downtown Las Vegas, lit up literally like a Christmas tree. Every year there were monumental traffic jams on our block because of the painstaking efforts my father took to be sure we had the best and most completely decorated house in the state.

Nineteen forty-two began for Dad like 1941—with a full work schedule. The entertainment industry was very much involved in the war effort. Clark Gable and Jimmy Stewart were notable early volunteers who shelved their careers for the duration. Bud Abbott was too old for the service. My father had some physical problems. President Roosevelt had other plans for them anyway. Mobilization of troops was only part of winning a war. Morale was of prime importance to the government in building a military force to fight on two fronts when we had precious little military strength at the outset. Abbott & Costello were immediately drafted by the USO and the Armed Forces Radio. Dad wired the President that he would do anything he could for his country.

Meanwhile, Louis B. Mayer, lionized head of MGM Pictures, was festering because Universal had "stolen" Abbott & Costello from under his nose. He always felt that the act belonged to Metro and that he'd been double-crossed by the William Morris Agency. In order to avoid direct conflict whith Louis B. Mayer, who had the clout to sink them, Universal allowed the team to be on loan to the larger studio. Louis B. Mayer didn't believe in giving percentages (which both Universal and Abbott & Costello wanted). Their biggest stars were denied such "outlandish" requests.

It was finally agreed that MGM would pay $300,000, half to Universal and $75,000 each to Abbott & Costello. This would be a picture-by-picture deal. Their first film at MGM, *Rio Rita*, was a remake of a Ziegfeld operetta that had been made into a motion picture at RKO in 1929. Although the reviews were kind to Dad and Bud, the picture (despite MGM's big production values) was not the bonanza their grade-B movies at Universal had been. The chemistry just wasn't good at MGM, where Abbott & Costello were welcomed like distant cousins—at arm's length. Although Dad initially was happy to be finally starring in an MGM picture, I think he was disappointed that his boyhood dream was not, in reality, as big as he had imagined.

MGM built stars on a production-line basis, developing each one by means of a highly calculated process known as the "star system." For Kathryn Grayson, the budding starlet MGM selected to work with Abbott & Costello, *Rio Rita* was just another step along the way to the major stardom she would eventually achieve. Miss Grayson tells us what she recalls most clearly about my father while they worked together on the film:

"I was young and somewhat inexperienced toward film making and it stands out vividly in my mind how much Lou seemed to enjoy being helpful. I'm very grateful to him and thank him to a great extent that it was such a happy film to work on."

The Abbott & Costello contract had been rewritten at Universal. They were now to be paid $150,000 a picture plus twenty percent of the profits. Back from their loan-out to MGM, Dad and Bud went right into *Pardon My Sarong*, which spoofed Dorothy Lamour's South Sea Island films at Paramount. Erle C. Kenton directed, replacing Arthur Lubin, their previous director. Kenton went on to direct three films in a row for Abbott & Costello: *Pardon My Sarong*, *Who Done It?*, and *It Ain't Hay*. He finally accepted other assignments because he felt my father and Bud weren't listening to him and were becoming somewhat bored. Arthur Lubin had left for the same reason. Alex Gottlieb comments about this trend:

"A director is the man who really makes the film *work*. When the actors don't put forth the effort, the director doesn't. I think that's what happened with Bud and Lou. Nevertheless, I feel that

Arthur Lubin and later on Charles Barton were two of the best directors for Abbott & Costello films because each had the ability to translate that comedy to the screen."

When Dad came to Universal Studios, Joe Elias operated a shoe-shine stand at the studio barber shop. They had developed a friendship, and Dad arranged for Joe to have a cigar store and newsstand on the studio lot. Joe had a stiff hip which was increasingly complicated by arthritis. An operation was needed, but there never seemed to be enough money. Dad was going out on the road for six weeks when he found out about it, so he went in to see Joe and pick up some cigars. "Joe," he said, "when I get back I wanna talk to you, okay?" Their conversation is still fresh in Joe Elias' memory:

"Lou came back from the tour, came in to see me and said, 'Have your doctor come and see me. I wanna talk to him.' My doctor was the head of Los Angeles Orthopedic Hospital and a very busy man. I explained that to Lou and then he said, 'I want a breakdown on costs. How much for your operation and hospital costs. I'd like the information by tomorrow.' I got it for him and he immediately phoned Dr. Lowman. When he got off the phone, Lou gave me an order: 'You be at the hospital Tuesday morning for the operation.' "

Not only did Dad pay for the operation and hospitalization, he shamed some of the executives at the studio into giving Joe's wife, Josie, a weekly check to take care of her expenses until Joe was back at his concession stand. My father maintained that support for ten weeks and when Joe came out of the hospital and returned to the studio, Dad bought him a golf cart outfitted with drawers to hold candy, cigars, soft drinks, and gum. Until Joe was able to maintain the concession stand, he used that cart to make his rounds and service the personnel at the studio, right on the sets.

Because of public reaction to *Hold That Ghost*, especially to Dad's incredible display of fright, Abbott & Costello starred in a series of ghost and monster films—always, of course, in hilarious situations. Following *Pardon My Sarong* the boys made *Who Done It?*, a very popular film in which they played a gamut of characters from soda jerks in a New York radio station to angels.

When the film was released, it established Abbott & Costello as the most popular box office attraction in the world, outdistancing all of the superstars at MGM.

Riding a crest, Dad was euphoric because Mom was pregnant again. Although Dad would be happy just to have a live, healthy baby, in his heart he fervently desired a male heir. My parents were not to be disappointed. On November 6, 1942, Mom gave birth to Louis Francis Cristillo, Jr. (who would forever after be known simply as "Butch"). It was a time of great jubilation in the Costello family. A son and a grandson! The Cristillos reacted in typical old-world Italian fashion—they celebrated, partied and toasted until there was not even a fourth cousin left to raise a glass of champagne.

Dad no longer seemed tired. The birth of Butch filled him with renewed vigor. It was the new Lou Costello who heeded President Roosevelt's request to join Bud on a cross-country tour in February 1943 to promote the sale of war bonds. It was to be a grueling tour, covering eighty-five cities in thirty-eight days, often in very bad weather. Bombers flew the troupe from city to city and state troopers sped them to their destinations, where they often performed on makeshift outdoor stages. They put on shows everywhere and in every conceivable situation: in small towns, large cities—always to overflowing crowds.

Uncle Pat was on active duty at the time but was able to accompany Dad on the tour by special permission of the United States Navy. He remembers the trip:

"It was interesting how they raised money. For instance, they'd split the crowd between them. Bud would say, 'Lou, I'll take this side over here. They're respectable people.' Lou would nod. 'Okay, I'll take this group. They're a bunch of crap shooters.' Then they'd proceed to see whose side could raise the most money in bond sales. It was very competitive—not just for the war effort, but between Bud and Lou. A pretty girl would stroll through the audience on each side, accepting pledges. After a few bonds were sold, Bud and Lou would reward the audience with 'Who's on First' or another routine."

At one stop during the bond tour—Omaha, Nebraska—two kids came up to Bud and Dad and asked them if they would do a show in their backyard for the neighborhood. Some official tried to chase the boys away, but Dad said, "Wait a minute. I want to talk to these kids." He turned to them and said, "You know we're here to sell bonds."

"Yes sir," one boy replied, "but don't you sell savings stamps too?"

"I don't know why not," Dad answered. "It's all for the war effort."

"Okay," the youngster said, digging into his pockets. "I've got $1.16 and I'll bet all my friends would pitch in too."

Dad looked at Bud, who nodded. "You got a deal, kid," Dad said. "Just as soon as we finish this show, you be right here and the next show is yours."

The kid must've gone through several neighborhoods collecting other kids and grownups as well, because his backyard was overflowing when Dad and Bud appeared for the show. They collected several hundred dollars—all because one kid had $1.16.

My father was notorious for his practical jokes and he didn't let up during the bond tour. Bud didn't like to fly and he kept insisting that flying once in a while was okay, but that they were pushing their luck with so much airborne time. One time, they were having coffee at the Chicago airport, waiting for a plane to Oklahoma City and Bud started in again about flying. Dad said, "Look, Bud, I'll bet you a hundred bucks that the minute you get on that plane and into your seat, you'll just fall asleep. I guarantee it." Bud reluctantly agreed.

Sure enough, the minute Bud sat down, he fell sound asleep. (Dad had simply slipped a sleeping pill into Bud's coffee.) When they arrived in Oklahoma City, a publicity man was there to meet them. Dad said, "Hey, Abbott's still in the plane, sleeping. Maybe you better go wake him up."

A short while later, when Bud had caught up with my father, he shoved a hundred-dollar bill into his hand. "Well, Lou," he beamed, "you were right. I went to sleep just like that!"

In spite of all the fun and games and working for Mr. Roosevelt, Dad missed his son. The tour finally came to an end on the steps of New York City's City Hall with an official greeting by "The Little Flower," Mayor Fiorello LaGuardia himself. Abbott & Costello had raised over $5 million in bond sales, an astronomical figure in 1943. It was March and extremely cold in New York. Not only had the tour been immensely successful, but their second picture, *It Ain't Hay* (shot before the tour on a very quick schedule), was released simultaneously with the termination of their bond promotion to cash in on all the personal appearances.

When Dad returned to California from the tour, his father went to Union Station in Los Angeles to meet the arriving train. As Dad got off the train, Grandpop held out his hand to shake Dad's. Dad said, "Don't press too hard, Pop. It hurts."

My grandfather was deeply concerned because he knew immediately that my father was out of sorts. Dad said he was just tired from the trip, but my grandfather sensed something far more serious.

Shortly after he got home, Dad's old friend Milt Bronson, who had arrived in Hollywood just prior to the beginning of the tour, came by to welcome him back. Milt took immediate action:

"He was ill and he knew it. I knew it too. He had pains in his leg joints and it pained him to walk. I asked him, 'Lou, what's the matter?' He said, 'My legs, Milt. I hurt all over.' I immediately put him to bed and began applying hot applications to help soothe the pain."

It was always difficult to know when my father was ill, because he wouldn't let on. He absolutely cringed away from doctors, having an almost abnormal fear of anything medical. Yet he never hesitated to suggest that somebody else see one for something so mild as a headache. Mom couldn't imagine what was wrong with him. Consequently there was a lot of apprehension as Mom and Milt ministered to my father while waiting for our family doctor. Those anxieties were well justified.

The Armory Five basketball team. Although small, Lou was a wizard on the courts in his native New Jersey. He is standing on the left.

CAROLE COSTELLO

Lou as boxer "Lou King" in Paterson, New Jersey.

CAROLE COSTELLO

Lou working as a stuntman on MGM's The Trail of '98, *during his first, unsuccessful trip to Hollywood in 1928.*

CAROLE COSTELLO

Lou Costello in his early twenties.

CAROLE COSTELLO

Abbott & Costello appearing with the Andrews Sisters promoting their successful Hold That Ghost *at Atlantic City's world-renowned Steel Pier.*

CAROLE COSTELLO

Lou and Bud during an early appearance on the Kate Smith Hour—*which catapulted them to stardom.*

CAROLE COSTELLO

Lou, Bud and the Andrews Sisters (center) pose with three other cast members of Buck Privates, *their biggest picture ever.* (1941) UNIVERSAL STUDIOS

During a break in the action at Universal Studios, Lou talks with Marlene Dietrich. UNIVERSAL STUDIOS

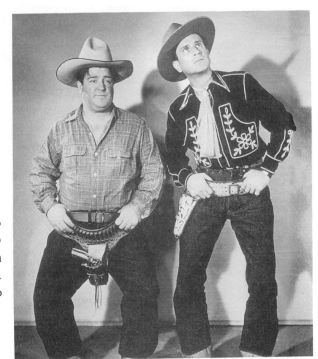

Abbott & Costello ready to saddle up for Ride 'Em Cowboy.

CHRIS COSTELLO

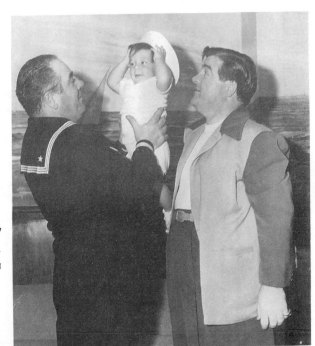

Uncle Pat, baby Butch, and Lou.

MARY FAILLA COLLECTON

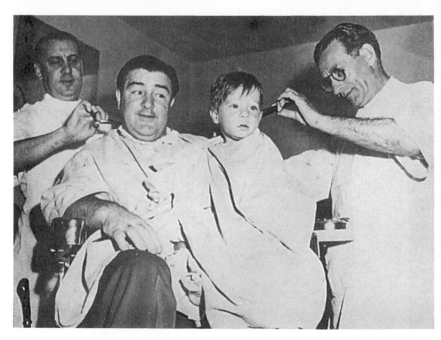

Butch's first haircut, within days of his tragic death.

PRESS ASSOCIATES, INC.

Lou gets Patricia, age five, and Carole Lou, three, into the spirit of Pardon My Sarong, *the latest Abbott & Costello film.*

UNIVERSAL STUDIOS, MARY FAILLA COLLECTION

Paddy, Lou, Anne, and Carole being photographed for publicity purposes in the mid '40s.

CAROLE COSTELLO

Lou and Anne stepping out.

UNIVERSAL PICTURES,
MARY FAILLA COLLECTION

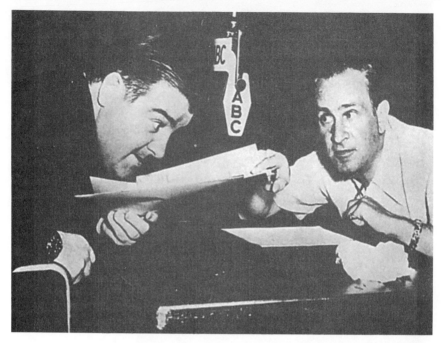

*Lou and Bud ad-libbing their weekly ABC radio show,
the* Abbott & Costello Program, *in the mid '40s.*

JEFF LENBURG COLLECTION

*Bud and Lou with
Leo Durocher and
the gold record of
"Who's on First,"
the first recording
ever to become
enshrined in the
Baseball Hall of
Fame.*

CAROLE COSTELLO

CHAPTER IX

Rheumatic Fever

THE RAPID PACE of life my father had maintained was brought to a halt. He had rheumatic fever and was ordered to bed, where he was to be confined for many months. His recovery was slow. He was a very sick man. I think Mom had ambivalent feelings about Dad's illness. She hated to see any of her family sick for a minute, but she loved having Dad home and being able to wait on him hand and foot—and she did just that.

In spite of the doctor's orders that he should have "quiet and bedrest," Dad found a way to combine convalescence with pleasure. Every night Mom gave him alcohol rubdowns to keep his body toned. One night Dorothy DiMaggio, Joe's wife, was over for a visit. Mom had just finished her routine. Dad, with a sheet over him, kept scratching his leg. He said, "Dorothy, I've got something on my leg and I don't know what it is." Dorothy looked askance at Mom.

"Let me see, Lou," Mom said, moving closer.

"Wait a minute," Dorothy said, "you can't see that way. Here, let me try." She bent down and lit a match to see closer. It was on the inside of his thigh. She got too close and accidentally burned a lot of the hair on his leg. Dad jumped straight up in bed, grinning from ear to ear. "How do you like that? Sonofabitch! She comes over to visit and tries to burn me up."

Dorothy looked at him deadpan and said, "It was the only light I had. Maybe if you'd learn to light your cigar with a flashlight, you wouldn't have these kind of problems." Dad did a pratfall right in the middle of the bed.

Some moments during his recovery were happy, some sad. Dad wasn't really worried about motion pictures because Abbott & Costello were still before the public. Another quickie had been shot (before Dad got sick) almost simultaneously with *It Ain't Hay*, called *Hit the Ice*. Every theater in the country wanted their films. Their pictures played neighborhood theaters for weeks at a time and in the big houses, often for months. Of course the radio show didn't work without Dad. Bud tried working with some other comedians, but the listeners wanted Dad. It had to be shelved while he was ill.

Alex Gottlieb, Abbott & Costello's producer, decided it was the right time for Dad to start looking for something else to do. He had wanted to do "other kinds of films" for some time and so it seemed that the circumstances called for him to make the move.

Alex, of course, was one of his frequent visitors once the okay was given (Dad had visitors without permission, ignoring the doctor's advice). Gottlieb's memories of Mom and my father are warm ones:

"I was crazy about Anne Costello and thought she was a darling woman. Even after I went to Warner Brothers, I kept in touch with Lou and visited the Longridge house. Sometimes we went out to dinner together. Anne was devoted to the man. I once asked her, "How do you put up with some of the capers Lou pulls?' She smiled and, in the sweetest tone, said, 'Because I love him, Alex.' I don't think she was ever jealous or had reason to be, except that Lou clowned around with the girls a lot. He enjoyed joking around with them and embarrassing the hell out of them—just for laughs. I think that was a carryover from his burlesque days. I don't think he ever cheated on Anne, but he could sure talk up a good situation."

Even the gambling and the money my father gave away were eccentricities that Mom accepted. Occasionally he'd raise his voice to my mother, but she never once criticized him in public. If she ever did at all, it was in the privacy of their bedroom. He hated to be interrupted or to be given an unsolicited opinion. One time Mom spoke up and Dad bluntly said, "Nobody asked you, Anne." That's all he said, but she was deeply hurt. He never knew that because she kept it to herself.

During his illness Dad had an opportunity to enjoy the mansion he had built. It was an amazing event, that house. Dad never stopped building on to it, adding another deck here or a new bath there. Our backyard was like Central Park. Anytime a visitor stopped by and hadn't been there for a month or so, Dad would proudly show off some new addition to the structure or grounds. One time, Alex Gottlieb was being shown some innovation and he asked Dad: "Lou, what do you need all these rooms for?"

Like a little boy showing off a new toy, he said, "I wanna big house, Alex."

Alex looked around, smiling, and turned back to my father. "You've got a big house, Lou!"

The carpenters in the crafts shops at Universal designed and constructed a special bed for my father that could be wheeled outside next to Butch's playpen in the patio area. The greatest joy in his life was having that bed lowered to ground level so he could reach out and play finger games with his son. Butch was truly "Daddy's boy," because every possible moment of the day he could be with his son, Dad was. He knew every finger movement, every whimper—and what they meant. As Butch started to crawl, Dad would get out of bed and crawl around on the patio with him, he too on his hands and knees. It was as though they were learning together how to crawl and then to walk.

Dad's illness seemed to bring the Abbott & Costello families closer together. Socially Dad had always been closer to Bud's brother, Harry, than to Bud. He was very fond of Harry. During the months he was away from work, Bud's sister Olive also became a frequent visitor—she lived nearby. She could see how difficult it was for my father to stay down:

"It was an emotionally and physically trying time for Lou. He was always such an active man and to be told he must lie flat on his back for months was very frustrating. I remember when he was finally able to move around in a wheel chair—he rode all over the house and *always* had a smile and a lot of optimism. 'I'm gonna beat this,' he'd say. 'Just watch my speed.' I never saw him display self-pity or depression over his illness. He was always joking around. Bud, Harry, myself, and my sister Babe often went up together to see him. Lou idolized Babe. When they were doing the Kate Smith show, Babe would sit in the audience, howling at their routines. Lou loved her laugh. One night he stopped in the middle of a joke and said, 'I gotta hire this girl.' Babe was very uncomplicated and Lou liked that. She was good for his morale."

Joe Elias and his wife, Josie, were frequent visitors during my father's convalesence. Dad was on a strict diet and was not allowed to eat many of his favorite foods. He loved candy but was not allowed to have anything with even a trace of salt in it. Joe kept him supplied with chocolates, especially Hershey's chocolate bars, his favorites. After he returned to work, months later, he went into Joe's concession stand and asked Josie, "How many pounds of chocolate would you say Joe brought up to the house when I was sick?"

"Gosh, Lou," she replied, "I really don't recall, but it must have been quite a bit."

"I thought so," he said. He walked straight to the candy section and bought up all the boxes of candy in stock, paid for them, and gave Josie a hefty tip. As he started to leave he said, "I know a lot of sick kids who like candy."

Close friends never had to knock at our house. It was a sign that you were considered part of the family when Dad said, "You know you don't have to knock. If we're not home, make yourself comfortable. Somebody'll be home soon." Joe and Josie Elias were considered in that family circle of close friends. Joe says:

"We always felt comfortable at Lou's house. I had the opportunity of being a guest at Bud Abbott's and other stars' homes, but it was never like Lou's. It was the way Anne and Lou talked with us. They never put on fancy or phony airs; both were very ordinary down-to-earth people."

Everything possible was done to make our home easy for my father to get around in once he was able to manipulate a wheel chair. Before his illness, through Associated Press photographer Frank Worth, Dad met Mac Brainard. Mac was an inventor and after a guided tour of his home (which included such finger-touch operations as putting a finger on a certain date on a wall calendar to make the linen closet swing open), my father asked Mac to install some of his gadgetry in our Longridge home. Mac remembers the boyish enthusiasm of my father:

"First of all, Lou's home was magnificent. When you walked in through the front door, to the left was the large formal living room, all in a cream satin decor. The family lived more in the den, which had an enormous bar and room for informal getting together. The home was unbelievable in its magnificence. Lou's train in the back of the house ran around the entire property with tunnels, lakes and streams (with live fish), doll houses, basketball and tennis courts, pool, and beautiful bird aviary. Everything was exquisite.

"Lou wanted dozens of my inventions installed and gave me carte blanche authority to rip out paneling or anything else that was needed to accomplish his desires. Anne would see me coming and pack the children into her car and take off for Palm Springs until I was out of the house. One of the first things we put in was a 'light organ.' Then we installed fluorescent lights behind the paneling where Lou had nautical wall scenes. That was connected to the radio which, when turned on, caused the lights to flash on and off. It was a very inventive idea of the times. Now it is more commonplace.

"One room had huge closets on both sides. I removed the doors and put in bookshelves. The shelves were filled with hollow-bound books that weighed very little. I then took an 8" x 10" photo of Lou and set it up on a table next to the bookshelves. When you put your finger on Lou's nose in the picture, the bookcases opened up to reveal the clothes closet. Lou played with these innovations like a kid with a new erector set. It was delightful just to watch the expressions on his face."

Mac also installed a complete alarm system throughout the house and property. It was set up so that if even one relay was broken a bell would ring. For instance, if a plate on a table were sensitized the mere laying of a hand against it would set off the alarm. A few nights after the complete system had been installed, Mac received a call from my father at four A.M. The alarm system had gone off and Dad couldn't get the bells to stop ringing. The whole neighborhood was awake. When Mac arrived, the police were not far behind. What had happened was this: It was a damp night and since the whole idea worked with the presence of a body (which is ninety-eight percent water) the system was very sensitive to water. Dad had been prepared for the worst. Mac found him in his robe, sitting in a chair with a shotgun lying across his lap. Not only were the bells ringing, but lights were flashing all over the place. Mac had to disconnect the system and later adjust it so it wasn't quite so sensitive. Mac shook his head remembering how Dad was with a buck:

"He always carried a large wad of bills in his pocket and when he wanted something new built he'd pull out his roll of bills and ask, 'How much will it cost, Mac?' I never charged him for my time—only the labor I hired and the parts. I enjoyed seeing him get such a kick out of it. But there he was, peeling off hundred-dollar bills and I'd be yelling, 'Hold it Lou! Wait a minute! It's not that much!' Lou wanted to set me up with my own lab, but I passed on that because I saw how people took advantage of him and I didn't ever want to be put in a position where my motives might be questioned."

Dad was always backing somebody in some kind of new invention. Few of them ever got off the ground.

While Dad was recovering, there was one affront he never got over. Dad had always believed in Dean Martin's talent and helped promote his career when Dean was just a nightclub performer in the East. He had gone so far as to pay for Dean Martin's getting a "nose job." Dean had no money of his own at the time. Dad said, "Don't worry about the money. You can pay me back some day when you have it." Dad never worried about money. But he worried about Dean not visiting him while he was ill. Throughout all the long months when Dad was confined, not one time did Dean come and visit him or call and ask how he was doing. It wasn't because he had done Dean favors, it was because he genuinely liked Dean and thought he was a dear friend. He never did get over that.

Dad learned that a lot of people he thought were friends were merely the sunshine variety. That's not to say the hangers-on evacuated. It was only during those periods when he was in so much pain and the house had to be kept absolutely quiet that the house was void of outsiders. There were times when legitimate visitors couldn't get through the pool and bar area because of the free-loaders. Although he had around-the-clock nursing, my mother insisted on doing everything herself when she was awake. She wanted to be near him, to make sure he wasn't bothered. She always said, "If he needs me, I want to be there."

No matter how many times the family was told that Dad must have quiet, they came. Especially his family. He could hear people talking and would say, "Oh, come on, Anne, send them in. It'll make me feel better." And they didn't just come to visit. Friends and family alike—one needed this and another wanted that. The fact that he wasn't working didn't seem to concern any of them—and certainly not him. Mom just shook her head and made notes, carrying out my father's orders to the letter.

It was a trying time for both my parents and if ever there was need to prove their love for one another, that proof was magnified during Dad's illness. Love conquered all.

As he started feeling better, Dad began to resume his screenings of motion pictures for friends and family. His bed was wheeled into the theater and someone would operate the projector for him. One night he phoned Dorothy DiMaggio and said, "I want you and Joe to come over tonight. I have a big surprise for you." When they arrived, they discovered that Dad had gotten hold of a copy of a film that had featured Dorothy during her acting days, before she was married to the baseball star. It was quite a surprise and Dad was delighted that he had caught them flat-footed with his little scenario.

Nick Condos and Martha Raye (who had married while Martha was appearing in *Keep 'Em Flying*) were often invited to screenings, as were Patti, Maxene and LaVerne—the Andrews Sisters. Dad remained close friends with the sisters after their three films together—and also with their parents. He'd often pick up the phone and invite them over for a big barbecue. "Bring your folks too," he'd urge, "and any friends you may have as guests. We always got room for a few more." Maxene describes Dad's understanding of a traveling trio:

"He was overly generous in opening his home to people. We always got along so well because Lou was such a family man, a real Italian family man who loved his home and entertaining in his home. Since our parents traveled with us, he was always glad to see them sit down to dinner and relax with us. He treated us like old friends from back home. We loved Lou and Anne."

Dad began to take up (slowly, by my mother's insistence) other activities. The first outside venture was with his train. He and David Rose would get together in our backyard and play trains. My sister Carole delighted in upsetting their efforts:

"I used to sabotage the train everytime it went under the tunnel and it would wind up jumping the rails and tipping over. Dad would get so irritated trying to find out why. He and David would have the butler help get it back on the track and start over. Each time the train reached that certain spot, it would tip over again. Meanwhile, I was hiding in the bushes, my hand over my mouth to stifle uncontrollable giggles. After a while I'd walk up to Dad and say, 'Watch. I'll fix it.' After removing the object of derailment (with Dad and Mr. Rose watching), I'd climb into the cab and ride around the track. Dad and Mr. Rose stood with puzzled expressions as I rode around the property with the greatest of ease. When the train came to a halt, Dad would be waiting. 'I can't understand it!' he once commented. I looked up at him, grinning and said, 'I'm just a mental giant, Dad.' He loved such foolishness."

As summer began to pass, Dad became anxious. He wanted to be back at work. But Dr. Kovner wasn't ready to release him and warned that taking on too much activity could result in a relapse, causing serious damage to the heart valves. Dad had difficulty accepting that prognosis. "Look," he complained, "I feel great. I've never felt better in my life. And well I should. I've been in bed almost as long as Rip Van Winkle." It was a difficult task to keep Dad away from the studio or the radio station. Inevitably he'd have to be accommodated.

Dad would spend hours with Paddy and Carole, asking questions, telling jokes—loving them. He liked to find out about their lives and had a way of getting out of them all the naughty little things they did or how they got around my mother's rules. Carole enjoyed discussing the movie stars who came to visit our house. Clark Gable was her favorite. She had a real crush on him (and later on Errol Flynn). She somehow never thought of them as stars—just visitors—and had the good taste to pick only stars as her heroes. She always wanted Gable to come up and kiss her goodnight if he stayed until her bedtime. One time Gable brought actress Veronica Lake to the house for dinner. Carole was in the kitchen when the cooks were carving the turkey. Even as a kid she loved to eat the crunchy skin, and as she reached for a piece of the skin, Veronica walked in, slapped her hand and said, "Don't do that!"

Carole, rebellious child that she was, looked at her and said bluntly, "It's my house!" Veronica slapped her hand again. Carole gave her a defiant look and suddenly kicked her in the shins. She then ran out of the kitchen and went tearing up the stairs to her room, certain Mom would be up shortly to really give it to her. Instead, a few minutes later, Clark Gable peeked his head in the door, smiled and winked and said, "Good work."

My father delighted in hearing such stories. Mom took a less enthusiastic view. One of her favorite expressions when one of the girls committed a no-no was, "Well, it won't be long before they'll be at Marymount and the good sisters will straighten them out."

That didn't stop Carole. One afternoon when Mom was having some ladies over for brunch, the dining room table was piled high with all sorts of goodies. Carole kept peeping over the table edge, staring at the donuts. Mom said, "Carole, don't touch the food."

"I won't, Mama."

"I mean it, Carole."

"Yes, ma'am." Mom walked out of the room and Carole quickly reached over and grabbed a donut. Just as she bit into it, the front door bell rang and she went to answer. Reaching up to turn the knob, she opened the door and there standing in full uniform was a policeman. Carole threw the donut on the floor and started screaming and crying. "I'll never do it again. I promise. I'll *never* do it again."

Mom ran into the hallway and looked at the policeman and then at Carole in hysterics. The policeman, a friend of the family, said, "Anne, I swear . . . I didn't even touch her!"

When my older sisters were small, Mom also threatened them with sending them away to reform school if they were bad. One time on the train during a trip back East, Mom warned that if one of them disobeyed she'd "just have to sell you to the Indians in Albuquerque." As a result, Carole couldn't be pulled off the train at Albuquerque. Mom was so serious Carole believed she'd actually sell her to the Navajos. Or worse, trade her for a blanket.

Paddy, on the other hand, seemed (to Carole at least) to get away with murder. But she always took up for Carole. Whenever Mom would threaten Carole with sending her to reform school, Paddy would say, "No, Mom. Don't send her. She's too little. Take me."

Carole, hiding behind Paddy, would speak up and say, "Yeah, send *her*, Mom."

Carole seemed not to ever be able to avoid trouble—and it always got her into hot water with Mom. Mom, who was one of the founders of SHARE, a Hollywood charitable organization, used to have meetings at the Longridge house with the SHARE people. One time, Mitch (our butler) had laid some mouse traps in the attic and Carole went up to see if any mice had been caught. Sure enough, she found one and proceeded to take it down to show Mom and the other women. She walked into the large den, where the women were assembled, holding up a squeaking, bloody mouse and announced: "Look what I found!" Needless to say the women scattered in every direction and Carole was in trouble again.

My father lovingly listened to his daughters relate these childhood capers, with Mom—very much a wife and mother during the summer and fall of 1943—shaking her head in despair. Dad would say, "Oh, come on, Anne, it's not that bad. It's all part of growing up." Later on, when the boys started coming around, it was my father who became the tyrant. No greasy-headed hot-rodder was going to defile one of his daughters.

If my father was dominant in his relationship with my mother, my grandmother Cristillo exerted a strong influence over him—all her life. There are those in our family who believe my father lived his entire life to please his mother. When he was really too ill to be out, he'd get up each day and drive down to his mother's house just so he could show her that he wasn't sick. It was a family joke how Grandma faked high blood pressure attacks when Dad didn't visit her every day. She'd even have her doctor call Dad and ask him to stop by, "just to make her feel better."

My grandfather spoiled Grandma rotten. It's the only word to use, because he did. He was a lovely man. He did the cooking for the family and was great. My grandmother, a woman born in the late 1800s, when women were expected to do everything, couldn't cook, couldn't sew or do much of anything else. Grandpa occasionally would get angry when she did something particularly selfish, but he took a lot from her before he reached his boiling point. My father never did know how to stand up to his mother.

Carole used to get on her bike on Sunday mornings and start for church, eventually arriving at my grandparents' house on Coldwater Canyon. She could never let Grandma know she hadn't been to church, because there would have been an all-day lecture. Yet, she always told Grandpa. He'd take her by the hand, sit down with her in the breakfast nook, and make coffee for her with lots of milk.

Aunt Marie, who had (and still has) a marvelous singing voice, was once asked to join the Modernaires, the singing group who became famous with the Glenn Miller Orchestra. My grandmother was so incensed, she laid down an ultimatum she never intended to keep, but it served its purpose. "Marie," she said, "I have one child in show business and that's enough! If you go, I'll leave your father!" First of all, she never would've left Grandpa, because in spite of her being so indulged, the two of them truly loved each other. But the threat worked and Marie did not become a Modernaire.

Grandma was forever telling Mom what to do while Dad was confined. Mom used to joke about it, after a particularly trying encounter with her. "You know," she'd laugh, "that woman will never die—they'll have to shoot her!"

Nevertheless, Dad continued to improve and was finally given the okay to start rehearsals to reinaugurate the Abbott & Costello radio show.

It was November and Butch would be a year old on the sixth. Dad told everybody who would listen, "You know, my son and I kind of grew up together this year. He's gonna have one hellova first birthday party. It's gonna be a party we can share together, because I'm celebrating getting back in harness. It's a good feeling."

CHAPTER X

Tragedy

THE COSTELLO HOUSEHOLD was in a festive mood. Dad, recovered from his long seige with rheumatic fever, was about to resume being an active part of Abbott & Costello. It was his first day back at work and the Abbott & Costello radio show was going on the air that night live, for the first time since the onset of Dad's illness. Add to that the fact it was November 4, 1943—only two more days until my brother Butch's first birthday.

Everything at the studio during rehearsals was normal. Dad was clowning around with the crew. The show, sponsored by Camel cigarettes, would air at seven P.M. PST, making it a ten to ten-thirty P.M. airing on the East Coast due to the three-hour time difference. They were all there for the rehearsal: Ken Niles, the announcer; Connie Haines, who had always been the regular vocalist on the show; along with the Freddie Rich Orchestra. The special guest for the evening was glamorous movie star Lana Turner.

Dad got up early that morning, joking and making light of the most serious problems, as he always did when he was feeling good. His outlook on the future was bright and he had every reason to be happy. His parting words to my mother as he left the house were, "Anne, keep Butch up tonight, because I want to see if he'll recognize my voice over the air."

Mitch, our butler, had driven Dad to the NBC studios in Hollywood. There was no reason for anyone to remotely suspect that, in spite of the warm Indian summer weather, it would be a day of such awesome tragedy. The Costello star was on a true course to even more spectacular altitudes. Who would dream that within hours it would come hurtling back to earth in such a devastating fashion? But it did.

Miss Feather, Butch's nurse, had the day off and Mother was caring for the baby herself. After Dad left for the studio, she gave Butch his bath and placed him in the playpen outside, which was the usual thing to do because he loved to look at the pool. Ophelia Watson, the maid (who was also Mitch's wife), was at the house as was Dad's new secretary, Marty Kertz (later Uncle Pat's wife), and of course Mom.

With Butch's first birthday coming up in a couple of days, Mom went over to Babytown in Studio City to pick up a new stroller she'd ordered for the occasion.

Marty, who had worked for Dad only a short time, was not familiar with the household routines, the baby, or household staff duties. She was there primarily to work, not to babysit. So she went back into the house to take care of some secretarial chores for Dad. However, she had stayed outside with Butch for half an hour playing with him and watching as he scooted across the playpen. She remembers that he was ". . . still in the crawling stage and would go lickety split across the pen. He was quite spirited."

Ophelia was busy with her household chores and Mitch had of course gone with my father. Most people with any knowledge of our family and Butch's habits agreed that he was fascinated with watching the leaves fall from the trees onto the glassy surface of the pool. The last time anyone remembered seeing Butch alive was through the kitchen window. Ophelia had prepared lunch and Marty, after having a bite to eat in the kitchen, looked out into the yard and remembers seeing Butch playing, dressed in a white shirt and blue shorts—obviously enjoying himself.

Ophelia later drove over to Brentwood to pick up my sisters Carole and Paddy at Marymount Junior School. Marty continued taking care of her secretarial work. Butch was still in the playpen near the pool.

Marty and Butch were the only ones at the house for a spell until Mom returned with the stroller. Marty, working in Dad's office, didn't know she was the only adult in the house. When Mom came in with the stroller, she asked Marty to help her assemble it. Their task completed, Marty suggested getting Butch so he could try it out.

Butch was not in the playpen. Marty immediately ran to the

pool, but saw no trace of Butch. Marty says, "I remember that vividly, because the filter had been turned off and the water was smooth and crystal clear. The bottom was clearly visible the length of the pool. Butch simply was not there."

Trying to hold back approaching panic, Marty yelled back to the house, "Anne, the baby's not here."

"Oh, my God!" Mom yelled back, "The pool! Marty, check the pool!"

Once again Marty went to the pool and scanned the length of it. She saw no trace of Butch. Quickly running her eyes across the yard she still saw nothing and raced into the house to be with Mom. "He's not in the pool, Anne, and I can't find him in the yard."

"Maybe Ophelia put him down for his nap before she left," Mom said, and together she and Marty raced each other up the stairs to the nursery. They found the crib empty. Mom led the way as they ran back down the stairs and out into the yard to the playpen. Mom continued on to the pool and Marty, by the playpen, heard the blood-curdling scream and the resounding splash as Mom jumped into the pool fully clothed. By the time Marty reached the pool's edge, Mom was clambering out of the shallow end with little Butch's inert form cuddled in her arms. Mom was caught up in shock, hysteria, tears, and an expression on her face of total incomprehension.

Mom stood in the backyard, silently rocking the baby back and forth in her arms as Marty rushed into the house and phoned the fire department, then hurried back outside, took the baby from Mom's arms and began giving him mouth to mouth resuscitation. A next-door neighbor had been hanging out drapes and saw what was happening. He immediately came over and said, "I've had experience with this. Let me help." He took over and began working on my brother.

Within minutes panic was replaced by the special kind of chaos that follows tragedy. The fire department's rescue unit arrived, followed by Dr. Kovner, our family doctor. Every effort was made to revive Butch—all to no avail. At five P.M. Anne and Lou Costello's son was pronounced dead.

By this time Aunt Marie and Dad's mother and father were there, and out of all the tears and confusion, it was Aunt Marie who prevailed with some sense of duty. My mother, in shock, sat surrounded by women, silent tears trickling down her cheeks and splashing onto her dress, her fumbling fingers catatonically clinging to her rosary beads.

Dr. Kovner, also wet-eyed, stood by the fireplace in the den. Marie did not yet know the baby was dead. She walked over to where the doctor was standing and asked, "Is the baby okay?" "The baby is gone, Marie." His voice broke. "How do we tell Lou?" It was a task he obviously did not relish or want. "Would you . . .?"

"I'll call him," Marie said unsteadily. "But— My God, how can I tell him a thing like that?"

Out of the sea of faces a voice spoke up: "Well, it has to be done!"

Dad's father went outside by the pool, where the baby's body was still lying, waiting for someone to make a decision as to what to do in the aftermath of so much turmoil. Marie looked out the window. Sadness overcame her as she watched her father pacing back and forth, hands clasped behind his back, head slowly moving from side to side in disbelief. She would now have to tell Lou. She hoped God would give her the strength not to cry.

When she phoned NBC studios, her instincts warned her not to talk to Dad directly. She knew he was just barely on his feet from his long illness and any sudden shock might cause him to have a heart attack. She didn't want that on her conscience. So she asked for Eddie Sherman, the team's agent and manager.

"Eddie, this is Marie. You'd better bring Lou home."

Almost by instinct he responded, "Is it Butch?"

"Yes, Eddie, it is."

Eddie hung up the phone, got Dad's coat and quickly ushered him out to the car. I don't think he ever told Dad what had happened, because when they arrived at the house and Dad walked into the den, he went straight to Dr. Kovner, who still had tears in his eyes. Dad mumbled, "Butch?"

The doctor bit his lip fighting back tears, reached out and squeezed Dad's hand hard. "I'm sorry, Lou. It was too late. I'm so sorry."

Dad went directly to his office and was accompanied by Harry Abbott, my grandfather, and Eddie Sherman. Dad closed the door behind him once they were all inside the office. Nobody is certain what went on inside during the time they were there, but in no time the phones began ringing off the wall. Every top name in show business was offering to take over for Dad that night on the radio show. Mickey Rooney and Lana Turner were two of the first to offer whatever help they could.

Dad finally summoned Aunt Marie to the office. He said, "Call NBC, Marie, and tell them I'll be doing the show as scheduled."

"But Lou . . ." she stammered.

He cut in, "Just do it, Marie. I asked Anne to keep that baby up tonight to see if he would be able to recognize my voice, and wherever God has taken my little boy, I want him to hear it."

Mitch had returned with Dad and went immediately outside, where the baby lay on the pavement at the shallow end of the pool. Mitch gently took off his new coat (Dad had recently purchased it for him) and with great tenderness covered the baby.

By now investigators were trampling all over the premises and nobody seemed to be in charge of anything. One of the detectives grabbed Mitch by the arm and harshly said, "Hey, you can't touch the body until the coroner arrives. Nobody touches nothing until the coroner gets here."

Mitch, grief etched into his facial features, still bowed over the spot where Butch lay and without turning to look at the investigator said, "I don't care who's coming. This baby is cold and I'm gonna cover him up!" Noticing a tiny white sock that had slipped off the baby's foot, Mitch reached out to pick it up. He numbly caressed it in his big hand.

Another detective brusquely accosted Aunt Marie and she was startled as he bluntly blurted out, "Could you help us on one thing?"

Marie said, "I'll try."

"Could there have been any reason for foul play?"

Marie, stunned, hurt, and instantly filled with anger, said, "Who? Who would even think of doing a thing like that? Foul play? Lou doesn't have an enemy in the world. Who would do such a thing?" She turned away from the man who proceeded about his business.

The house was rapidly filling up with friends and relatives as the news of Butch's death reached more people. Ophelia returned from picking up Paddy and Carole at school and was near a state of collapse when told what had happened during her absence. Carole went to Mom, who was still sitting in the same chair with people around her—crying hard now. At five years of age Carole didn't totally comprehend what was wrong, but she hugged Mom and said, "I'll be your baby, Momma." It touched Mom so deeply that she sobbed even harder and was nearing hysteria when some of the women helped her out of the room into seclusion. Carole, wondering what she had said to cause such an outburst, said, tears starting to cascade down her own cheeks, "I just wanted Momma to know I'll be here with her." There were no dry eyes in the room.

Paddy, on the other hand, went directly to her room. At the top of the stairs she paused and looked out the windows that overlooked the pool and patio area. Seeing all the people milling about she—(as she has since described her actions)—". . . almost by instinct went to my blackboard and began drawing a tombstone. Afterward I went back to the window and saw some men carrying a small box out to a car."

Everybody who had been at the house before the accident was questioned. Ophelia defended my mother. "Anne never would have put that baby outside in the playpen if she thought he'd have gotten out. Never! I think the baby shook the playpen loose at the corner where the little hooks held it together." She explained that it had been his habit to shake the crib when put down to sleep; it created a rocking motion that helped him fall asleep." The investigators did discover that one of the hooks was loose.

Nevertheless, there was a lot of confusion. Why couldn't the baby be found when Marty first raced outside to look for him? Why were there no scuff marks on his knees since he would've had to crawl across the concrete apron around the pool to reach the water? Members of the household who were at the funeral home that evening making arrangements noticed this oddity and commented about it.

I suppose all of this was taken into consideration when the investigation was completed and the coroner's report filed, because the official statement following an autopsy was simply inked in: Death caused by . . . drowning.

During the days that followed, even after the funeral, Mom had the women of the family with her, and Dad's very close friend, Milt Bronson, hardly ever left his side. In the interim things had to be done. Life went on. My father did the Abbott & Costello radio show that night. At the end of the show, Bud Abbott, choking back his own personal grief over our family tragedy, stepped before the microphones at the NBC studio and addressed the audience, both in the room and all over the country. "Thank you, Ken [the show's announcer]. Ladies and gentlemen, now that our program is over and we have done our best to entertain you, I would like to take a moment to pay tribute to my best friend and to a man who has more courage than I have ever seen displayed in the theater. Tonight, the old expression 'The show must go on,' was brought home to all of us on this program more clearly than ever before. Just a short time before our broadcast started, Lou Costello was told that his baby son—who would have been one year old in a couple of days—had died.

"In the face of the greatest tragedy which can come to any man, Lou Costello went on tonight. . . . so that, you, the radio audience, would not be disappointed. There is nothing more that I can say except that I know you all join me in expressing our deepest sympathy to a great trouper. Good night."

That was not only an announcement to the world that there had been a tragedy in our life, but a great tribute to the man my father was—a man who knew and understood his responsibilities and discharged them although it broke his heart to do so.

Among others, Milt Bronson accompanied Dad back to the house from the studio. The minute the show was over, he was taken to the car, protected by studio security from the mob at the artists' entrance seeking photos and autographs. Hustled into the waiting car, he collapsed in the back seat. At the house Dad was given a sedative and put to bed. He'd handled more in one day than most men face in years.

Nobody recalls that Mom and Dad saw much of each other that day or that there was any embracing and words of comfort. Each had their own thoughts and their own way of expressing them. The next few days would set the tone that would eventually split our family and for all practical purposes sound the death knell to the warmth that had always existed between Mom and Dad.

The rosary for Butch was held the following night at Steen's Mortuary in North Hollywood. Mother brought with her a pair of shoes—they would have been Butch's first pair of hard-soled shoes. With the tenderness of mothers throughout the ages, she slipped them onto his tiny feet in the open casket. Over and over again she kept tying and untying the shoe laces, each time repeating through her tears and exhaustion, "This one was always my little angel."

Mother was all but ignored from the moment my father arrived home that fatal day until after the funeral. Dad's mother, at one point, said to Mother: "Why did you allow my son's boy to die? What have you done to my grandson?" In her eyes my mother didn't count, only my father and his male heir. It was cold and cruel, but Mom must've gotten a lot of that attitude from certain members of my father's family over the years and learned to live with it—as long as she had Dad on her side. Now even he seemed to have deserted her. At a time when they should've been closely united in a common loss, they were not.

The funeral was held on what would've been Butch's first birthday at St. Francis de Sales Church in Sherman Oaks. Both my grandmothers had been given tranquilizing shots. Aunt Marie, still the strong one, walked into the church with my parents, one on each arm. Dad used a cane. He'd been walking with it as a part of his rehabilitation from rheumatic fever and seemed now to lean on it for much more than that. Mom and Dad still were not communicating with each other. Aunt Marie sat between them during the funeral. She recalls, "Things were just so tense. There was so much emotion. I expected either or both of them to really crack at some point. It wasn't right."

Dad shook with hurt, not even bothering to take a dry handkerchief to the constant flow of silent tears that ran endlessly down his chubby cheeks. He was engulfed with emotion, like a little boy who had just discovered the *real* Santa Claus on Christmas Eve, who had been forced before his time to accept adult values, who had kissed childhood good-bye. Mother, as she had done from the beginning, took solace in her rosary throughout the service. Father Burbage spoke from the altar:

"God realized that Mr. and Mrs. Costello had everything as far as money and fame. He knew that they were good people. He chose to take their only son and make him an angel."

With those words of comfort, a change took place in my father. He lifted his head, sat up erect in the pew, and was apparently interested in what was going on for the first time. The words of the priest seemed to be what he needed to help him shed his feelings of guilt. My father did not accompany Butch to his final resting place at Calvary Cemetery. Wisely, he was taken home and put to bed, where he collapsed from exhaustion. Mom took over the task of taking that last ride behind Butch to East Los Angeles, where he was laid to rest in the mausoleum.

I doubt that Mother went home and drowned her sorrows in a bottle that night, but nobody would've blamed her. Butch was *her* son too, she loved him like life itself. Actually Mom was a lot closer to Butch than Dad was, although Dad, being the total Italian father, got all the publicity. Friends and family *always* spoke of Dad and Butch, but seldom of Mom and the baby.

It was totally unfair for anybody, much less my father, to cast any shadows over my mother's care and attention of her baby. Her whole life was wrapped up in her family and making us comfortable and happy—especially my father. His contentment was paramount in everything she did. She was given a black mark as a mother because of what happened to Butch—a mark that grew from family gossip, was picked up by friends, and after a while became legend—a totally false one. It eventually became too much for my parents to handle, although no one remembers specifically any arguments they had about it.

After his son's death, my father gave vent to outbursts of anger and temperament that had never previously been part of his personality. It was really a shame that all through the biggest years of his career he was emotionally nettled by the reality of not having a son to carry on his name. In traditional Italian families *name* is as important as *family*. It would be a while yet, but my birth would further emphasize the percentages of Dad's not ever having a male heir. I think he took Butch's death so seriously, it clouded everything else he did for the rest of his life.

CHAPTER XI

Aftermath

THERE IS A BEGINNING, a middle, and an end to a career. Dad had his beginning, and the second half would never have the glitter the first half had. Oh, Abbott & Costello went on to make films and their films made money, but not as much money as their early ones. They would go on to years more of radio and television—and even Las Vegas—but my father lost a lot of his lust for life when Butch died. Everybody around my father could see the difference, from family to set workers at the studio. One of the reasons our entire family was incensed when the book *Bud and Lou,* and the subsequent TV movie made from that book reached the public, was because it represented the characterization that was only a part of my father's life—*following the drowning of his son.*

His manager, Eddie Sherman, practically dictated that book. He'd first gone to the well-known writer and editor, Leo Guild. Mr. Guild turned Eddie down because there was too little money involved in the project. Eddie then went to the William Morris Agency and through them obtained the services of writer Bob Thomas. Eddie denegrated the relationship he had with my father and destroyed, in my opinion, whatever integrity he had left as a human being. So much for Mr. Sherman at this point.

Although there was never a blunt statement, I know my father blamed my mother for the baby's death. He agonized over his feelings because he truly loved my mother. I believe the feelings of love mingled with those of suspicion actually shortened his life, which, from then on, became a Jekyll-and-Hyde existence.

It is important to hear what others have to say in retrospect about the feelings my father had about my mother, the baby's death, and himself. Howard Christie, assistant director and producer on many of the Abbott & Costello films, recalls:

> "For years following the baby's death, Lou wore a bracelet that was welded together so that it would remain a permanent reminder of Butch, whose name was engraved on it. Even in scenes where no jewelry should've been worn, he refused to take it off. Makeup men taped or camouflaged it. That's an example of the depth of his sorrow."

Bernie Sheldon, a boyhood friend who often was a guest in our home when he was in Hollywood on leave from the Navy, saw the change in my father:

> "The baby's death knocked the hell out of Lou. It knocked the hell out of all of us. But Lou changed as a man. It seemed that with the baby's death he was zapped of all inner life and purpose to go on. I don't think he could've cared if the world had turned to ashes."

Connie Haines who, for four years, was the singer on the Abbott & Costello radio show, also saw the change:

> "A side of Lou emerged which I'd never seen before. At the time I wasn't sure whether it was the baby's death and his sorrow that caused him to slightly change, but in some ways—not all of the time, but occasionally—there developed an almost sadistic cruelty in his humor toward Bud Abbott. I was so shy I didn't understand anything that was going on in Lou's life really, but those are my recollections."

Milt Bronson remained close to my father, even closer following the drowning. He was one of the first to see the growing rift between my mother and father as a direct result of Butch's death:

> "I know that for some time following the baby's death, Lou made suggestions that Anne's negligence contributed to the child's demise. Anne had her own sense of guilt and grief and it was then that she started drinking more than merely moderately. There were times when Lou and Anne would fight and argue just a little

bit more. Yet, in spite of all that, I believe there was still a deep love between them. I must add, however, there were times I felt Lou stood more with his mother than with his wife."

Olive Abbott, always Mom's friend, became a better friend. She remembers a lot of confusion, emotion, and grief, and that on their nights out together it was pleasant but strained:

"Regardless of what people might have said so far as to what went on between Lou and Anne after the tragedy, when Anne, myself, Marie, Betty, and Babe all got together, we never really sat down and had intimate private conversations. Anne tried to put all of that behind her. We'd just all jump in a car and maybe go out and have some dinner and a few cocktails. We tried to concentrate on having a good time."

Julia Boutee, a longtime friend, was employed by Alexis Smith (who was appearing in a show in New York) at the time of Butch's death and flew out to the Coast for the funeral. After she returned to New York, Mom spoke to her on the phone often:

"Back in New York I sensed that Anne seemed to need me more. Things were getting to her. She was drinking more than she should but I never really talked to her about that. She would have had to want to stop herself. Drinking was not Anne's problem 'problem.' She hid from her guilt feelings by drinking. I knew she absolutely adored Lou and couldn't understand that he would ever in any way associate anything she did with the baby's death. That child was not Lou's alone. Butch belonged to both of them. It was an accident that could've happened with a hundred people around. I know Lou loved all of his children, but the boy was a male heir—there simply is no way to get around that.

"I also believe Anne went through hell with Lou's mother following the accident. I'm sure she suffered greatly. She also expresssed in so many words that she felt like an outsider in her own family at times. I sensed a deep feeling of loneliness in her. I once approached Lou and said, 'Lou, don't hurt Anne. She's been hurt enough. Try to understand *her* grief and *her* sorrow in the loss of a child.' I think Lou, in his own way, understood what I was saying."

Mom would've taken out her heart and given it to my father if she thought that could ease his pain. She carried her own cross in her own way, and drinking eased her pain. Everybody tried to understand my father, but Mom seemed to be lost in the rush to him. There were people around all of the time, but mostly they were acquaintances. Only with her true friends did Mom let any of her inner feelings show.

Allan Jones, who co-starred with Dad in *One Night in the Tropics*, hadn't seen Dad since sometime before the baby's death. When he did come on one of the sets where Dad was working, the change was evident immediately: "Before, Lou always took relish in kidding around with you, but he had become somewhat more subdued. He didn't appear to be as ebullient and overflowing as before."

Bobby Barber probably was one of an exceptionally few people who ever heard my father express how much grief he felt. One day sometime after the funeral, Bobby came by the house. He found Dad standing beside the pool, hands behind his back, with tears in his eyes. He said, "Bobby, all my life I wanted to make it big. I promised myself that when I made money I was going to have a big swimming pool, because as a kid growing up, we weren't wealthy and that's all I wanted to have when I made it big. I wanted a swimming pool. Isn't it ironic that the swimming pool I now have also took my child from me?" Nobody really recalls Dad saying much beyond that; he couldn't stand to talk about it.

Dorothy DiMaggio, always close to Mom and always in and out of the house, often heard my mother's feelings spill out when they were alone together. Dorothy knew that my father had turned more to himself than to others, that he'd often go into quiet moods that lasted for days, and that he accused Mom of negligence. One night, according to Dorothy, my father made the mistake of commenting about that to my mother. It so angered her, she picked up a small radio and threw it at him. She missed, but Dad got the message.

Although Dad was always calling the Andrews Sisters to invite them over for a barbecue or a screening of a new film, they came less and less as time went on. Maxene remembers how she saw Dad change:

"We began to stop calling because we thought we might be bothering Lou. He didn't seem to be as fun-loving and as warm. I think it was just a conglomeration of things that contributed to his change in behavior. He seemed to anger easily, but he was certainly nothing like the character he was portrayed to be in the movie of the week, *Bud & Lou.*

"He was very generous in loaning us films from his library but it got to the point where I'd drive over to his home and the place would be overrun with strangers—people everywhere. I'd wait until someone brought me the film and then I'd leave. Lou was not as attentive as he had been before. Maybe having the crowds of people around helped him forget the pain he felt—or maybe it was just that we had all gone our separate ways. But there was a difference in his attitude."

My aunt Marie understood Dad's feelings. There was a special chemistry between the two of them, a special kind of love. Aunt Marie understood everybody's problems; she still does. She understood and cared for my mother too. From the very beginning she and Mom were close, always palling around together. Even when Dad bought the home in Florida in the thirties, before moving to California, I can remember Mom talking about how she and Marie would fly or drive down there together and have a fun time. Aunt Marie was a leaning post for Mom after the baby's death, more than anyone else on my father's side of the family. Mom loved Aunt Marie.

Uncle Pat enjoyed a special relationship as Dad's older brother. Nobody could understand why Uncle Pat, who had a brilliant talent as a fine saxophone player with his own band, packed up and moved out to the West Coast, where, from that day forward, he worked for my father and gave up his own ambitions. You'd think an older brother would feel some form of sibling rivalry, but nobody ever saw it if it existed.

Dad and Uncle Pat were built exactly the same size. Except for the difference in their facial makeup, you'd have thought them to be inseparable identical twins. Dad would take Uncle Pat with him to his tailor once or twice a year and have Uncle Pat pick out the fabrics for Dad's suits. Then Uncle Pat would go in for the fittings in Dad's place, knowing that after they'd been worn once or twice—maybe not at all—they'd become his. The fierce loyalty between them seemed to intensify following the baby's death.

Dad had always tried to keep his family involved in his work.

Uncle Pat did his stunt work (except when my father insisted on doing it himself). He was employed by Universal Studios, not by my father. Uncle Pat never had Dad's athletic background but he performed what he had to do in journeyman fashion. Uncle Pat even flew with famed pilot/stuntman Paul Mantz in *Keep 'Em Flying* (1941). In one scene where Dad was supposed to be riding a runaway torpedo, it was actually Uncle Pat. He describes that scene with clarity:

"The scenes at the airstrip, including the one where Lou is riding on the runaway torpedo, were all shot at Cal Aero Field near Ontario, California. I believe it was the assistant director who got a friend of his to drive the torpedo mockup. It was driven from inside. (The driver, however, was no stunt driver.) It was about a seventy-yard run, cadets on both sides. The man was lying on his stomach inside the shell of the torpedo steering it. Before we shot the scene, I said to this guy, 'Go straight and ride out of the camera's range. That's it.' Inside the torpedo the set up was like a miniature car, only the clutch was toward the back. I instructed the fellow how we'd do it and said, 'Let's try it.' At first he went about five miles an hour, so slow I kept sliding off. Then we tried it at fifteen miles an hour and when we finally got it up to forty, I did it without falling off.

"When we were ready, Arthur Lubin, the director, said, 'Let's see how it's gonna look for the camera.' I got on the torpedo, the director yelled 'Action,' and away we went. One thing went wrong, however. Instead of just riding out of camera range and then slowing down until it stopped, the driver made a turn and flung me through the air.

"Lubin wanted to retake the shot, so I pounded on the shell and said to the guy, 'Keep the damn thing straight this time. No turns. Okay?' Okay. We started over and somehow I just felt this guy was going to make a left turn out of camera range, but instead he turned right and away I go again. I got up, brushed myself off, and went up to the assistant director and said, 'Either you get somebody else to drive that thing or get somebody else to ride it!' It was useless. Every time we did it, he either went left or right—never straight. The assistant director gave me a dirty look and brought in a professional stuntman from Hollywood to take the driver's place. I explained to the stuntman: drive it out of the picture, slow down, and just stop. The stuntman said, 'No problem.' Then he said to me, 'You know, Pat, get this torpedo to go another five miles an hour faster and I think it'll look great. Then we can go to the assistant and bargain for more money.'

"Well, at forty-five miles per hour the steel prop on the end (for visual effect only) was spinning up a storm and looked really authentic. God certainly must've been on my side because my nose couldn't have been more than one inch from that twirling propeller. (In the film Lou appears to be riding it backwards.) After he brought it to a stop, I got off the thing and said, 'Let's go back to forty miles an hour. I can do with less money.' "

Meanwhile, my father was standing on the sidelines, doubled over in laughter.

In *Rio Rita* (MGM) Uncle Pat nearly drowned doing a stunt for my father. It was a scene with Dad in a washing machine—a big, old-fashioned washing machine with an agitator that moves up and down like a plunger. What nobody seemed to realize was that the woolen blankets to be put in the machine would be very heavy when they were soaked. As the machine started to work, Uncle Pat somehow got to a position in which the blankets were over his head and weighing him down. He almost drowned—for $300 or $400. In order to make sure Uncle Pat got additional money, my father went to the men's room and clocked the time, returning to the set only after he knew it was assured. Time meant money—and the longer Uncle Pat took to do the stunt, the larger his pay check.

During the shooting of *It Ain't Hay* at Universal, Uncle Pat, doubling for Dad, was rigged up in a body harness that held him as he flew back and forth in the air. Each time he was stopped, it was worth an additional $75 to him in salary. Director Erle C. Kenton kept yelling "Cut!" and Uncle Pat rang up another $75. During a rest period he went to Dad and asked, "See how long you can keep this thing going, Lou." Dad said okay and Uncle Pat went back to work. The next time he was rigged up, he was in midair and heard a "ping"—it was the wire breaking. He came crashing to the ground and made his last $75 for that day.

On one picture, Uncle Pat reported to the location site at seven-thirty A.M. ready for work. The cast and crew were all standing around having coffee and rapping, but Dad wasn't to be found. It got to be eight, nine, ten o'clock and still no Lou. Arthur Lubin finally sent one of his assistants out to the front gate of the military base where they were shooting to see if Dad had gotten lost enroute. He found Dad arguing with two guards at the gate, who had refused him admittance. One of them telling Dad, "Lou Costello went through these gates at seven-thirty this morning. I have him checked off."

Dad was yelling back, "Me? You have me checked off? That was my brother!"

The guard wasn't convinced. "You could be his brother trying to crash. But Lou Costello went through these gates." Of course the assistant finally identified my father and Dad was admitted to the location site.

It was now the year 1944 and in addition to the series of Abbott & Costello pictures my father was working on at this time, he began to devote more of his time and effort toward raising the funds needed to establish a youth center in Los Angeles, in memory of Butch. That summer, *In Society* was released. It was considered the best film Abbott & Costello had done in some time. Well directed by Jean Yarbrough, it also brought the veteran burlesque comic Sid Fields into the Abbott & Costello fold. Dad wanted Fields, because he knew Sid could "add some zing" to the script. Later on, Sid became known as the grouchy landlord in the Abbott & Costello television series. Dad never forgot his old vaudeville and burlesque cronies, nor did Abbott. Murray Leonard was another old pal from New York who came to Hollywood to work in several of my father's films.

Having plunged himself back into a slave-driving pace with radio show, films, and personal appearances, Dad stepped up his efforts for servicemen. He opened up his home to the military. One night while dining at the Hollywood Brown Derby, he noticed a young sailor being turned away by the maître d' because he didn't have a reservation. Dad got up from his table, followed the young man outside and invited him back to sit at his table for dinner. Later, finding the young man had no weekend plans, Dad invited him out to the house, where he spent not only that weekend but several others thereafter. My father gave more of himself to the war effort than just USO bond tours—he was committed to the mobilization heart and soul.

John Grant was now getting co-screenwriting credits on the Abbott & Costello films. Dad kept him busy revising old burlesque routines. Every time one of his old buddies from the early days hit town, Dad would ask, "Tell me your favorite burlesque routine." He would then relate it to Grant and say, "John, this is great. Let's use it in the next picture."

Following *In Society* the team went back over to Metro to do *Lost in A Harem*, which costarred Marilyn Maxwell, the blonde goddess. Dad found a spot in the picture for Murray Leonard just as he had for Milt Bronson in *In Society*. It was 1944. The big push was on in Europe. General Eisenhower's troops had landed on the coast of France at Normandy and it would turn out to be a long hard winter for the American forces bogged down in snow, rain, and mud.

It was also the year my father ventured into his one and only attempt at producing a film. The picture, *A Wave, a Wac and a Marine*, was released through Monogram Pictures. It was no blockbuster and may have even lost money, but it cured my father of any ideas he may have had to become a Hollywood movie mogul.

Dad's company, Biltmore Productions, lasted just long enough to make a mess of my grandfather's pension—something my father never would've done intentionally. He was trying to let my grandfather make some extra money, so he put him on salary with the production company. Some not-so-well intentioned clerk with the insurance company that paid Grandpa's pension found out about the job and due to some fluke ruling, his pension was stopped. Dad felt terrible but he made sure Grandpa didn't want for anything.

By the end of 1944, things at the Longridge house had come back into some kind of focus. Although the baby's death was always in the back of my father's mind, he did have to go on living. Business took up a lot of his time. Family took the rest—not so much his immediate family, but his mother, father, and other relatives. My grandmother more and more kept pressing her will on Dad and he humbly accepted it.

Christmas of 1944 was the usual open-house affair and my father's enthusiasm was as high as ever. If he was quietly feeling the sadness of 1943, it didn't show on the surface. He went out and bought everything in sight, and invited everybody imaginable—including a contingent of servicemen—to the annual Christmas party. Of course, the entire country—especially popular music lovers—was saddened with the news that Glenn Miller had disappeared over the English Channel on a routine flight from England to Paris. A lot of Miller music was played during the holidays of '44—at our house as well as throughout the country. Our family spent more time with the servicemen than with other guests—which included many movie stars and old personal friends. I think Dad wanted to be their father away from home.

It was during this time that my sister Carole first began to sense that my mother was becoming an alcoholic, although my sister didn't know it at the time. What she saw was Mom drinking "too much":

"They say that every alcoholic has one person in the family they will pick on and I guess with my mother, I was that person. Perhaps she sensed in me a little bit of herself. At that time I think I hated Mom more than anyone will ever know. It was a long time afterward that I started to understand there were reasons for her drinking. All I could see then was that lovely lady for whom I had such high ideals letting me down. I'm sure I aggravated her beyond any patience she might've had with me by just demanding, through all sorts of devilishness, that she please notice me—here I am; see me. Mom loved me deeply. I know that. She was always there for me, yet we seemed to clash.

"I know now it wasn't just the baby's death that increased her romance with the bottle. It was that plus a lot of other things. My father's family for one. When she drank, she was like a Jekyll and Hyde. For instance, when we went on vacation, she never touched a drop, but when we got back home, she'd drink. Every home we had it was the same after the baby's death. Mom, faced with everyday family life, found escape in drink from the problems that went with that. But she was really such a neat lady. If only she'd been allowed to be herself—not a movie star's wife. So much was expected of her that I don't think she was either capable of or amenable to being.

"She loved my father in an incredible way. It was difficult for either of them to express that love when every time they turned around they were surrounded by fans. Then at home we had the hangers-on and leeches that seem to have nested at our home. I think the only time they were truly alone was when they went to bed each night.

"I don't ever remember seeing our parents hug and kiss. I fault my father for that. He was not the type who could show affection that way. His upbringing had been very sterile in that respect and it just carried over to his own family. Mom could, though. She was a very touching woman. The lack of a physical affection at times deeply put a void in her life—not the physical side of making love—but common little gestures between man and woman. A hug, a squeeze—a kiss. It was very hard for my father to do that. Still I know he loved my mother and no other woman."

All in all it had been a year of healing and learning to cope with a missing member of our family. There were scars, but the family learned to walk again, to laugh—even to love. It was a seasoning of endurance. It was survival.

CHAPTER XII

Dissention

WHILE FILMING *Here Come the Co-Eds* and *Naughty Nineties* at Universal in quick succession in 1945, signs of tension between Dad and Bud Abbott again began to appear. It started with little things. Often a joke between them would become severely sarcastic. It wasn't just my father. Bud was quite capable of handling his end of any argument. He'd been in burlesque before my father ever stepped out of the high chair and occasionally would remind him of his seniority in the business. They had their trial separations, as in marriage, often to the consternation of others around them, but Eddie Sherman was always around reminding both (especially my father) that there were a long string of contractual commitments that provided for a team—not a single.

Nonetheless the two of them were bickering more and more. Then Eddie Sherman added salt to the wound. My father, Bud, and Uncle Pat were having lunch one afternoon at the Universal commissary. Eddie Sherman joined them. After he sat down he said, "I want to talk to you alone—just the two of you," indicating that Uncle Pat was excluded. Dad just kept on eating, ignoring the request. Sherman looked at Uncle Pat and said, "Just Bud and Lou."

Uncle Pat started to get up and Dad put his hand on his arm and said, "Sit down, Pat. You ain't goin' nowhere." He then turned to Eddie and said, "This is my brother. There is nothing we got to discuss he can't hear."

Eddie saw that he had irritated my father and he put his hand up as if in defense and said, "Okay, Lou—if that's what you want."

"Now," Dad asked, "what is this great secret you want to talk about?"

Bud said nothing, just sat and listened to the cross-conversation between the two men.

"Well, I think I ought to take over both management and artist representation of the team. That would cost you twenty-five percent of your gross, but it would be worth it."

My father exploded. "Look, you little sonofabitch! If I wanted a manager/agent I'd say so. You just keep managing and take your ten percent. You're asking for something like a quarter of a million dollars a year and I don't think I'm willing to give up that kind of money to anybody. Now if you want to make a deal with Abbott, fine. But leave me out of it."

I believe Dad somehow saw Eddie and Bud in some sort of conspiracy against him. He knew that neither of the men liked the idea that he had insisted on having the larger cut, but he didn't care. Eddie dropped the proposition and never brought it up again. There were several times afterward, though, when Dad would tell Eddie he was fired and the following week they'd patch up their differences. But the relationship between my father and Eddie Sherman always seemed to have a cutting edge from that time on.

As for Dad and Bud, their first split came shortly afterward, over the silliest thing. For whatever reason, my father had felt justified in dismissing one of our household servants. He later found out that Abbott had hired her and her new husband as part of his staff. Dad was infuriated. He remarked angrily to my mother that there was only one reason one person employed another's ex-maid—to spy on them. Mom dismissed the whole thing as childish. She neither agreed nor disagreed with my father, but she knew there were other reasons for the coming blowup between Bud and Dad. The maid incident was merely the catalyst.

Dad called Bud and insisted he had been betrayed and if Bud ever wanted the two of them to work together again, he'd get rid of her immediately. Bud stubbornly declared that he lived in a free country and being master of his own castle would hire anybody he liked.

There was an impasse, because my father was just as adamantly swearing never to work with Abbott again. He called Eddie Sherman and said, "Either you make him fire her or I won't work with him no more, nowhere!"

Eddie reminded Dad that it would not only cost him contractual commitments but lawsuits that could run into the millions. "And frankly, Lou," he advised, "you don't have that kind of money." Dad had sense enough to know that Eddie was correct and that he'd have to honor his obligations. He would have anyway, but he tested the water as far as he could before accepting the temperature of things.

"Okay, Eddie, but I won't speak to him except when we work. No more card games. No more anything. You got that? You tell him that!"

Eddie said he'd relay the information but hoped he and Lou would iron things out between them. They didn't—not for a long time. They worked together and nobody heard a cross word between them. There wasn't—they didn't talk. They came on the set from opposite sides and left the same way. It was a routine duplicated at the radio station and onstage when they toured. Still Dad never lost track of the fact that he and Bud were a team whenever he felt Universal or anybody else was giving them short shrift on money. He'd pick up the phone and say to Eddie Sherman, "That deal stinks. We can do better. Get it for me, Eddie—for Bud too." It was always Dad who pushed for better contracts. Bud just went along with whatever he said, because he knew my father would insist on the most and the best there was to be obtained.

Dad was excellent at that type of business. He knew a good movie or nightclub contract but would go out and invest his hard-earned money in some of the most outrageous schemes invented by man—and believed in them like a kid being conned at a carnival sideshow.

Even though he and Bud weren't speaking, he never interfered with Mom's relationship with Betty Abbott. They remained the best of friends throughout the rift. Betty Abbott remembers how close they were:

"I loved Anne. We were good friends and very close. One of the reasons why, I guess, we had such a good relationship was because she never knew my life and I never pried into hers. We never involved ourselves in the relationship between our husbands. To me, Anne was quite a lady, but so much fun to be around. We always managed to have a ball.

"I remember one night that was a beaut. Bud and Lou were out of town and she called and said, 'Come on, let's go out.' Her older sister, Irene joined us. Anne drove and we picked up some other friends—there were five of us girls finally. We stopped at Bud's place, Abbott's Backstage, and had a few drinks. Anne was restless. She said, 'I know a place,' which led to several other clubs, where we drank and they refused to accept our money. Everybody knew we were Bud's and Lou's wives. After a bit of this, Anne said, 'I know another place.' I said, 'Anne, it's too late.' She said, 'It's an all-night spot.' I said, 'Okay, let's go,' and the other girls agreed.

"Away we went and Anne started driving on the wrong side of the road and scared us all half to death. I couldn't take the wheel because I didn't know how to drive, but we did get to this place, which turned out to be an all-night speakeasy. Anne had been there before, because she knew all about it. She knocked on the door and a guy opened up a little peephole and said, 'Yes?' Anne answered, 'I'm Mrs. Costello and this is Mrs. Abbott and we'd like to come in.' 'I'm sorry,' he said, 'no ladies without an escort!' Bang! The window came down. It was our last resort. We started home and the more we talked about the incident, the more hysterical we became. Imagine a carful of women, feeling no pain, with the giggles. That was us. Well, we laughed so hard Anne ended up on the wrong side of the road again and none of us noticed it we were so broken up with mirth. However, a traffic cop did and pulled us over to the side of the road.

"The policeman very politely approached the driver's side of the car and asked Anne for her license, which she produced. As he proceeded to write up the ticket, she said, 'What's your name?' He ignored the question, and Anne pulled herself up to all of her small height and asked it again. 'I'd like to know what your name is, because I'm Mrs. Lou Costello and this lady next to me is Mrs. Bud Abbott. You see, Abbott and Costello do all of the policemen shows and from now on I'm going to make sure they don't work for you!'

"He gave us the ticket anyway and very politely told Anne to drive home carefully. Well, we were in even more hysterics all the way home. It was funny listening to Anne, ever the lady, suddenly trying to pull rank on a traffic cop. Fortunately we did all get home all right, but that's the kind of fun we had when we got together. What Bud and Lou did was their problem—not ours."

Mom was lucky she was only ticketed for driving on the wrong side of the road, because she'd obviously had too much to drink. In the beginning, of course—like anyone who drinks—it didn't interfere with her routine as a mother and wife. That would come years later.

Dad and Bud had one more picture to do at MGM and then the studio dropped the deal with Universal. I believe both sides had fulfilled whatever trade-outs the studios had agreed to in the beginning. The picture was scheduled to roll later in the year. In the meantime Dad and Bud were in New York appearing at the Roxy Theater. It was summertime and the radio show was on vacation. Gossip columnists were reporting with regularity that the Abbott & Costello team had split up and yet, here they were appearing together at the Roxy. Appearing together, but not speaking offstage. Publicity people were giving out ridiculous press releases about the team—none of it worth an ounce of truth. The public was satisfied with Abbott & Costello. It never saw what went on behind the scenes.

When Dad had anything to say to Bud, he communicated through his attorney, as did Bud Abbott. The press hounded their performances backstage but came away empty-handed. At stops along the way wherever they performed, it was the same scenario—more press and fewer answers to their questions. Dad and Bud traveled separately and even returned to Hollywood separately. It was ridiculously obvious they weren't getting along, but neither would confirm that publicly. Their radio show sponsors and the hierarchy at Universal breathed nervously, expecting the bomb to drop any day. But it never did.

Mike Mazurki, the professional wrestler turned actor, worked with Dad on several films and was in *Abbott & Costello in Hollywood,* their last film in the MGM/Universal deal. He was close to my father during that picture and saw the strain in Dad's relationship with Abbott. He also saw other sides of my father's personality:

"Bud was a drinker, and Lou was not: one big reason for not having too much in common socially. They tiffed and went in opposite directions, but on the set they were very professional during this picture. Each had his own circle of friends. They would even joke a little bit before the takes, then Lou would maybe say, 'Okay, Bud. Time to go to work now. We gotta get serious.'

"Apart from their working relationship, which did not appear as strained as their personal involvements, it was best they stayed apart, because there were times when Bud would get slightly sarcastic toward Lou, especially when he started to drink. Yet, Lou never appeared to be affected by that. Lou was a fun guy to be around and was always joking around and laughing. Bud, off camera, played the straight man—very quiet, very within himself, and very serious. Lou had a lovable quality about him and we developed a strong friendship.

"I'll never forget the time he went to bat for me. Somebody on the set made a remark about 'that punch-drunk wrestler, Mazurki.' Lou overheard it clear across the set and came right over to the guy and lit into him: 'What the hell are you talking about? Punch-drunk wrestler? Do you know that he's a college man and has a bachelor of arts degree? He also went to law school for a year. You ought to be ashamed of yourself.' The guy said, 'Well, he sounds like a moron when he talks.' Lou said, 'If you took time to find out, instead of mouthing off, you'd know that's because he was hit in the Adam's apple in a wrestling match.'

"That was true and when I started playing gangster roles—roles that didn't seem to communicate a lot of intelligence—people began to actually think I was a moron. I'll always be grateful that Lou, the star of the picture, stood up for me. That was part of his serious side—speaking up for what he believed in—but when he was 'on,' Lord, he could make you laugh.

"Lou loved sports and when I wrestled in Los Angeles, he always came down with his friends to see the matches. The old Hollywood Legion Hall was a place where many of Hollywood's top stars came in those days to see sports events. Lou also loved the prize fights and I doubt that he missed any major card while he was alive. He always wanted me to show him various wrestling holds. He was a serious student who really wanted to know how it worked.

"Although he loved to pal around with his buddies, he was ever the family man. Someone might say after shooting, 'Hey, let's all go over across the street and get a drink,' and Lou might come along for an hour or so just to be with the guys—but you always had the impression that he really wanted to get home. He was a family man inside and he loved his home."

MGM didn't publicize this last effort with Abbott & Costello as well as they had their previous films. Consequently it was a box-office disappointment. Universal was worried about profits too and cut Dad and Lou down to two pictures for the following year. The war was over and the major studios weren't doing as many comedy films, perhaps because people were being reunited and there was less need (in the minds of the movie executives) for that kind of picture. It would, of course, all turn around in the fifties, when many comedy teams and films would become a large part of the American scene—and with Abbott & Costello as important contributors to the revival.

With less work scheduled, Dad spent more time relaxing. The race track became a favorite oasis. Sid Fields has some beautiful stories about my father at the track, which are worth repeating as Sid remembered them (with a very special thanks to Jim Mulholland, who collected them for his own book):

Costello had bought this mare but it had *always* finished last and Lou could not figure this out. One day another horse owner asked Lou how the horse was doing and Lou explained how the horse was always finishing dead last. "When are you going to pump her up?" asked the owner. Lou said, "What do you mean, 'pump her up'?" The owner said, "Don't you know that the horse has a collapsed left lung? You have to pump the lung up so that she can get air into it." Lou was furious and called his trainer, yelling, "How can you claim a horse for me that has a collapsed lung?" The trainer knew nothing about it and then Lou got an idea. He said, "We can make a killing with this horse." He sent the trainer with the mare to New Jersey. When they got to New Jersey Lou called the trainer and told him to enter the horse in the last race on Saturday. "Pump her up and don't tell anybody! Do you hear me?" The trainer replied, "I could hear you without the phone." Saturday came and Lou bet $4,000 across the board. The mare had never won a race and so the odds were 20-1 in the New York papers and 20-1 in the scratch sheets. That night, Lou sat by the radio and listened for the results. The mare won. As soon as he heard that Lou switched off the radio, got a pencil and paper and started to figure out how much he had won for $4,000 at 20-1. The next morning when he got the newspaper, the horse paid $4.00! Never won a race before. Lou again got on the phone with the trainer and yelled, "What happened? Didn't I tell you not to tell anyone?" The trainer said, "I didn't tell anybody. *You* must have told somebody. Well . . . on the way to the track I stopped off at a little Italian restaurant and told the waiter to put a few dollars on the horse." Costello hollered into the phone, "*When you tell one Italian in New York—you tell Italy!!!*"

At the Del Mar race track on a quiet afternoon, Lou bet $4,000 on a long shot. Because of the size of the bet, the odds on the horse went down, and the horse ultimately became the favorite. The horse lost but Lou was pleased with himself because he had almost single-handedly controlled the betting in the race.

Lou had bought a horse sired in Ireland, named Bazooka. A great sprinter. One day we were at the studios and the horse was running at Bay Meadows in San Francisco. Everybody yelled when Lou walked on the set. "Hey, Lou! Your horse is running today. We all bet on him." Lou said, "Wait a minute! I haven't talked to my trainer yet!" He immediately got a racing form and saw that it was a mile and sixteenth. "My horse is a sprinter!" Lou said. "What's he doing in this race?" He got on the phone and called his trainer in San Francisco and the trainer explained to Lou that he put the horse in the race for a sharpener. "He can't win, but he needs the workout," the trainer told Lou. As it turned out, the race was run so slow that Bazooka won, paying $82.00. Everybody in the studio had won—except Costello!

Many people helped fuel the differences between the two men by carrying tales and spreading rumors. Charles Barton directed eight of their films, the first of which was *Time of Their Lives*, during which time they were at the height of their first separation. He saw the relationship as a somewhat on-again, off-again partnership:

"Bud was a very easy-going man and a pleasure to direct. Of course, after four in the afternoon Bud would start drinking and then no one could reach him. Nobody really knew Bud like Lou did.
"When I started working with them and directing their films in 1946, I could sense an animosity between them. In one film they wouldn't even speak to one another. In another they'd have a riff one day and the next day it would be completely forgotten. Lou went through spells when he wanted to reverse the billing of their names. I don't think it was ever Lou's idea as much as the henchmen that were around him (Bud had his cronies around too). They'd say, 'Lou, you're the guy that's getting all the laughs. Your

name should be first.' Lou would blindly follow their advice. When Bud heard about these things, you could tell that he was deeply hurt, because he loved Lou so much. It was over one of these arguments that the two of them stopped speaking on one of our pictures. After a while the whole idea blew over and things got back to normal again."

My father would go into real tirades when somebody approached him (while he and Bud were on the outs) and ask, "Can I have your autograph, Mr. Abbott?" Kids often got them mixed up, but if they were fighting, look out. Dad, for instance, was in New York once and out on the town with Ann Corio, a good friend to both my parents. One night in a club a guy came up and asked for an autograph, addressing Dad as "Mr. Abbott." Dad ignored him. The guy, getting a little huffy, said, "Okay, Abbott. I knew you when you were in burlesque. Now you don't recognize me."

Dad looked at the man and said, "I honestly don't remember you and you don't know me very well either if you think my name is Abbott!"

However, no matter the disputes and differences, if anybody said anything about Bud Abbott to my father, all hell broke loose. What he said was one thing, but he didn't allow anyone else to make direct comments about Bud. It was okay if somebody said Bud was a better comic and deserved the laughs or more money, but he wouldn't allow any attacks on Bud in any fashion. He once decked a fellow who said Bud drank too much, yet during their feuds Dad lashed into Abbott about the amount of booze he consumed. Bud very pointedly told him it was none of his business what he did after four o'clock.

My father and Bud had a lot in common—their vaudeville and burlesque background and their career together. Unfortunately both men were naive and plainly ignorant when it came to investments. For that reason they would later both be hit hard by the Internal Revenue Service. They trusted and had faith in all their business advisors and managers, allowing them to handle their money and invest it without ever questioning what was going on.

One time Dad was all excited about an invention and put money into it. It was an ice machine. Dad, wanting to show off the model he had, invited Charlie Barton over to the house to see it one day. My father was beaming like he'd just become the father of twin boys when he turned it on. It made ice all right, but the machine was shooting the cubes in every direction. Barton and Dad ducked, but the cubes kept spitting out. To top it off, Dad couldn't get the machine to stop. Eventually he pulled the cord. What turned out to be pure slapstick began as a serious demonstration and the sad part is, it cost my father a lot of money.

Yet it was what most people expected of my father. He trusted so fervently and was so naive, he was constantly being gutted in the pocketbook. Barton asked the question, "Did anybody really expect him to be a big business tycoon? This funny little man with the cigar?"

Abbott had his share of bad investments and often was his own worst enemy. For instance, when he got off work he'd go home at four o'clock and start to drink; then later that night he'd have someone drive him to Abbott's Backstage (the club he owned) and proceed to throw all of the customers out so his friends could come in to eat, drink, and play cards. Barton was there one evening when Bud arrived and said, "Okay everybody. Ya gotta leave now 'cause my friends are comin' in." A hell of a way to run a business, and it cost Bud. He took a loss on the club, which was written off on his taxes—some say because of bad business management too much was written off—but, like Dad, he paid little attention to the details of business.

Still, Dad was the biggest sucker of all. Texas Guinan, the famous speakeasy owner, always welcomed her guests with the gusty expression, "Hello, suckers!" She would've loved my father. He was the perfect sucker for a con artist with a get-rich-quick scheme. He'd go right off the deep end and sock a big bundle into these fly-by-night projects. Obviously there were a few greedy bones in his chubby little body.

Nonetheless, my father and Bud each had their weaknesses and one of them was listening too much to hangers-on. They were both hurt by that many times.

It was Bud and Dad's fondness for children and for helping kids that brought them back together to end their first split. Dad had been working on an idea since his son's death: a youth foundation, established in honor of Butch. Bud wanted to help

Dad promote money for the project and Dad agreed. Immediately the two of them were buddies again and peace in their career seemed assured—at least for the forseeable future. Their families breathed easier—as did dozens of hangers-on, who one minute were ready to do hatchet jobs on the other side but deep down inside knew they'd all be out if the team broke up.

CHAPTER XIII

A Memorial, a Death, and a Birth

AFTER COMING TO California my father's life seemed to have been filled with grief of one kind or another. During the time when he should have been happiest—career booming, raising a family, progressing—so much happened that was of an unhappy nature. Naturally the death of his son was the most tragic event in his life, but his own illness had come at a time when his career was peaking and it kept him out of work for almost a year. Then, two years later there was the first split between him and Abbott, which made them both (and everybody else involved) miserable.

Throughout all of this kind of hardship, Dad never hesitated to give of himself and his money to those who were in trouble or need. While the first feud with Abbott was being seeded, Mom's mother suffered a slight stroke and was to a degree paralyzed for nine months. My father paid all her medical expenses—and insisted on doing so. This included nurses, around the clock, for a long time. He had previously purchased a home for her, which, upon her death, went to my aunt Mayme. She and her husband, Jim, continued to live there for many years afterward.

I don't know if her mother's death increased my mother's drinking, but her sister Mayme realized Mom was increasing her intake:

"... I could see that Anne was drinking more. She never confided to me why she drank and I never asked, but I think Lou's family contributed to her growing unhappiness. I remember when Lou gave Anne a beautiful mink stole and certain members of his family were openly upset—until he gifted them with one also. That sort of thing was a strain on Anne and she couldn't cope with it. All too often Lou's generosity created problems."

As Mom stayed out of Dad's problems with Bud Abbott, she was also not caught up in the Hollywood scene. For instance, when it was the maid and butler's day off, she'd clean house like mad. She took great pride in having the help out of the house so she could cook the things she knew my father liked, without being interfered with. On Thanksgiving she could always be found in the kitchen making the turkey stuffing my father liked—regardless of how many cooks they had. It was a recipe that her mother had handed down to her and Dad loved it.

Where Dad had a tendency to spoil us, my mother had the common sense to inject discipline with all that love and indulgence. If my father said yes to something she knew wasn't right for us, she had the most unique ways in the world of rescinding his generosity with a firm no, without seeming to have offended him or upset us.

Little Giant and *Time of Their Lives* were the only films Abbott & Costello made in 1946, but that did not mean Dad wasn't busy with business enterprises and personal appearances. Although he had promised Mom a long vacation, that was put on the back burner. The usual Christmas soiree was held that year, and the house was filled with friends and strangers alike. Then, in early 1947, Abbott & Costello made *Buck Privates Come Home*. Universal hoped the picture would have the same charismatic effect on audiences that the original *Buck Privates* generated, and although the film grossed a great deal of money, there was a missing ingredient: the Andrews Sisters. They made great chemistry with Abbott & Costello, and why Universal didn't continue to use them in my father's pictures is anybody's guess. Nonetheless, Abbott & Costello were again to reign as the top comedy team in films and their fans stood in lines for blocks to see this new picture.

Tragedy came again on May 9, 1947. The day before, my grandfather Cristillo had gone over to Universal, where Dad was beginning to shoot *The Wistful Widow of Wagon Gap*. It was his custom always to be on the set the first day the cameras rolled on my father's films. That day, he went to the studio barber shop and got a shave, haircut, pedicure, and manicure. Dad felt it was good luck to have his father around at the beginning of a picture. They had a great time together, lunched at the commissary, and when Dad dropped him off at home that night and said goodnight to him and my grandmother, it was the end of a happy day.

My grandfather retired early and seems to have slept well, arising early. He put on his overalls, which he called his "happy clothes" and puttered around outside in the garden. The only difference in his behavior from any other day was that he started to cough a lot. That worried my grandmother, who followed him out into the garden to make sure he was okay. He dismissed her concern. "It's probably something in the air," he said, "but if it'll make you happy I'll come in and get a glass of water and lie down for a while." He got as far as a rattan sofa in the living room, where he collapsed. By the time the doctor and Uncle Pat arrived, it was all over. Although he'd never had any problems with his heart, the cause of death was coronary thrombosis.

My mother was six months pregnant with me. It was a terrible blow to my father. The night before his death my grandfather received a call from Eddie Sherman. Someone had come to him complaining that Dad wasn't being cooperative about something or other. Eddie said, "Well, the quickest way to get to Lou is through his father. I'll give Chris a call." Grandpop, in turn, called Dad and relayed Eddie's concern. Dad was angered that Eddie went to his father. He said, "Don't worry about it, Pop, I'll clear it up tomorrow."

Dad was on the set when word came that his father had passed away. Very emotional and upset, my father got Eddie Sherman on the phone and screamed into the mouthpiece, "You sonofabitch, you're fired! You're fired! You killed my father!"

Robert Arthur, producer of *The Wistful Widow of Wagon Gap* was called to the set. He realized my father was distraught and made the announcement: "Okay fellas, wrap it up. That's it for today."

Following my grandfather's death, my grandmother decided it was she who should run the family. My mother had given birth to three children before me, but to listen to my grandmother it was Mom's first time out and she was doing everything wrong. She'd corner my father and say, "Lou, Anne's going to hurt herself—and the baby. You better pay close attention to her." That went on and on and my father felt caught between two women.

Mom was doing fine and didn't need any help. My grandmother, in addition to being somewhat dictatorial, was now a very lonely widow who was reaching out for a world that seemed to be slipping away from her. Mom understood Grandma's despair, but wasn't about to abdicate her own position merely to satisfy my grandmother's demands.

Whenever Grandma visited our house, my sister Carole would do somersaults or handcarts across the floor, just to get Grandma's reaction, which was always negative. Carole's memories of my grandmother's interference in our family's life are often brittle ones:

"There were times when Dad would give Mom a gift and as soon as my grandmother found out he'd have to go right back out and buy her the same thing. You simply could not fight his family.

"Aunt Marie, though, was great and we all flocked to her as children. Even today, we go to her when we have a problem. Grandma never let Aunt Marie live her own life and, as much as I love her, to this day Marie is a very intimidated woman. But she is a very wonderful human being who was probably the only member of my father's family who never meddled and kept to her own personal life (as much as she could with Grandma being around)."

In retrospect I too have a lot of resentment about the way my grandmother fueled the differences between my parents. My mother had enough grief without any outside help.

Dad's secretary, Marty Kertz, married Uncle Pat just before the end of World War II and was replaced by a lovely lady, Aida Polo, who we all affectionately called "De De." Dad was delighted when he discovered that De De was the niece of Eddie Polo, a very famous silent actor. De De recalls that Dad was easy to work for:

"He generally left me alone with my work. One of my functions was handling all checks and doing his personal banking. That meant I wrote out the checks, deposited the money in the bank, and made sure that everybody was paid. I also handled the abundant fan mail."

Dad's business manager at the time was Al Blum, who also handled Errol Flynn. When Blum died of cancer in the early fifties, he left a letter for Flynn (who was in Europe) that said, "You owe the government only $18,000. You have nothing to worry about." Shortly thereafter the government notified Flynn he owed $840,000 in taxes. Flynn was distraught. He said, "He was dying of cancer so he lived it up on my dough!" Blum died and left his own private plane, two Cadillacs, a house in the country, and a big home in Beverly Hills. It was all that affluence that caused everybody to suppose he was such a great business manager. According to Blum's secretary, he had said (shortly before dying), "Tell Errol I'm sorry."

Like Flynn, my father never made out income tax returns. He signed whatever papers his business managers handed him, which would later prove quite costly.

De De recalls how difficult it was to handle my father's financial affairs:

"No one could really handle Lou when it came to his business affairs. He used to go over to Universal and pick up his check before the business manager could get hold of it and then spend it on the horses or gambling, or through any number of avenues available because of his generosity. When it came to his family, he never asked how much—he'd just peel off the bills and turn them over to whoever had the need. It was the same with outsiders if they were down and out or had a convincing story. Anne used to tell me, 'If only Lou had let his father handle his money, he'd have been a lot better off.'

"I got to understand Lou after a while and got to know his habits. It began to dawn on me that he spent money like the nouveau riche. He had all the wrong people handling his money—and that includes himself. It appeared to me that spending money was his way of entertaining himself, his family, and his friends."

During the early part of 1947, Dad purchased an eighty-foot sub-chaser from the government—one of the few bargains he ever got for his money—and refurbished it into an elegant yacht. The inside was re-done in Philippine mahogany.

Also, just a week prior to my grandfather's death, Dad's dream of doing something to honor his son became a reality. On May 3, 1947, the Lou Costello Jr. Youth Foundation officially opened in East Los Angeles amid great fanfare, plus Abbott & Costello to give it a good beginning. It was a time of very mixed emotions for my father.

When Mom had discovered she was pregnant again, there was no denying that both she and my father prayed for a boy. During that wait for my birth, De De often found Mom alone in her room with photos of Butch spread out over her dressing table, crying and sobbing with grief.

Two weeks before my birth, Dad flew back to his hometown of Paterson, where he was being honored in a tribute dinner. My grandmother accompanied him as did Bud Abbott. All of the city fathers turned out and my father was deeply touched. Needless to say tears flowed freely.

Four days later, back home on the West Coast, Dad invited the entire family plus as many friends as he could get aboard the yacht—now officially christened *Lolly C* (after his mother) by my mother—for a shakedown cruise. He even thought to bring along Estelle Ronaine (one of his nurses during his illness with rheumatic fever) to take care of Mom or her sister Mayme (also pregnant), in case one of the babies came too soon. Publicity man Joe Glaston was there to take pictures. It was an hilarious boat ride. Everybody got sick except Mom and De De, who were sitting out on the deck drinking highballs and laughing and talking with no concern for what was happening to the others.

On August 14, De De drove Mom to the Good Samaritan Hospital in Los Angeles, where she was scheduled to deliver me by Ceasarean section the following morning. The morning I was born my father came to the hospital at seven A.M. and walked along beside the stretcher while Mom was being taken to the operating room. As they wheeled her through the big double doors, beyond which my father couldn't go, Mom waved to Dad and De De. "Bye. See ya in a while," she said.

An hour or so later Mom was wheeled out with me. Dr. Robert Fagan, who delivered me, approached Dad and said, "Well, congratulations, Lou. You have another girl."

Dad and De De hovered around mother and the new baby

until it was suggested Mom needed some rest. Dad and De De left the hospital then and drove back to the Valley. At the house Dad went to the bar and, for the first time, De De saw him pour himself a straight shot of Scotch. He sat down on one of the barstools and said, "I know of some people that will be glad she's a girl." That was it. The only thing De De could make of what he said was that maybe some people would be happy that the baby was a girl and not another Lou Costello, Jr. My father never did explain the meaning of his statement.

Both my parents indulged me unbelievably from the very beginning—if possible, my father even more so. In his mind I had replaced the lost baby, so it didn't matter whether I was a girl or boy. I was destined to be one spoiled brat—and I was.

Not too long after my birth Dad suffered one of his many relapses from the bout with rheumatic fever. He had always been afraid of doctors and one day, when he had complained of not feeling well while he and Mom were out on the *Lolly C*, Mom pleaded with him to see our current family doctor, Dr. Stanley Immerman, but Dad continued to put it off. Mom finally resorted to threats. "Lou," she said, "if you don't go *now*, I won't be home with the girls the next time you leave this house."

Dad consented and Dr. Immerman immediately hospitalized him. The doctor told my mother, "If Lou had waited just twelve more hours, he would've been dead." Dad was confined again to bed for several weeks.

It was also about this time that Dad changed business managers. De De remembers the changeover and how she felt about it:

"A young man approached Lou and explained that he was an accountant and would love to work for Lou. Lou said fine, he could share an office with me in the Longridge home.

"I guess it was intuition, but from the moment he started to work for Lou I didn't trust him. At that time my office was moved out to the pool house area in the back. I had a desk on one side of the room and he had his desk on the other side. I thought it unusual that he'd always manage to come to work around four in the afternoon, just when I was ready to go home.

"When I worked for Lou I was the only person authorized to

sign his name on checks, photos, and bank deposits. I had strong suspicions about what was going on after I went home but really couldn't prove anything."

De De came to know our family quite intimately and saw things that perhaps no one else did—especially the relationship between my father and his family:

"Of course Lou's mother wanted to be doted on—anybody could see that—especially after her husband died. She often used her high blood pressure to bend Lou to her will, and he seemed blind to her manipulation of him. Anne saw it and whenever she'd say something to Lou about it, he'd brush her aside with 'You're just building this all up.'

"Marie stayed pretty much to herself unless she was invited. The others, however, just seemed to horn in. Anne never had a day alone without someone at the house and at that bar. Lou's brother Pat was at the house every single day, as if to see what was going on. Of course I wrote out the weekly check to Pat too, because he was on Lou's payroll. I think it really got to Anne after a while, feeling as though she had to compete with Lou's family. In spite of what she felt, I never once saw Anne treat Lou's family any way but first class.

"During all the years I worked as Lou's secretary, I can't really say I ever saw him kiss Anne good-bye when he left for the studio in the morning or ever kiss her hello when he came back after the day's shooting. Nevertheless, I always felt theirs was a *love marriage*.

"Lou spoke to me only one time about Anne's drinking. It was after Christy was born and he asked me to drive him over to Ventura Boulevard to do some Christmas shopping. While we were driving along he asked, 'De De, do you know what makes Anne drink?' I was honest. I said, 'She's never really told me, Lou, but I feel it must've been because of losing the baby.' I turned and looked at him. He never said anything, just shook his head and looked away. He not only didn't reply to me, he never brought the subject up again."

I think Mom's drinking became more noticeable to my father after I was born. He was so careful about me, so afraid that something would happen. At my christening Mom got a little bit tipsy but none of the guests were aware of it. She calmly left the room and went to bed. There was a big mob at the house and after Mom disappeared, Dad, in a rage, singled out Ann Corio and told her Mom had been drinking. Ann said, "It's harmless. Everybody's drinking and celebrating today." Still, Dad carried a dark look over his face for the rest of the day.

After my grandfather's death, Dad seemed to seek out the company of Bobby Barber more and more. They did silly things together. For instance, if my father wanted an ice cream cone at eight o'clock in the morning, he'd insist that Bobby have one too. Dad would just smile and say, "Aw, come on, Bobby, have an ice cream cone with me." It was not just an invitation; it was the sharing of a very special moment and Bobby always succumbed to Dad's impishness. Bobby, like Dad, loved doing anything that would make other people laugh, which is why the two of them probably had such wonderful times with each other kibbitzing around on the set, throwing pies, pulling off gags. Bobby helped keep Dad's mind off problems and kept his energy up for the scenes he had to shoot.

One morning when it was quite cold Bobby picked up Dad on his way to the studio. As they drove along, my father said, "Jesus Christ! It's cold in here. Don't you have a heater in this thing?"

Bobby kept driving. "Naw. Don't need one."

Bobby kept old receipts and a lot of miscellaneous papers in his glove compartment. Dad began to rummage around, found a match and set fire to the papers in the glove compartment. As he held his hands over the growing blaze, he winked at the astounded Barber and said, "Now ya have a heater."

On another occasion when Bobby was driving the two of them to the studio, a motorcycle officer pulled the car over. Bobby asked, "What did I do, officer?"

Dad, sitting on the passenger side, said, "Aw, give him a ticket."

Bobby, looking back and forth from Dad to the officer, again asked, "But what did I do?"

Dad was having fun and kept on agitating the situation. "Don't listen to his excuses, officer," he said. "Just give him the ticket."

Bobby, now exasperated, turned to Dad and said, "Will you

keep your big mouth shut!" Dad, puffing away on his big cigar, had a smirk on his face as the panic-stricken Barber again asked the officer what was wrong.

As soon as the policeman recognized my father, he put his pad away and told Bobby to forget the whole thing and just move along. As the grateful Bobby drove away, my father said, "You see, I got you outta trouble again."

So close was their friendship, that following my grandfather's death, for a long time my father would hardly even go to the bathroom unless Bobby waited outside the door. Since my grandfather had dropped dead with such suddenness (and Dad having had so many problems from the rheumatic fever), I think my father was afraid of dropping dead and being all alone.

CHAPTER XIV

A Time of Growth

GOVERNMENT BY COMMITTEE is too communistic to be both peaceful and successful at the same time. For quite a while there had been a lot of in-fighting going on at Universal Studios and because *Little Giant* and *Time of Their Lives* hadn't taken in the profits the committee expected, some of the fallout from the dissension landed on Bud and Dad. It wasn't long before a management overthrow took place at Universal and not only were top executives fired and replaced, but so was the studio's name, which became Universal-International Pictures.

The Universal changeover had taken place in 1947 and *Buck Privates Come Home* and *The Wistful Widow of Wagon Gap* were both made under the new banner. Robert Arthur produced and Charles Barton directed—and the combination of Arthur, Barton, Abbott & Costello created a charisma on film the public couldn't resist. They came in droves to see the revival of Abbott & Costello and the profits Universal eventually grossed were outstanding. Nevertheless, the new hierarchy hadn't been in power long enough to see these returns and they were still disgruntled with the showing *Little Giant* and *Time of Their Lives* had made.

The new bosses of Universal-International, Leo Spitz and William Goetz, were not true Abbott & Costello fans. Spitz, an attorney, had paid no dues as a filmmaker and was in his new position more on administrative ability than because of any great knowledge of the motion picture industry. Goetz, on the other hand, was the son-in-law of Louis B. Mayer, the mighty

139

lion of MGM. Coming from that kind of filmmaking background and being a man of sophisticated tastes, Abbott & Costello did not attract his interests personally. He had taken over a studio that was known as a "distant cousin" in the movie world and was determined to eventually bring Universal's product to heights that would compete with the other major studios, including his father-in-law's empire.

Although he didn't really want Abbott & Costello, Goetz was aware that they were valuable assets to the studio. He saw Abbott & Costello films as a vehicle for promoting money to make the pictures he really wanted to make—serious dramatic films that said something. Under the firm hand of Goetz, during his first year at Universal-International, the studio released several quality pictures. One of those was *A Double Life*, which won for its star, Ronald Colman, an academy award for best actor.

Dad, who never had great love for the studio heads at any point in his professional career, was not enthralled with the future he saw at Universal-International. He was still embittered by the treatment he'd received at MGM and so far as he could see, Goetz (being Mayer's son-in-law) was part of the bad taste in his mouth.

Even though there was disenchantment on both the part of my father and Universal-International, the studio had scheduled four films for Abbott & Costello in 1947—an increase of two from the previous year. Taking Goetz's point of view, that would mean more Abbott & Costello films—more profit—more "quality pictures." However only two were completed that year, in spite of the great expectations.

Dad was totally unimpressed with the new bosses at Universal-International and told them so. Bill Goetz said the feeling was mutual. Under the new regime Universal-International was losing money. Goetz and his associates had dropped a lot of the grade-B pictures that were sustaining the studio. My father immediately saw through Goetz's scheme to sacrifice the talent that had kept the studio in business so that his artistic films could be produced. Dad complained bitterly about Goetz's new policy. After all, Abbott & Costello pictures (shot in ten to twenty days) were making money while "quality pictures" were still on location in Europe and losing money for the studio.

Despite the fact that Abbott & Costello's *Hold That Ghost*

(1941) had been the highly successful forerunner of a number of films based on supernatural themes, it was with a great deal of reluctance that Dad agreed to do *Abbott & Costello Meet Frankenstein*. Every monster on the lot was thrown in for good measure. Dad's reluctance notwithstanding, the film put the team right back at the top of Universal's moneymakers.

Seeing how well the film turned out and the profits that Universal would be making, Dad insisted on $25,000 more per picture or he wouldn't be on the set when they started shooting *Mexican Hayride*, their next project. Universal-International, through Goetz, suspended the team. Even Bud Abbott, who rarely complained about anything (he let my father handle complaints) had a beef with the new script. To wit: "This script stinks!" My father, to the contrary, thought it was a good script, but he simply refused to do another picture without more money.

The fans won. There was such a clamor against the suspension from the moviegoers and exhibitors, the studio gave in to my father's demands.

Dad decided he'd like to see the team get all of the rights for 16mm on Abbott & Costello films—otherwise he wouldn't appear on location in Calabassas for *Mexican Hayride*, which was already in production. Obviously they couldn't shoot without the stars and this time Abbott backed my father. He refused to come on the set until Dad did. Again the studio succumbed to what turned out to be quite legitimate demands, considering what stars were getting within a very few short years later. Once the agreement was made, both Dad and Bud appeared in the middle of the afternoon, at Calabassas, ready to shoot the picture.

There was a series of monster pictures that included *The Noose Hangs High, Abbott & Costello Meet the Killer, Boris Karloff, Abbott & Costello Meet the Invisible Man*, and other fright films such as *Abbott & Costello Meet Captain Kidd, Africa Screams, Abbott & Costello Meet Dr. Jekyll and Mr. Hyde*, and *Abbott & Costello Meet the Mummy*, with other pictures tossed in here and there for variety. All the films were designed to scratch the public's funny bone and all succeeded.

There were some very hang-loose moments during the filming of *Abbott & Costello Meet Frankenstein*, reminiscent of the early films of the team. In this picture Bud and Lou did a routine they called the "Pack and Unpack" bit. It wasn't new and they'd done it several times. Director Charles Barton quickly recognized that their time-worn joke needed freshening up and he went directly to John Grant with the problem. John, a man easy to get along with, said he'd come up with a new routine, but along the same line and Barton gave him the go ahead. When it was completed and presented to Barton, he told Grant he'd done a superior job.

Dad and Bud never really looked at a script as many actors do. I mean, they never memorized scripts, but merely scanned them to get the general idea of what they were expected to do. Of course my father never did the same thing twice, so a few verbal points from the director ordinarily would suffice. Be that as it may, the day came to shoot the revised routine John Grant wrote, and rehearsals got under way. After they'd been given their scripts both Bud and Dad looked at Charlie Barton as if to say, "What the hell is this crap?"

Dad made it verbal. "Charlie, what is this we're doing? I mean, this skit's a variation of Bud's and my 'Pack and Unpack' routine."

"You're right, Lou," Barton said, "but, this one's got a fresher feel and it won't be the same damn thing over and over."

Dad frowned. "Oh, come on, Charlie. Bud and I aren't going to sit here and learn this whole new routine. We'll do the old one."

Charlie sat down, which he rarely did when directing, and said, "Okay, Lou. You want to do the old 'Pack and Unpack'? I'll have another camera brought in, set it up, and then you and Bud can go ahead and do the old routine." The director halted production, ordered another camera set up on the team, and put his chair directly in front of them and asked, "Are you ready?"

"Right," Dad said, explaining where they'd be moving so the camera could follow.

Barton yelled for quiet on the set, then, "Action!"

Abbott goes to the window and says, "Ah! They're leaving. We can go ahead and unpack." Then Dad starts unpacking and throwing his clothes into the drawers, when Abbott suddenly says, "Oh! They're coming back, Lou. Quick! Pack the suitcase." Dad pulls open the drawers, scoops out his clothes, and dumps them into the suitcase. The routine goes on—Dad throwing his clothes back and forth—to the point where Dad gets more and more exasperated every time Abbott changes his mind. The routine was scripted for six minutes, but after the cameras had been running three minutes, Dad stopped in the middle of the routine, turned toward Barton, and said, "Aren't you gonna say 'cut?' "

Barton leaned back in his chair and replied, "I'm waiting for something funny."

Dad was so irate he grabbed Bud by the arm, left the set, and went home, where they stayed for three days without speaking a word to Barton. On the fourth day they returned to the studio, walked onto the set, and had the entire new routine down pat. No one ever mentioned the incident again, and the front office never could understand how Charlie Barton got them to do it *his* way—nor did Charlie.

Nevertheless, they still did a lot of ad-libbing in their films. It was a great credit to Bud Abbott, because there were times when Dad would start to do a scene and then suddenly break out into left field, completely away from the story line. Somebody had to bring him back, and Abbott could do it within seconds. There were other times the two of them would ad-lib so much, the scene would have to be edited out of the film. When they both got going on their own, that was it. A smart director would let them go and then shoot what he wanted later.

Barton recalls how it was to work with my father:

"Something funny was going on every single minute and the crews loved him. We all loved him. But if he got upset and started to demand things, then we more or less left him alone until it blew over. But, oh God! Everybody adored working with Lou Costello. Abbott, too, but Abbott was quiet and more subdued. Lou was always kidding around and doing funny things to break you up."

Because of his genius, Dad could be, and sometimes was, unmanageable, whereas Bud never bucked as Dad did. Bud would always follow Dad's decision if there was some argument with a director or with the studio. All Dad ever had to say was, "Come on, Bud, we're goin' home," and Bud would walk off with him.

However, my father was a gentleman when it came to taking

on the studio moguls. He did everything through his manager, who in turn went up to see whoever was in charge. Most always that duty fell to Eddie Sherman. In fact, neither Goetz nor Spitz wanted any personal confrontations with either Bud or my father. When they took over the studio, my father already had a reputation of being "the executive's enemy," so they carefully avoided this *enfant terrible* from the very beginning.

Both Bud and Dad knew they were making money for Universal because they kept up with the profit statements on their films. Whenever Dad thought the studio was making too much and Abbott & Costello too little, he'd take it out on Eddie Sherman. "Look what the hell you've done to us, Eddie," was his standard accusation.

Charlie Barton thoroughly understood Abbott & Costello's differences with the new bosses at Universal-International:

"It wasn't unusual for Bud and Lou to tear up their contracts if they thought they had been given a bad deal. I'm not saying Eddie was selling them short—he always tried to get the best deal he could—but there were times Lou thought Universal was making out like bandits on his and Bud's success. Remember also, that Abbott & Costello were keeping the gates open at Universal.

"There was the studio's side too. Bud and Lou were burlesque comics—brilliant and talented ones—but burlesque comics, nevertheless, who had branched out into radio. Until Universal signed them, they were still a radio team—getting exposure, but not the superstardom when Universal pushed and promoted them.

"I don't think Bill Goetz or Leo Spitz—when they took over the studio—fully understood comedy, because Bud and Lou were still Universal's top moneymakers. Goetz had been a very fine independent producer and both he and Spitz were truly charming men, but they just didn't know anything about comedy."

But my father was becoming somewhat bored. He felt that Universal-International had him on a treadmill and he wasn't really growing.

Even if Dad thought he wasn't growing, I was—every day. My coming into his life when I did gave impetus to his energies and money that went into the new Youth Foundation. The youth center was a large complex with equipment and space for a myriad of sports and other endeavors. It was Dad's desire that underprivileged children from Los Angeles—and especially from the East Side—would come to the center and get off the streets.

Dad didn't just open the foundation; he became an active part of it. He loved that youth center because it was a constant reminder of his dead son. He went there as often as he could, to make sure things were okay, to visit and joke with the kids. Sometimes he even got out on the baseball diamond and batted balls around with the youngsters. If he went overboard on the project, it was because he wanted "his" kids to have the best recreation facility in the world—and it was. There was a wood-carving shop, a machine shop, a swimming pool fully equipped with lifeguards and swimming instructors, an ice skating rink, a baseball diamond, basketball courts, and a movie theater. A nurse was on duty at all times and a very large staff served the children. The original cost of the facility was $95,700. Today it would cost several million dollars.

There were disappointments as well as satisfaction with the center. People Dad had counted on to donate funds to keep the center open failed, one by one, to do so and the responsibility eventually fell completely on Dad's shoulders. Once, he was late paying the electric bill and the Department of Water and Power threatened to cut off service to the center. By the time everything was installed, the center was worth about $350,000 and cost $80,000 a year to operate. Eventually my father turned the youth center over to the City of Los Angeles and it is still operated by the city as the Lou Costello Jr. Youth Foundation. Recently there has been effort on the part of myself, my sisters, and others to rejuvenate the center and get it back into top running shape again.

Dad also worried about the welfare of his mother. Not long after my grandfather's death, someone robbed the Coldwater Canyon house. My grandmother was in the living room talking to a relative when some guy came right in through the front door, grabbed both their purses, and went on to scoop up some jewlery in the bedroom. My grandmother's total loss was $12,-000. The police believed it was someone who knew of my grandfather's death. Dad was so concerned, he asked Milt Bronson, his old friend, to give up his apartment in Hollywood and move in to live with my grandmother. Milt did. Not only that, he drove Grandma wherever she wanted to go, took her out to dinner, and did the chores around the house.

No matter how hard my father was working at the studio, with Grandpop gone, Dad spent more and more time at my grandmother's house—every single day after work he'd stop to have a cup of coffee with her. Mom never seemed to mind that he did that. She objected only when Grandma directly interfered in our family life. Even then she more often than not bit her tongue rather than say something to upset my father.

In the meanwhile, Mom found a unique way to help the youth center—through gambling. Actually it was Lois Van's idea. Lois was Frankie Van's wife. Frankie, of course, ran the gym at Universal and was a very close friend of my father's. It happened while Dad was on one of his fund-raising campaigns. Mom, Lois, and another friend, Lorraine Miliron (who was very in with the socially elite around town) were having lunch and Lois said, "Why don't we girls do something to raise funds for the center?" to which my mother and Lorraine responded, almost in unison, that it sounded like a marvelous idea. They formed a group, calling themselves Los Costalitos and went to work. What they did was hold poker games and charge entrance fees, which went into the youth center's kitty.

Mother and her friends held these gambling fund-raisers at Hugh Herbert's home and after my father found out what was going on, he just had to get involved. So he went to Universal and "borrowed" all the necessary gambling equipment, tables, etc. A big truck from Universal backed up to Hugh Herbert's home in Encino and unloaded enough equipment to stock a Las Vegas casino. The crowds were large and were there to have fun and spend money for a good cause. The games were paid off in chips (as required by law) and the chips were exchanged for prizes, all of which had been donated through solicitation by the Los Costalitos club. They managed to raise several thousand dollars for the club and Dad was so proud of Mom.

My mother had to do things to keep from going crazy, because inside she was a very lonely and sad woman. Truly, she was the best dressed, most bejeweled lonely woman in Hollywood. Dad was far more attentive to us children than to our mother, but I think he found it easier to express love to a child. I'm sure he showed me warmth and affection beyond what he showed others in the family, simply because of Butch's death and his concern that something might happen to his "baby." I wasn't around when Butch drowned, so I didn't have the fears the rest of the family had. I'm certain Mom carried a sense of fear along with the guilt she felt. Otherwise she would never have put herself into the position of being almost a servant to my father.

I remember how attentive my mother was to us girls. She'd drop everything to attend a school function, help organize a school bazaar, or take one of my sisters to a dancing class or to the riding academy for lessons. How many times she would look down at me and smile and say, "It won't be long, Christy. Your turn is coming soon." She was a natural mother and delighted in being with and doing things for her children.

My sisters, I must admit, received more discipline than I did. For one thing, they were older and secondly, I was the baby. When someone would tell Dad he was spoiling me or overindulging one of my whims, he'd say, "So what? You only get to be a kid once. So let her have fun."

If I wanted something it was like having a fairy godmother. My father performed magic with my wants much to my delight and—later on, after my parents were gone—to my sisters' consternation.

I was still a baby when Dad and Abbott made their first independent film, *The Noose Hangs High*, for a new studio: Eagle-Lion. I've been told they breezed through that shooting schedule, because my father was so elated with his new daughter. There were no flashes of temper or walking off the set. Universal had shut down while the management changes were taking place but once everything was corporately transferred over to Universal-International, it was back to business as usual.

Africa Screams, one of Abbott & Costello's best films, was not a Universal-International picture. It was made in 1948 and released through United Artists. That year, my mother's stepbrother, Walter Battler, moved in with us. He was fourteen and like a big brother to my sisters and me. He was closer in age to Paddy and Carole and I can remember them swimming in the Longridge pool together a lot when I was quite young. Dad treated Walter like his own son.

Walter was eleven when my grandmother Battler died in

1944. He had a natural mother but he always looked upon my grandmother as the only real mother he had ever known. The day she died, Walter was brought over to our house and my father, having sensed a deep feeling of death only a year earlier, said to him, "Come on, Walter. Let's take a walk in the yard." Walter tells it better:

"Lou was a very sensitive person, a private man who kept many thoughts to himself. Yet he cared a great deal for people. We had always talked at great length but rarely alone. It was usually in the home and with other people around—group conversation, never in private. This one day, though, we did. As we walked through the backyard area, he remained quiet at first, just being there with me, his arm around my shoulder. I sensed something was wrong, but didn't know as yet what. He began to talk about our family, how large it was, and how everyone helped each other. Then, in a very gentle way, he told me that Mother Battler had passed away. He explained to me that she'd been very ill for a long time and that she was now in heaven with God."

Thereafter, although Walter was living with my Aunt Mayme and Uncle Jim, he was a constant fixture around our house. He moved in with us because Aunt Mayme was traveling a lot with her husband, a career Naval officer, and it was felt that he needed to be in one place rather than uprooted every time Uncle Jim was transferred to another base.

Walter was offered a bedroom in the main house but chose to live in the pool house, with my father's approval, where he had access to his own small kitchen area, a front room, bath, and dressing room. Not bad for a kid just turning fourteen:

"It was neat to think that Lou would let me have a place like that all to myself. I did, however, spend a lot of time in the main house and ate all my meals there. I can remember Paddy, Carole, and me getting into all sorts of trouble, but having a great time. I especially loved having dinner in the huge dining room at the Long-ridge house. Lou, after having had rheumatic fever in 1943 (plus his weight problem) was always on what seemed to be a restricted diet. The maid would bring in a tray heaped with roast beef, potatoes, rolls and all of that good stuff—and there would be poor Lou with a hamburger patty, cottage cheese, and skim milk. He would stare at the rest of us as we ate and then start to kid us, pretending he was going to steal our food. He always made light of the human condition—even if it was his own."

Dad always stocked the bar area with soft drinks and lots of candy. A favorite was Hollywood candy bars, which he bought by the gross and kept around for the "kids." Whenever Mom or Dad found an open box down to the last couple of bars, my father would ask, "What happened to all of them?" Of course, nobody ever knew—except perhaps himself.

Education was number one on my father's list of rules for success. Consequently, Walter would go to a good school. Mom wanted him to attend Notre Dame High School in Sherman Oaks, one of the best Catholic high schools for boys in the country, where he was enrolled as a freshman and graduated. Dad financed his entire education and never once mentioned it. Walter was one of "his" kids and nothing was too good for his kids.

During the summer months, you could always find Walter, Paddy, and Carole on the set with Dad when he was shooting, and it was vacation time for the kids. They used to sneak around the lot, going from one soundstage to another watching them shoot, having a great time. In the morning there was always big boxes of donuts on the coffee cart and they'd stuff their mouths. Eventually it became my turn. The others were older and into other things. I loved being turned loose so I could slip into the prop department, makeup and wardrobe areas to look around, certain that I was totally alone and unwatched. I wish! My father knew where I was every minute of the day when I was on a movie set—just as he had with Walter and my sisters. We were "show biz brats" and I'm sure studio workers often would've liked to wring our necks.

While we kids were having fun, it was a grueling day for my father. Here's a sample of his daily schedule when he was working on a film:

Up at six A.M. He'd pick up the script from his dressing table and go into the dining room in his robe to have coffee, a boiled egg, and piece of toast. Only he and the cook would be up that early. During the school year, we got up in time to see him leave for the studio. Mom always got up to make sure that Walter and my sisters were dressed properly for school and fed a nourishing breakfast. Dad arrived at the studio about seven-thirty A.M. and went directly to makeup and wardrobe. He was usually in front of—or ready for—the cameras by eight A.M. It was usually six or seven P.M. when Dad arrived home, and often even later. He never wanted the family to wait dinner for him. If he wasn't home by seven, we sat down and started dinner. Even when he was there for dinner, it was a quiet time. We always respected his time of relaxation at the dinner table after a hard day at the studio. It was obvious by the strain on his face that he was too exhausted for petty conversation.

After dinner and a hot bath he'd always come into the den to visit with the family, a much more relaxed and less tense man. The den with the big bar always was a favorite of my father's—a place to sit alone and reflect or to gather with his family. I remember he had a big recliner and even today I can see him leaning back in that chair, me perched up on his lap—God, those were wonderful family affairs that I'll treasure forever. Around nine o'clock Dad would pick up his script, tuck it under his arm, and retire for the night—but never without giving his children a hug and kiss and warm goodnight. Mom went into the bedroom to make sure he was okay and would then come back out and join us before she tucked us into bed. My father was a hard-working family man.

Those were the wonderful years when I didn't understand about adult problems—only that I had Mommy and Daddy, that they loved me, and that we lived in a big house with a lot of rooms and a lot of hugs and kisses.

CHAPTER XV

Kissing the
Forties Good-bye

UNIVERSAL-INTERNATIONAL had been in the process of developing competition for Abbott & Costello by the end of the decade, so in 1949 the executives didn't mind loaning the team out to United Artists for *Africa Screams*, a Huntington Hartford Production, produced by Edward Nassour and directed by Charles Barton.

The only description that aptly describes the making of this film is that it was a slapstick, chaotic, free-wheeling production. "Bring 'em back alive" big game hunter-actor Frank Buck and circus owner/lion tamer/actor Clyde Beatty were added to the film to lend authenticity for the public's imagination. It was a waste of talent and money, because Abbott & Costello are what the film was all about. It wasn't a classic Abbott & Costello picture. Much of the blame for that can be placed at Universal's doorstep. Dad felt the studio was trying to kill off the goose that laid the golden egg, while giving more and more attention to Francis the Talking Mule along with Ma and Pa Kettle pictures.

Eddie Nassour and my father did not get along from the start. Nassour sent out memos that if anybody on the picture caught Lou Costello playing pranks or practical jokes they were to report directly to him. He would "truck" no foolishness on his picture. That was not the way to start an Abbott & Costello picture. Melvin Joseph Bassett, who managed Nassour Studios, recalls the making of *Africa Screams*:

> "It got so we were calling the picture 'Nassour Screams.' Hardly a day went by that Eddie didn't find something wrong with Lou. He

thought Lou was goofing off too much and not following the shooting schedule. Of course, the fact that he had a lot of his own money in the picture may have contributed to his attitude.

"I worked for Eddie Nassour for thirty-five years and knew him to be basically a nice guy. His brother used to egg him on a bit, but Donald Crisp instigated a lot of the friction between Lou and Eddie. Donald was controlling the financing and was known to be very tight with the buck. The picture was scheduled to be shot in sixteen days. It took twenty-seven. I can still hear Eddie trying to soothe Crisp. 'Just one more day, Don,' he'd say. 'Just one.'

"Every day after sixteen Eddie would start having fits. One day, unable to contain himself any longer, Eddie went screaming out of his office with a gun in his hand, yelling, 'I'm gonna kill him!' "

Eddie Nassour brought on the gun incident by an action he had taken earlier. For whatever reason, he had ordered a set to be painted, and then charged the cost to Abbott & Costello. Dad refused to pay any part of it. Eddie made charges; Dad countered them. Finally the feud got out of hand and Eddie came racing onto the set waving a pistol and threating to blow Dad's head off. The head cameraman, Charles Van Enger, took the gun away from Nassour. It was a disturbing act, by a man who seemed unable to handle the frustrations of day-to-day film production. It was reported that Nassour, some years later, took his own life.

Bobby Barber was working on the picture as was Joe Besser, whom Dad had known and worked with in burlesque. Consequently a lot of shenanigans took place. The pie-throwing sequence reached its peak in *Africa Screams*. Before the film was completed, not only Bobby and Dad, but everybody on the picture, had been caught up in tossing the gooey pastries. Dad ordered custard and cream pies from a baker in the San Fernando Valley and Bobby would pick several dozen up each day on his way to the studio. These were not the tasteless prop department imitations, but the real honest-to-goodness luscious treats, fresh from the ovens daily. Dad assumed the posture that if Eddie Nassour wanted to be "an old sourpuss," then they might as well have a good time doing the picture.

As always, Dad wanted to work with people he considered part of the Costello family. Joe Besser was one of those he liked to have aboard. Not only had he known and worked with Joe in burlesque, but also in radio, including his own show. Joe had moved out to California in 1948, after the *Abbott & Costello Radio Show* went from NBC to ABC (1946). In addition to their regular weekly radio spot, Dad and Bud hosted a kiddie show called *The Abbott & Costello Children's Show* on Saturday mornings over ABC radio. It ran for three years. In March of 1949, following one of his perennial relapses, Dad asked Joe Besser to take over his spot on the children's show, which he did for one week. As good a comic and actor as Joe Besser was, people wanted Abbott & Costello—not Abbott & Besser.

Martin Ragaway and Leonard Stern were signed on as writers for *Africa Screams.* Neither of the two men was a stranger to my father, since they had both been writers on the *Abbott & Costello Radio Show.* Both men have excellent recollections of their experiences with my father. Martin Ragaway:

"Lou wanted a lot of jokes on the radio show. I remember the time he held up a script that had been submitted and said, 'Nope. It won't work. There's only ten jokes on this page, which means only ten laughs.' He wanted scripts that were machine-gun fire rapid with jokes and skits for the show. I recall one joke which really embarrassed me. Lou was talking to some high society woman:

LOU: You're hoity-toity.
S.W.: No! I'm sorry, I'm *houtee* toytee.
LOU: You might be hoytee, but you'll never see toytee again.

"I was against using the joke. I said, 'Lou, you can't possibly do that on the radio.' Lou looked at me with a smile and said, 'Watch.' When he did it on the air with a studio audience, it got the largest laugh of the night."

As I've mentioned earlier, Dad didn't like to use jokes or routines that hadn't been time-tested in burlesque or vaudeville. One time there was a joke Ragaway and Stern were anxious to get into one of the Abbott & Costello radio scripts. In order to pass Dad's standing rule about what jokes to use, they lied to him and told him that Fred Allen had gotten a big laugh with it on his radio show. When Dad heard that, he immediately changed his mind after previously rejecting the skit. "Oh, okay," he said. "If Fred used it, we'll keep it in."

One of the greatest jokes that Dad and Bud ever used was contrived by Ragaway and Stern. Here are two versions of it that give an indication of just how much mileage can be gotten out of good basic material:

> LOU: I'm going out to do the chores.
> BUD: What chores?
> LOU: I'll have a Scotch and water.
> $\qquad$ and
> LOU: We're going to take this boat to some foreign shores.
> BUD: What shores?
> LOU: I'll have a Scotch and soda.

These two writers were also responsible for creating a take-off on *Sam Spade, Private Eye,* which was dubbed "Sam Shovel" on the radio show. When Dad did it on the air, it was an immediate hit. It also gave him a chance to spoof every detective show that ever appeared in comics or on radio, and it became a standard part of the show for quite some time.

My father had offices on Sunset Boulevard in West Hollywood in The Lou Costello Building. Script meetings were held there every week for the radio show—and often for films when Dad felt the necessity. Bud Abbott seldom was interested in such meetings unless Dad initiated them. On the day of the show the team would meet with the head writer and whatever other writers were involved for the week. The script would be discussed and everybody would make comments about what to keep in or changes to make, if any. Leonard Stern recalls those early meetings:

> "Marty and myself were the babies on the show which had writers like Eddie Forman, Sid Fields, Harry Crane, Hal Fimberg, Don Prindle, Ed Cherkose, Parke Levy, Paul Conlon, and John Grant, their main gag writer. Because we were new, Bud and Lou were somewhat protective of us, always referring to us as 'The boys' or 'The kids.' Bud called everybody 'Neighbor' and Lou called me 'Toots.' It became a standing joke for Lou to see us coming into a meeting and say, 'Well, here come Toots and Neighbor.'

"The first meeting we ever attended upset me quite a bit. I learned something about Hollywood that day. I was new to the show and Bud wasn't there, for whatever reason. Right away some of the writers were making changes in Bud's lines and I thought it was unfair to do that with him missing, but I couldn't say anything.

"It was a rather impersonal beginning for us, but once I got to know how the Abbott & Costello team functioned and knew the two of them better, I realized what professionals they were. I never really got to know Lou well until *Africa Screams,* which was the first of three films I worked on for them. Lou never forgot you if he liked you and was satisfied with your work. He had great loyalty."

As I mentioned, a lot of pies were thrown on the set of *Africa Screams,* and Hillary Brooke, the female lead, nearly left the picture before it even got started. Having never worked with actors who didn't follow cue-lines, she was totally unprepared for Abbott & Costello. After the first day of shooting, she went home and phoned her agent, Ed Henry. "Ed," she cried, "I just can't do it. I can't keep up with them. I never get cues and I'm a maniac at this point!" The agent was sympathetic, but said, "Stay with it, Hillary; it'll be okay." Hillary says that it was indeed all right:

"Ed was right. I fell absolutely in love with Lou as a friend and had a great time on the film. The secret was, you just had to learn how to work with them. Once you mastered that, it was a ball! I was a tall, blonde, straight lady—not a comedienne—and he could be so funny. On *Africa Screams,* the first picture I did with Abbott & Costello, I got a good example of Lou's sense of humor. This was after Nassour had been screaming about production costs. One morning Lou tacked up some pictures of Nassour around the sound stage. He said, 'This is the way he looked two months ago, but you should see how he looks now!' "

When Hillary again worked with Abbott & Costello in *Abbott & Costello Meet Captain Kid* (1952), she was able to pass along her experience to Charles Laughton, who played Captain Kidd in the film:

"In the beginning Mr. Laughton found it very difficult to work with Bud and Lou because of their ad-libbing. After all, he came from the legitimate theater, was disciplined, and relied on proper cues. So I said to the great man, 'You'll do fine. You just have to know how to work with Lou.' "

Neither Dad nor Bud ever played tricks to actually hurt anybody. It was more a matter of keeping the energy level high in between takes, so there wouldn't be any letdown when shooting resumed. Hillary Brooke was one co-worker who understood:

"There were some who thought their pranks were very unprofessional—especially producers. But it is very important when you are dealing in comedy to keep up that peak of energy, particularly when it is comedy in films. Bud and Lou were easy to work with and such fun. It was the type of experience in which you couldn't wait to get back on the set the following morning and you never wanted to leave at night. I believe that every actor and actress should be allowed to do at least one Abbott & Costello film—it's a shame they're both gone now."

In spite of the tension, traumas, fights, and side-splitting antics, *Africa Screams* was finally completed much to the delight of everyone concerned. As usual, there was as much or more going on in Dad's private life as at the studio. Ophelia and Mitch Watson had left our employ and for two years were replaced by Mae and Sven. Following their departure Mom decided that it was wise not to hire another couple. Instead she employed Ophelia MacFashion, whose sister was our laundress. Mitch had always doubled as our chauffeur, so Dad asked Ophelia if she'd be his "chaufferette." Ophelia's answer was no. Driving scared her half to death and she'd given it up. Of course that didn't deter my father. He simply encouraged Ophelia to go to driving school and learn all over again. Ophelia took the course and passed the test. When Dad got home from the studio that day, his first question was, "Well, show me your license."

Although Ophelia didn't become Dad's personal chauffeurette, she inherited the assignment of taking Paddy and Carole back and forth to Marymount School in Brentwood—and she did it quite well, despite her fear of driving over the canyons to get there and back.

Ann Abbey, my nurse, had a routine. She would put me down for my nap in the afternoon, then get me up, dress me, and fix my hair before Dad got home from the studio. It was almost a ritual that I appear in laces and ruffled dresses, hair combed and curled, and looking all spic-and-span to greet my father when he got home every day. Poor Ophelia spent hours pressing the ruffles on my dresses.

After our annual Christmas soiree on Longridge Avenue, we spent the waning days of 1949 in Palm Springs, where Dad always took the family to spend New Year's, returning to the San Fernando Valley in time for my sisters' first day of school in January. It was around this time when Dad purchased the two-acre parcel he named the "L.C. Ranch," located in North Hollywood near Roscoe Boulevard and Whitsett. It was here that Dad began to show an interest in raising his own thoroughbred racehorses.

Through Aunt Marie's husband, Joe Kirk, Dad met and hired Ruth and Russ Grose as caretakers of the ranch. Ruth says:

"I remember that you would turn onto a dirt road and the barn and main house were tucked away from the street. There was a two-bedroom home on the property, where Russ and I moved in with our two children, Jim and Pat. Also there were some small stable areas, where we housed Lou's horses. At Lou's request, Russ drew up plans for a new barn, which Lou approved and Russ built, providing adequate space for Lou's horses. He was just starting with thoroughbreds, but purchased horses for Paddy and Carole, and later a pony for Christy. Before long there were additional ponies for her friends to ride."

All of Dad's racehorses were kept at the ranch, unless they were running; then they were transferred to the track stables until after the races. Dad had Bazooka, Lolly C, and another horse named Blue Baby that never ran in a race. Many of our thoroughbreds were bred there at the ranch, including *Bold Bazooka*, the only horse he *really* made money on from racing.

Dad had never seen a horse born. One day Russ told him one of the ponies was about to give birth. Dad's eyes lit up with excitement and he asked Russ to call him at the house when he knew it was going to happen. Dad went home, and about four in the morning Russ telephoned him. "Lou, the pony's in labor. You better get right over here." My father broke speed limits driving out to the ranch, where he found the pony in one of the stalls at the barn, almost ready to deliver. He stationed himself in the doorway (Ruth brought him a chair), where he could see everything and there he waited, like an impatient mid-wife, for the birth. When it finally happened, his eyes grew large and he danced about as tickled as he could be. Yet all he could say was, "I'll be damned. Did you see that? I'll be damned!"

We also raised chickens and turkeys, and one time Dad called Russ and said, "I have some Jewish friends I wanna give some turkeys to, so I'm sending over a rabbi. I don't know what he wants, but do whatever he says, because these birds have got to be kosher. They're for eatin' and I want them to be the kosherest turkeys he ever saw."

Dad was train crazy, so it surprised no one when he decided to put in tracks at the ranch, all the while repeating, "I want it finished by Christmas so Christy can have it as a gift." Everybody knew Dad loved that project so much it was doubtful he would share it with anyone. Professionals were hired to lay the tracks around the property and a miniature train consisting of a front engine with a seat, plus several cars, was set up. Needless to say, there was a great to-do on Christmas about my present. My father sat down on the engine seat and placed me in one of the cars. He said, "Since it is her train, Christy gets the first ride." Then he started the engine and drove me around the ranch. Ann Abbey brought me over to the ranch during the week for a train ride but it was a long time before I was ever allowed to operate it by myself.

I spent a lot of afternoons during my early years on that ranch—time spent with my mother, who loved to get away from the Longridge house and take me to the ranch to ride the ponies and see our animals. Dad would often quite unexpectedly show up with a number of friends for lunch, which sent Ruth to the chickenhouse to collect eggs for egg sandwiches. It was the only thing she could prepare on the spur of the moment.

It was during this time in our lives that Mom became suspicious that Dad was seeing another woman. She never could prove it, but somehow or other she had it implanted in her mind. She began to drink more and she became more easily depressed. She confided in De De, who recalls her own convictions about my mother's concern:

> "Whether Lou was or wasn't seeing someone else, I don't know now and didn't know then, but in show business it happens every day. You always hear of women throwing themselves in the path of some successful man. Lou was not only successful, but extremely popular. It would not have been surprising if women threw themselves at him—and I don't doubt some did. But there was never any evidence I ever saw that gave credence to any 'illicit romance' on the part of Lou."

Ann Abbey, my nurse, didn't help matters between Mom and Dad. Well aware of my mother's drinking, she waited up one night until my father came home late, prepping herself to "give him the facts about his wife." She told De De what she had in mind, and the following day when De De asked Ann if she had talked with my father, she said yes, she had.

"What happened?" De De asked.

"Nothing. He never even answered me when I told him."

With all her suspicions, plus the everyday pressures of raising a family, Mom felt the world was closing in on her and that my father no longer cared. She spoke to De De about her frustrations with my father and how cold he was toward her. "De De," she confided, "I just can't take it anymore. I'm going to take the girls and rent an apartment in Beverly Hills." De De did not take her threat seriously, knowing how much Mom's marriage meant to her. "You know something, De De?" she said, "I have tried to have pillow talks with Lou, but he just turns over on his back and doesn't say a word."

De De assured her that what the whole family needed was a vacation together away from Hollywood. She remembers Mom saying, "If we only could. . . ."

Although Dad may have been uncommunicative with our mother, he was always involved in something with us girls—as was Mom. He was extremely affectionate with me—and always concerned. I was young and didn't know about Butch or what had happened to him, and one day while splashing around in the shallow end of the pool, I started playing make-believe. I yelled out, "I'm drowning, Daddy. I'm drowning." Then I burst into childish giggles. Dad grabbed me up from the water and looked at me in the most stern manner I ever saw. "Young lady, don't you *ever* let me hear you say that again unless you are actually having problems in the water, because if you do I will personally give you a sun-burned bottom with my bare hand. Drowning is not something you joke about." That's one time my hurt feelings went unattended. He meant business.

Whatever problems my parents were having between them, Mom devoted most of her time to making us happy, and Dad over-indulged us with things until it was ridiculous. Nothing was ever too expensive if one of us girls wanted it, though for our own good Mom would occasionally veto his approval. In spite of Mom and Dad's differences, I saw us as a very happy and loving family.

CHAPTER XVI

New Adventures

F OR SEVERAL YEARS negotiations had been going on to bring Abbott & Costello to England to play the world-famous Palladium. Several agents had been involved in the transactions—in America as well as in the United Kingdom. There was a lot of in-fighting over who would set the deal, with numerous cancellations, charges, and countercharges. Dad waited until he had the financial arrangements *he* wanted rather than relying on the back-slapping assurances of wheeler-dealer theatrical agents and entrepreneurs.

This was to be no ordinary trip, for accompanying the two stars were their business and professional representatives brought along to buffer fans and the media. I'd say we were a bit like Barnum & Bailey, moving from one continent to another, as both Dad and Bud Abbott each brought along an enormous entourage, which included their families, their families' family, plus the usual coterie, who always seem to consider themselves necessary to administer to the needs of a star. Boarding the *Super Chief* in Los Angeles, Mom, Dad, and we girls were joined by my grandmother Cristillo, her sister Mae, Dr. Immerman (Dad's doctor) and his family, a governess for me—and my godfather, Joe Bozzo from New Jersey. I mean, we took all the comforts (and some of the drawbacks) of home with us. Dad wanted Aunt Marie to come along, but her boys were still too young to leave behind even though they had a nurse.

Of course, there was a side-trip from New York to visit Joe Bozzo's home on Lake Erskine in Jersey. Italian families are very large on exchanging visits with one another.

We finally boarded the *Queen Mary* and departed New York harbor with great fanfare and, for me at least, lots of excitement and confusion. Dad promised Paddy and Carole that if they were good girls they could go horseback riding in London at Windsor Park with "Princess Margueriette." He couldn't simply say Princess Margaret; he had to jazz it up.

On board with us was actor Clifton Webb. Carole had been an enthusiastic Webb fan after seeing him in *Titanic*. When she heard he was sailing with us, she instantly bombarded our parents with requests for an introduction. "I gotta meet him! I just gotta meet him!" Among Dad's collection at our Longridge home was the film *Mr. Pennybacker*, which starred Mr. Webb. Carole was forever asking Dad to run that picture "just one more time."

Dad told Carole he'd see what could be done. "Mr. Webb is a very private man. I'm not sure he wants to be disturbed by fans." Eventually Carole did meet Mr. Webb and it was all contrived quite theatrically. One afternoon, when she was on deck leaning over the railing, she heard Dad calling out, "Carole, I'd like you to meet someone." On the deck, just below where she was standing, she saw Dad looking up and waving. "Here's a gentleman," he said, "who's just dying to meet you." Clifton Webb turned around, looked up at Carole and smiled at her. Of course my sister broke into hysterical giggles, not very elegant behavior for a twelve year old trying to act sophisticated. Dad played it for a laugh and that's exactly what he got.

Val Parnell, impresario of the London Palladium, rolled out the welcome carpet for Abbott & Costello. When our ship docked in Southampton, we were greeted by the press in droves. Dad and Bud entertained them with a litany of their famous routines. Abbott & Costello had been extraordinarily popular during the war in England and the welcome at the Savoy Hotel in London was equally generous and genuine. The English audiences went wild at the Palladium. Night after night the rounds of applause rolled across the concert hall like thunder. It seemed that Dad and Bud could do no wrong.

An old friend from the press, columnist May Mann, was staying at the Grand Hotel when the Costello entourage arrived in Rome, taking the city by storm. Miss Mann tells of our impact from firsthand knowledge:

"I, by this time, had established a relationship with Lou and Anne. When they arrived in Rome they seemed to revolutionize the whole city. During that time of year it was extremely hot and there were no fans in the hotel rooms—only in the elevators. Well, leave it to Lou. Someway, somehow, he managed to scrape up twenty electric fans! He *needed* them with the troupe he was bringing along. It was one of the largest Hollywood parties ever to hit Rome. The luggage alone would almost fill a railroad baggage car. But the Italians loved Lou and would follow him down the streets. It was a mob scene wherever he went."

While Dad was playing show dates around the continent, we girls did things with Mom and sometimes with my grandmother, who was visiting Europe for the first time. We all went to Scotland, where Mom was born, and we visited with relatives we had never seen before. Mother, to our delight, had a wonderful time hugging, kissing, and touching kin she hadn't heard from since coming to America with her father many years earlier.

Good times somehow always seem to be followed by bad ones. While we were in Europe, De De suspected even more strongly that something was wrong with Dad's new accountant—and the books:

"I knew some mischief was going on and I started to get nervous about things. Checks were going through the bank account that I didn't recognize and I was still the only person authorized by Lou to sign checks. I finally decided to write Lou in London, explaining things to him and tendering my resignation from his employment. I knew something was going to happen and I didn't want to get into the middle of anything shady that might be going on."

Dad received De De's letter while we were at the Savoy in London. He called Los Angeles. De De quickly explained her feelings to Dad. He said that he understood and would talk to her when he got home, but he was depressed for several days. He trusted De De and felt she should've stayed at the house until he returned. He felt it was wrong for somebody who was "part of the family" to abandon him. De De saw it otherwise.

De De went to work for a friend for three months, but when we returned from our European tour one of the first things Dad did was call her and ask her to come back to work for him.

163

She immediately answered, "Yes," admitting that she missed working for Dad.

"How soon can you start?"

She said, "Monday. But Lou, I can't return for the same money because I'm making more with this job I have now."

There was silence on Dad's end of the line for a moment before he said, "Okay, you got it. See you on Monday."

Dad was very quick when he made up his mind he wanted De De back. He never liked the idea that anybody could woo away any of his employees.

On Monday morning Dad welcomed De De back and asked her to call the Bank of America in Studio City and have them send all of his statements and cancelled checks over to the house by special messenger. Once they were received, he very carefully went over all the signatures on the cancelled checks. As he pored over the checks he asked, without looking up, "De De, how many of these are there?" It was obvious that his signature had been forged.

"About $18,000 worth, Lou."

Dad called a meeting that same night in the pool room at our home with Max Fink, himself, De De and the accountant. The young man was confronted, found to be at fault, and fired by my father. A few days later his wife came to see Dad and pleaded with him to give her husband one more chance, that they had two children and would be destitute if her husband had no employment. Dad, always a softie when it came to the welfare of children, couldn't hide his sympathetic feelings for the woman and finally decided to give her husband his job back with conditions: He would never take another penny he hadn't earned and would repay the funds he had embezzled from Dad's account. The man agreed.

A few months later Dad again caught him not only forging Dad's name on checks, but also stamping the back of payroll checks and depositing them into another account. The only explanation Dad and De De had was that he must have opened a joint account in his and Dad's names by forging Dad's signature, and was depositing the pay checks into it.

Shortly after this financial fiasco Dad asked De De to take some cash over to the Studio City branch of the Bank of America. It was not unusual for Dad to let his bills go to the very last moment, have De De write out checks, and then rush over to the bank with a deposit to make sure everything was covered. On this particular day he handed De De a big wad of cash— $48,000 to be exact. De De was scared to death. "How on earth do you expect me to drive over to the bank with that much cash, Lou? What happens if I'm in an accident?"

Dad joked, "Just don't wreck my limousine."

Dad phoned Mr. Flynn at the bank and advised him that De De was on her way over with the cash. He looked at De De and winked as he spoke to Flynn: "If she isn't down there in twenty minutes, then she's on a boat to Panama!"

The incident with the accountant was not unique in my father's career. Later there was an actor (an ex-cop from New York) who approached Dad while he was in the throes of his problems with the Internal Revenue Service. He assured Dad that for $25,000 he could straighten the whole problem out for him. Dad, anxious to have his name cleared with the IRS, gave the guy the $25,000. Of course the man was never heard from again, until he was arrested for embezzling in the San Francisco area and sent to jail. Dad never tried to have him prosecuted for what he did to us.

Dad also had some funny experiences with his underworld-type friends—people who were on the shady side of the law but who liked to rub elbows with movie stars even though they had ambivalent feelings about them. Dad had many "influential" friends who absolutely adored him. When he owned the Band Box nightclub, one night after closing the place was robbed. Intruders took everything—cash, furniture, and liquor. When Dad was apprised of what had happened, he got on the phone to one of his "friends" and told the guy he'd been "taken to the cleaners."

"Now Lou, I'm sure this wouldn't have happened if they'd known it was *your* club they were robbing." Within a matter of hours a truck pulled up at the back entrance of the club and *everything* taken was safely returned, with apologies.

Another incident had Dad sweating. A powerful and extremely wealthy mogul invited Dad and our family to his son's wedding reception, which was to be held at the Biltmore Hotel in downtown Los Angeles. Dad completely forgot about it and instead took Mom and us girls on the yacht to Catalina. The reception turned out to be a lavish affair costing thousands of dollars. Doves with thousand-dollar bills clasped to their legs were released and flew into the air over the wedding party. De De attended and recalls how hilarious it was to see grown people climbing up the woodwork to catch those doves.

The following day the gentleman called my father to ask why he hadn't shown up. Dad, suddenly remembering, said "Oh! Well, you see . . . I took the boat over to Catalina and it broke down over there."

All the man said was, "All right, Lou," and hung up. He then phoned De De and asked her if Dad's story was true. De De, loyal employee that she was, assured the man that Dad had told the truth.

Dad may have forgotten that wedding, but he never once forgot me. He and Mother would take me out—and it didn't matter if we were at a studio or in a restaurant, there was never any objection when I decided to stand up and start singing. Once Mom took me to lunch at The Tail o' the Cock in Sherman Oaks. I stood up in the middle of my meal and started singing "Surrey with the Fringe on Top" from *Oklahoma*. I had a voice just like Dad's—high, piping, and shrill—and I sounded just like him when he used to say, "He—e—y—y A—b—b—o—t—t!"

De De loved my mother and the feeling was mutual. Although she worked for Dad, it was not unusual for Mom to call him and say, "Lou, I need to do some shopping. Mind if I take De De with me?" He always said yes and the two of them would go out for lunch and have a ball. Usually I went along because I wasn't in school yet. De De retains bright memories of my mother:

"I can't stress just how much Anne possessed that wonderful wit and humor. She truly loved to laugh. She was very domestically oriented and referred to herself as a *Scotch Guinea*. Sometimes, when the help was off, I'd come into the house and be unable to find Anne anywhere. After searching around, I usually located her in the little laundry room off the kitchen, where she would be sitting behind this big iron presser, ironing sheets and pillow cases. It was a great quality in her personality—she wasn't too big that she couldn't put her hand into anything that needed to be done.

"Ever the lady, Anne knew how to entertain and always asked questions when she wasn't certain about anything. Never a phony, she gravitated toward people who were sincere and real. Anne was never the type of woman who flocked around other stars' wives. She much preferred taking her children to lunch, the zoo or a park to being a part of the Hollywood ladies' auxiliary."

Mom always made certain she had money around the house when she needed it, and because she was confiding more and more in De De, she let her in on one of her most intimate secrets. In Dad's large semicircular dressing room off the master bedroom, he had a safe that was almost big enough to walk through. Mom, in her dressing room off the master bedroom, had a strong box. One day she asked De De to accompany her to her bedroom. "I want to show you something that will give you a big laugh." She took De De in and opened the strong box. Inside she had $10,000 in cash. "Lou," she said laughingly, "is so thrifty with his money that it makes me feel good to have this here. It's my mad money."

Although my dad squandered thousands of dollars, he was extremely frugal around the house. He gave my mother an allowance and expected her to run the house with it. He was not stingy, but he certainly valued the home expense dollar. The $10,000 was the result of Mom's ability to save from her weekly allowance.

Dad and Universal were at odds again in 1950. This time it was nothing petty. He received a letter from: "Just a fan who loves you dearly for all the joy you've brought to the world." The fan confidentially revealed that Universal was selling 16mm prints of Abbott & Costello films through a bootleg distributor who, in turn, was merchandising them through retail outlets—and that, as a matter of fact, one of these stores was in Hollywood. The name and address of the establishment was given.

Dad got Eddie Sherman on the phone. He was absolutely beside himself, thinking that Eddie was somehow involved in a scam to beat him out of money. He'd never fully trusted Sherman since his father's death. "You little sonofabitch!" he screamed into the receiver. "What the hell are you trying to do to Bud and me?"

"Calm down, Lou," Eddie said. "You're not making any sense. Start from the top."

"What the hell kind of deal you got goin' with Universal to

cheat us out of our 16mm rights," Dad hollered. "We had a deal and you know it. Those prints belong to Abbott & Costello. Not to you and not to Universal. Now I want a stop to it right now and I want an accounting. I wanna know how long this has been going on. I wanna sue Universal!"

When Dad calmed down, Eddie finally got out of him what he was talking about and swore to my father he knew nothing about it, but would investigate it immediately. Dad demanded that he do just that. He hung up the phone, never doubting that Eddie Sherman was in some way involved in the piracy of the Abbott & Costello films.

Then Dad got on the phone to Bud Abbott. Bud tried to soothe him. "Maybe it's just a crank letter, Lou. Maybe it's from somebody trying to cause trouble."

"I don't think so, Bud."

"Well, I'll go along with whatever you say. You know that. So let's see what Eddie finds out."

Eddie reported back to Dad that indeed the films were being sold in 16mm and that Universal was the culprit.

"I'll sue them for every goddamn penny they ever made," Dad roared, totally out of character.

Eddie was adamantly against suing the studio. "Lou," he said, "that will accomplish nothing but hard feelings and bad publicity."

"Hard feelings for who? Bad publicity for who? Not for Abbott & Costello. Maybe for Universal. I sure as hell hope so. I'd like to sink those sonsofbitches for all the shit they've put us through for the last ten years. They got some nerve."

Nevertheless, Sherman prevailed, and Dad went to his grave believing that the only reason Eddie didn't want to sue was because he had his own hand in the till along with Universal. Dad once told Mom there was no way Universal could sell their pictures in 16mm without Eddie Sherman knowing about it. "I really wish I could nail him on this."

Mom never liked to believe bad of others. "I think you may be mistaken, Lou."

Dad just grumbled under his breath.

Meanwhile Eddie Sherman went straight to the heads of Universal, but they laughed at him. Executives refused to see him or to discuss the issue when he finally did get in to see one of them. He brought that bad news back to Dad.

"Okay, Eddie, I did it your way. Now we're going to do it mine. Sue the bastards!" Abbott & Costello filed a five million-dollar damage suit against the studio. Additionally, they found out that Universal was reissuing old Abbott & Costello pictures in order to undercut the team's independent production of *The Noose Hangs High*.

The studio stood silent until it became obvious that Dad and Bud intended to air it all in open court. Nate Blumberg, president of Universal, called Eddie Sherman in to negotiate a compromise to legal action. Eddie was tough; Dad insisted that he be. Abbott & Costello settled for two million dollars plus, with Universal's guarantee to never again undercut the team.

Dad's final comment about the issue was to Bud Abbott: "I wonder how much Eddie made on the deal from the other side?" He never trusted Eddie Sherman again.

CHAPTER XVII

A Potpourri

(Universal Theft, Gambling, Horses and the Track)

OVER THE YEARS, as my father's legend has continued to grow, three subjects almost always come up in any conversation regarding Lou Costello. They are: removing things from movie sets without permission, gambling, and horses and the race track. This is a good time to shine a little light on those often exaggerated but usually hilarious facets of the collected memorabilia of Lou Costello.

Removing things from movie sets without permission: Universal was quite chintzy when it came to furnishing sets—essentially because they were in the business of producing low-budget, grade-B films. Throughout my father's career at Universal, he helped himself to items of furniture or other objects from his film sets. He never had any pangs of guilt about what he was doing, because so far as he was concerned, he was underpaid by the studio, Universal was using his talents in low-budget pictures, and he wasn't taking anything that expensive. Stars had always taken things from the set at the end of filming, including expensive wardrobes, without a lot of fanfare. It was "customary," as they say in the industry. Consequently the following anecdotes are related without rancor or regret. They were part of the ongoing love-hate relationship that existed between Dad and Universal.

The way my father was built, it was impossible for the studio to fit him, as they did the Andrew Sisters, from the wardrobe department racks. His wardrobe *had* to be tailored. He would go to the studio tailor and order three of each item of clothing to

Anne Costello posing in front of the famous wishing well at the Longridge house.
CHRIS COSTELLO

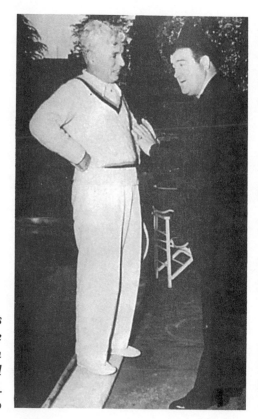

Lou meets with his idol, Charlie Chaplin, in Hollywood around 1946.
CAROLE COSTELLO

1947: Lou gets his first look at baby Chris. CHRIS COSTELLO

Carole, Paddy, and Lou in the kitchen, cooking for Mother's Day. CAROLE COSTELLO

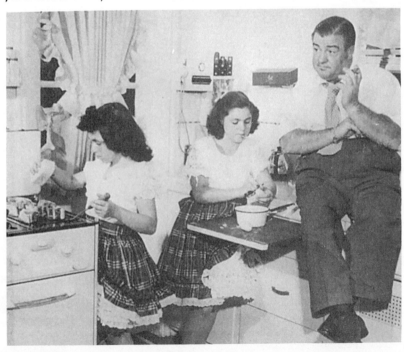

Anne and Lou at the opening of the Lou Costello Jr. Youth Foundation.

MARY FAILLA COLLECTION

Lou's mother with baby Chris. CHRIS COSTELLO

Chris and Lou on the set of Africa Screams.

CAROLE COSTELLO

Lou escorts daughter Paddy down the aisle at her wedding to James Mobley.

MARY FAILLA COLLECTION

Romeo Lou woos the fair maiden in a dream sequence (which was later deleted) from Buck Privates. UNIVERSAL STUDIOS

The first grandchild, Paddy's son Butch, and his doting grandfather. COLLECTION OF PADDY HUMPHRIES

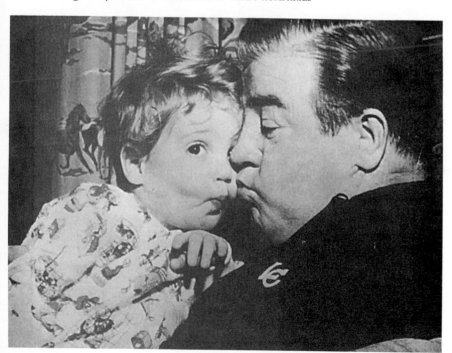

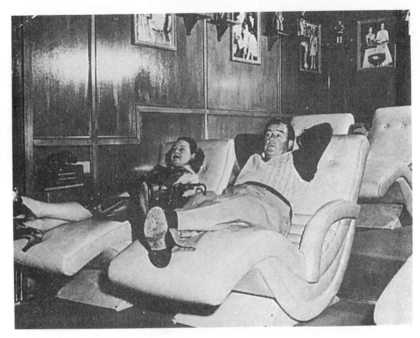

Anne and Lou watch a film in their home theater.

CAROLE COSTELLO

"Bazooka," Lou's first thoroughbred racehorse, at the Whitsett Ranch. CAROLE COSTELLO

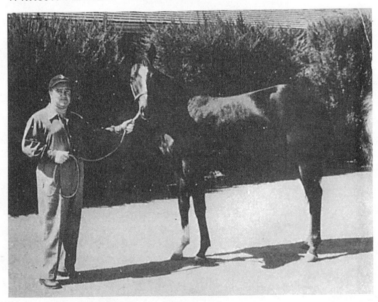

Joe Kirk (Marie's husband), Carole, Paddy, Lou's mother, Lou, Chris (in Anne's arms), Anne, and Marie (Lou's sister) at Thanksgiving dinner in 1947. CHRIS COSTELLO

Ward Bond and Lou rehearsing a scene for Wagon Train.
UNIVERSAL STUDIOS

Bud Abbott reads of Lou's death. U.P.I. COURTESY OF JIM MULHOLLAND

be used in a picture. He would immediately start kidding the wardrobe man. "Of course," he would say, "you're gonna let me keep all these clothes, aren't you?" He kept them regardless. His defense was, "It's better to give them to me than to the moths. Who else has a body like mine?"

One night Dad came home from work, joined Mom in the den, and placed a big box on the coffee table. He sent for Ophelia MacFashion and told her to turn around, which she did, used to my father's horsing around. He opened the box and placed a mink stole around her shoulders. "This is yours, Ophelia."

Mom's eyes popped. "Lou, have you lost your mind?"

"Mr. Costello, do you want me to have this?" Ophelia asked.

"I do. It's yours," Dad replied.

My mother knew exactly where my father got it. "No he doesn't," she said, her voice rising.

Dad was bent over double from laughing. "Yes I do, Ophelia. You take it on home with you tonight. It's yours."

Mom took out after Ophelia, who was by this time running around the table and out of the den, still yelling, "Oh, no she's not." Ophelia ran into a room off the kitchen and locked the door. Later in the evening when Ophelia was preparing to leave for the night, she went to Mom's bedroom and said, "Mrs. Costello, do you want me to have this mink stole? If you don't, I'll hand it back."

Mom smiled and said, "Yes, Ophelia, I want you to have it, so take it home with you. Okay?"

Ophelia suffered for taking it though, because while Dad was around that weekend, Mom didn't say anything, but when he left for the studio on Monday morning, she gave Ophelia hell for accepting the stole.

It was part of his nature to give and he had always been most generous with employees.

On another occasion Dad brought home a beautiful piece of crystal from the studio and gave it to Ophelia. Mom said nothing. She, too, was extremely generous with the help, yet on that one particular occasion she had taken exception.

Milt Bronson spent a lot of time on the set with Dad and helped him several times in getting set furnishings from the studio to our home on Longridge. Universal was aware of what was missing and knew who had taken it. When they were looking for a prop that had disappeared overnight, it increasingly became routine for them to either call Dad or send someone from the prop department over to our house to bring whatever Dad had taken back to the studio in order to finish the film. Milt claims Dad's mind was so quick that before Universal knew what was happening he had them agreeing that they could *borrow* it, provided it was returned right after the set was struck.

Universal wasn't the only studio to fall victim to Dad's chicanery. In 1944 he and Abbott were on loan-out to MGM to do *Lost in a Harem*. On the set they used very large, colorful stuffed pillows in a harem scene. After the shooting was completed, Dad was caught tossing pillows like crazy into the back of a delivery truck. Nobody said anything to him, but the following day the prop department was frantically searching for their pillows. They needed them for another scene. Someone tipped the front office and Dad was approached. "Please, Lou," the executive asked, "bring them back so we can complete shooting—then you can have them."

Charles Barton, who directed the disastrous filming of *Africa Screams* at Nassour Studios, remembers an incident that probably contributed to the Costello-Nassour conflicts:

"Lou never did anything to retaliate against a studio. Anybody who says he did, just didn't understand Lou. He was like a little boy. If he saw something pretty and liked it, he'd take it home with him. He was never malicious and even if he made it tough to get an item back, he did it in fun—not to hurt anyone. On *Africa Screams* we had some river scenes. In one situation we had the construction people build us a jungle set on a big sound stage with an actual water tank camouflaged to resemble the Congo River. There was a canoe in the scene made of beautiful buckskin with which Lou fell immediately in love. I knew his reputation and we all kept an eye on him to be sure the canoe stayed in place.

"One day we had to halt shooting because one of our actors, Shemp Howard, got seasick and he was part of the scene. We shut down for the day and in the confusion nobody thought to keep an eye on Lou. The following day when we resumed shooting the canoe was nowhere to be found. It had disappeared.

"We discovered it in Lou's front yard. Our men got there just in time to rescue it from his gardener. It was destined to become a rose planter."

Producer Robert Arthur tells one of the all-time classic Lou stories:

"We were doing *Abbott & Costello Meet Frankenstein* and had been shooting a scene in Dracula's castle. We wrapped one day [closed down the set], planning to pick up the same scene the following morning. The next morning an antique clock was missing from the mantel. Nobody could understand it because a Universal guard had been assigned to the set to prevent just such an occurrence. It meant we'd have to go back and reshoot all the scenes from the previous day—a very costly and time-consuming obstacle. I went down on the set and Joe Kenny, the assistant director, said to me, 'I think Lou took it home.'

'Did you ask him?' I said.

'Yeah, and he claims he didn't.'

We all knew that Lou had been admiring the clock, so when he came in that morning, I walked right up to him and said, 'Lou, did you take the clock?'

He looked at me impishly and asked, 'What clock?'

'The clock that used to be on the mantel over there. It's missing.'

He took his cigar out of his mouth and with a twinkle in his eyes replied, 'You're kidding! It is?'

We both knew he had the clock, so I finally said, 'Lou, tell you what I'll do. I'll make you a deal. Anybody who will bring back the clock so we can get this scene finished can have it after we have completed shooting.'

Lou looked at me with a gleeful grin of victory and said, 'Will ya put that in writing?'

That was Lou Costello—a rascal. Peck's bad boy, if you will, without a malicious bone in his body."

On another occasion, Charles Van Enger, the cameraman for a dozen or so Abbott & Costello pictures, recalls a similar incident:

"In this picture Lou and Marjorie Reynolds come back as ghosts. To get those ghost effects, we'd first photograph the set with nobody on it and then cover everything in black velvet. Next, we photographed the scene with the people. This was overlapped so that it looked as if, when somebody sat down in a chair, you could see right through them, giving the illusion of ghosts.

"We worked practically all day doing one of those ghost sequences and left word that *no one* was to touch anything on the set when we broke for the day. That night, however, Lou sneaked back in and took a lot of items off the set that he'd been casing during the daytime. As a result, we had to retake all of those scenes, which was costly, because even when we got the stuff back from Lou, we couldn't put them back exactly as they had been before. I don't think Lou ever understood the signs we posted all over the set following that incident which read: NOW DON'T MOVE ANYTHING!!!'"

Joe Kenny, the assistant director on several of my father's films, laughs when he recalls one of Dad's kleptomaniac forays:

"We had a beautiful garden set on one of the big sound stages. I remember there was a giant sleigh and it was brimming over with all sorts of beautiful flowers. We had finished shooting late one evening, and the next morning, when we all walked onto the set to resume where we'd left off, every stick of garden furniture, including the sleigh filled with flowers, was gone. There wasn't anything left on the stage—wiped out completely!

"I got hold of the prop man and set dresser and told them our predicament. They were dumbfounded. 'Joe,' I was assured, 'when we left last night, *everything* was in place.'

"I called Robert Arthur, our producer, and said, 'Bob, I think we've been had.' I explained what had happened. It was now about eight in the morning and it was costing the studio money to hold up production. I suggested perhaps Lou might know something about it. 'Why don't you call him at home? I'm sure he hasn't left for the studio yet, because he isn't scheduled until later in the day.' Bob did just that. He said, 'Lou—look, do me a favor, will you? I'm sending a truck out to your home to pick up the furniture you took off the set last night. When we're finished with it you can have it back. Is that all right?' It was. Evidently Lou had confiscated a studio truck and transported the load to his house. We found everything intact, all neatly arranged around his swimming pool area. Lou thought it looked great in his backyard.

"Lou, in his impish way, would never openly admit to taking something, but everyone knew that if Lou had his eye on something, it would eventually disappear. He'd go around the set saying, 'That's mine! That's mine!' "

Universal had a few tricks up its sleeves to deal with my father's shenanigans. Evidently, at one point someone in the front office said, "That's it!" They couldn't outright call Dad a thief, because he would've walked off the set and created more headaches than the items were worth. But one time, after a particularly bad week and when Dad had confiscated everything in sight, Universal devised a plan to get their property back. The paint department was asked to paint a sign on one of the studio trucks so it looked like a piano-moving truck. This done, they drove to our house and told Mom they were there from some piano-moving company to take Dad's piano out. Mom thought Dad had either sold or traded the instrument, so she let them in, commenting, "I'll bet Lou is trying to surprise me with the new piano he promised me." She accommodated the "piano movers" as much as possible, and they walked away with Dad's grand piano.

Dad went home for lunch that day, and when he got back to the studio, he had a look of grave concern. "You won't believe the thieves that are around this studio! Somebody walked into my house in broad daylight and stole my piano. It just had to be someone from the studio. I know it!"

Someone from the executive department took him aside and said, "Look, Lou, if you bring back the stuff you took off the set, then we'll make sure you get your piano back." The ploy worked and somehow or other I'm sure my father chuckled that the studio could be that sharp. It was not often that he was outwitted in the game, and it was just that—a game, Lou Costello being the little boy he always was.

Gambling: God knows my father was a gambler. Not a very good one, I might add, but he had fun doing it. Still, it was a costly pastime. There have been various estimates of how much money he lost playing cards, but a round figure of $1 million would be as good a ballpark figure as anybody could come up with. My father was compulsive about gambling—and so was Bud Abbott.

Dad's gambling began while he was in burlesque and vaudeville. In the early days it was nickel-and-dime stuff and nobody got hurt. Also, it was just he and Bud playing gin or seven-card stud backstage or between shows. George Raft, who knew Dad both in New York and Hollywood, recalled my father's compulsion:

"I remember how Lou loved to gamble. I always felt that led to his tax problems later on. He'd get into poker games at unbelievable stakes and with heavy pros, which was a big mistake. When he and Bud were gambling for thousands of dollars at the turn of a card, it got downright scary. There was a guy named Lewis that Lou used to invite to his poker games. This gentleman was a good card player and always won from Bud and Lou. Lou, though, would try to outdo Bud by raising and by trying to draw on an inside straight. Lewis, however, would play only if he had the right hand."

Dad was known to play a hand out even when he knew he couldn't win. There was something about staying in the game and being "one of the boys." He was very much like an adolescent kid who feels big because the older boys allow him to spend his money on them.

Actors, directors, producers—*strangers*—all were gambling partners of my father and Bud Abbott. Many of them made good money at their professions and some made an equally good amount of money from gambling with my father. He was an easy mark for any con job, so much so that Howard Christie was even able to devise a way to make sure Dad would be on the set on time.

"A fellow actor named Nick, who came from Chicago, often played poker with Bud and Lou. If I wanted to make certain Lou was on the set at a certain time, I simply put Nick's name on the daily call sheet for that time and I could be assured of Lou's punctuality. If I put Nick's name down for an eight o'clock call, you can bet Lou'd be there, along with Bud, eight o'clock sharp— to play poker! Then, if they were all in the middle of a poker game and we needed them for a scene, Joe Kenny and I would literally lift Lou up off his chair and carry him onto the set."

Maxene Andrews was the only person who wasn't involved in the card game that Dad allowed in his trailer back in 1941, when they made *Buck Privates*.

"Bud and Lou and a couple of their cronies would sneak away from the set and go into one of their trailers to play poker. Often their producer, Alex Gottlieb, would be in there with them! On one occasion I remember looking at the pot on the table and there must've been close to $30,000 in it. I had never seen that much cash! I was sworn to secrecy, and if they were wanted on the set and somebody asked me where they were, I always acted dumb."

Associated Press Hollywood reporter James Bacon was another old and dear friend from the early Abbott & Costello days on the burlesque and vaudeville circuits. Jim had better sense than to gamble with my father and his friends.

> "I never gambled with Bud and Lou. The reason being, when they started playing cards, they went for big stakes. I watched them tossing $100 bills into the pot like Halloween confetti. Often they were badly taken by professional card sharks who feigned friendship. Lou told me once that, after some twenty years, Bud had only managed to win something like $200 back."

Producer Howard Koch, who has gained so much fame for his magnificent productions of the annual Academy Award presentations, held the job of first assistant director on *The Noose Hangs High* (1948):

> "I hadn't met either Lou or Bud until *The Noose Hangs High*, which Abbott & Costello were producing independently. It seemed to be a low period in their career, but we all had a good time. Everyone enjoyed working with the team, but the big problem on the picture was their gambling. For instance, they'd be heavily into a gin rummy game when we had the set lit and ready to shoot. Whoever was winning would say to the other, 'Come on, let's go to work.' The one who was losing would reply, 'Screw you! I wanna finish this hand!' Because we were on a short schedule, I used every ounce of personality and persuasion just to get them out on the set. If they were unduly reluctant, I'd remind them that they were the producers, which worked when nothing else did. They didn't mind spending money on cards, but the idea that their production money was going down the drain got them moving."

There were a lot of good poker players in Hollywood, and Dad made the mistake of becoming involved with most of them. Often these guys would invite Dad into their games with the promise that he could have half his losings back. He fell for it until the IRS came on the scene. It was only then that my father eased up on gambling. In the meantime, it was "Katy bar the door!"

Dad and Bud held poker games at their homes, too, and I remember the times they played late into the night, and I could smell the different aromas of tobacco from cigarettes, pipes, and cigars. If someone walked through the room who was not a sit-down player, he was pressed into service to bring sandwiches and drinks to the players. The butlers cleaned up. There was an older man who used to come on Saturday mornings. He and my father would sit in the breakfast room and play cards all day and all night, the games breaking up on Sunday morning before Mom got up. This man always won from my father.

One morning Ophelia MacFashion walked through the room and Dad asked her for coffee and sandwiches. When she returned, his money was all lined up in front of the other man. Dad reached into the man's pile, picked a $20 bill off the top, and handed it to Ophelia. The man looked at Dad and shouted, "Hey, wait a minute! What the hell do you think you're doing?"

Dad laughed. "Take it, Ophelia," he said, "take it and run."

Ophelia recalls the aftermath of one of Dad's gambling ventures:

"One time Lou came back from Las Vegas with a satchel full of silver dollars. Anne found out where he hid it and kept going in and taking silver dollars out of the bag. Each time, she'd give me a few of them. One morning Lou decided he'd take the satchel of silver to the studio with him to play cards, but when he lifted the bag, there were only two or three dollars left in it. Anne had siphoned it all off. Lou looked everywhere for his silver dollars but I don't think he ever knew it was Anne. He went around the house for a week mumbling, 'What the hell happened to my money?!'

"When Bud came to the Longridge house to gamble with Lou, all hell would break loose. When Bud started to drink, he loved to argue, and I remember those poker games when all he and Lou would do is argue across the table. When Bud put his money down on the table, you could hear him all over the house. Anne never commented or expressed her feelings about Lou's poker games. I guess she accepted the fact that, outside of his passion for television, those poker games were his life on the weekends."

Gambling was unquestionably a compulsion. Dad and Bud even gambled over the telephone. Dad would call Bud and say, "Toss you for $100. You got the coin, Abbott? Okay, toss it."

Dad might say heads and Abbott would reply, "Right, so now I owe you $200."

"Okay Bud, now I'll toss." Then, "Okay, Bud. We're even. Now once for $200." It got to be that the phone would ring and

Dad would pick it up and say, "Okay, Bud—once for two hundred."

Dad played poker with a fellow by the name of Mike Potson. Potson always won, yet Dad always had him on the set, just as he often had gambling figures like Nick the Greek fly in from Las Vegas for a game. Dad was no match for these men at a card table. Sometimes they'd get so rowdy, Joe Kenny would threaten to have them barred from the set:

> "I once approached Mike Potson and said to him, 'Potson, I'm gonna bar you from the lot.' Well, I couldn't bar Potson from the lot. I didn't have that kind of clout. Mike just stood there looking at me, with a silly grin on his face. Like all the others, he knew Lou had the last word on who came and went on the set."

It was easy to tell when Dad had really lost a bundle. The following week he was on the phone with Eddie Sherman asking that Universal renegotiate their contract with a big raise in pay and money up front.

Aunt Marie often went to Las Vegas with Mom and Dad. Once, Bud and Dad were playing at the Dunes Hotel in Vegas, and the crowds left other tables and gathered around to watch Dad play blackjack. It was hysterical. He always got rid of Mom and Aunt Marie, as she recalls:

> "He would tell us, 'I got your table reservation for the show. You're sitting right down front—right in front of the stage. Go on. Don't do anything till you hear from me. Just stay put.' Pretty soon we could hear Lou all the way out in the casino yelling in his high-pitched voice, 'Hit me! Hit me!' I knew nothing of cards. I turned to Anne and asked, 'Why is he asking someone to hit him?' Anne doubled up laughing. She couldn't believe I didn't know what 'hit me' meant in a gambling casino."

One time at our home in Sherman Oaks, Dad had some of his gambling buddies in from Chicago for a poker game that ran several days. After the game was well under way he phoned Julia Boutee and said, "Julia, I want you to run down to the bank for me and bring some money over to the house."

Julia said, "Of course, Lou. How much?"

"One hundred fifty thousand dollars. It's all arranged."

Monday morning my father was broke. When Milt Bronson

cautioned him about his big losses, he replied, "I'll get 'em, Milt. Just you watch. I'll get 'em."

Only once does anybody remember Dad backing out of a poker game—even if he was losing every hand. He told Harry Von Zell about it:

"Lou was riding in the club car between Philadelphia and New York. He'd been playing cards with some strangers, and they were knocking him out, right and left. Finally he said to himself, these two guys are working together, and so he called the conductor over to the table and asked, 'Does this railroad allow gambling in transit?' The conductor told him, 'No sir, it does not.'

"Lou took one look at the two guys who were beating him, rose up to his fullest stature, and said, 'Drop dead!' With that he left the club car and went back to his compartment."

I'm sure there are dozens of other stories about my father's compulsion to risk thousands at the card table, but they would all illustrate the same theme: He wanted so much to be counted among the big-time players, and it turned out to be an expensive desire, for sure.

Horses and the track: My father's first thoroughbred was a horse named Bazooka that he purchased from a farm in Ireland. He later bought more horses and we began to raise our own. By the time he moved us all to the big ranch in Canoga Park, he was well into the racing scene, as an owner as well as a bettor. Bazooka was raced but never was a winning horse. It was Bazooka's son, Bold Bazooka, that started to make money for Dad. He was our only champion and raced until a knee injury put him out of competition. Joe Kenny has good reason to remember Bazooka:

"Lou had Bazooka running at one of the Southern California tracks, despite the fact that the horse had gone down the tubes three times in a row. I'd told him I was going up to San Francisco and he said, 'Watch the racing form and bet on my horse. Bet Bazooka.'

"On this one morning I got up and there's a telegram stuck under my door that read: BAZOOKA TODAY. I didn't know any bookies in San Francisco, so I asked a bellhop to handle it. 'Bazooka,' I said. 'Ten to win.' He pulled out a scratch sheet, checked the race, and said, 'You gotta be kidding.' I said, 'I'm not kidding.' Then he said, 'Okay, I'll take it.'

"Much to our surprise the horse won and paid $45 on a $2 ticket. It was the longest price the horse ever paid, so I did all right. Lou's tip paid my hotel bill with money left over. It was one hell of a surprise, though.

"I remember another thing about Lou and his horses. At one point Universal bought some limousines with the telephones in them. We were working out in Calabassas on *Mexican Hayride* in 1948, I think. Bud and Lou came out to the location site in one of those phone cars. Every time we got ready to shoot a scene somebody had to go look for Lou. In one particular instance I went to find him. Someone had seen him getting in and out of the limo. Sure enough this time both Lou and the car were gone. We found it parked up the hill with the antenna pulled up and there is little Louie sittin' in it, just yackin' away on that telephone to his bookie!"

Dad took his friends Ted Lewis and James Bacon to Santa Anita òne afternoon and had he listened to Bacon he would've saved himself some money:

"Lou always doubled his bets. For instance, he might start out with a $50 bet in the first race and then in the second he'd go up to $100. Before you knew it, by the ninth race he was eager to place $5000 on some horse—usually a long shot—trying to recoup his losses. On this one day when he wanted to place a five-grand bet on a long shot, I looked over the racing form and said to Lou, 'There's only one horse here that's got even an outside chance of winning this race.' I pointed out the horse, but Lou kept with his long shot. Lou's horse finished way back in the field. Mine won. Poor Lou. I put $10 on a horse that paid $99 for a $2 bet. If he had listened to me, he would've needed a Brinks truck to carry home his quarter-million dollars."

Dad always had a box at the track, as did Robert Arthur, and occasionally they'd frequent the track together. One afternoon when both were at the track, Dad was very involved with a racehorse he'd purchased, trained, and was running in one of the day's races. He had his bookie sitting right in the box with him and he was placing his bets with the bookie rather than at the betting windows. Bob saw what was going on and said, "Lou, go bet the horses at the window."

Dad turned around and said, "You kiddin'? And bring the odds down?"

Photographer Frank Worth was another of Dad's friends who often accompanied him to the track. He didn't mind sending Frank to the $100 window to place bets for him. He trusted Frank and never asked to see the tickets unless he won. One day the two of them were at the track together, and the track handicapper, a close friend of Frank's, stopped him and asked, "What's Lou betting on?" (Dad was known to bet on long shots.) Frank gave his friend the name of the horse, and the handicapper shook his head. "No way can he win with that horse." The horse Dad liked was a long, long, long shot.

The handicapper said, "His horse doesn't have a chance, Frank, but mine does. It's a three-to-one bet."

Frank was holding on to $700 in cash that Dad had given him to place on the long shot. If his friend's horse won, that would bring in $2,100. If Dad's horse won, it would be thousands and thousands. He bet Dad's horse. The handicapper's horse won as Frank guessed it would, but he just couldn't go against Dad's wishes.

We went to Del Mar every summer after Dad bought the big ranch. He'd rented a home right on the beach near the track, and every morning he'd leave for the course and not come back until after the last race. At the far end of the beach Desi Arnaz and Lucille Ball owned a home, the very last house on the north section of the beach. One day my cousin Susan (Uncle Pat's daughter) and I got bored and decided to take a walk down that way. We met and played practically the entire day with little Desi and Luci, the Arnaz children. I don't think anybody missed us. Their parents were at the track too.

When Dad took us to the track, we sat in his reserved box at the Turf Club and I remember him slumped over the table with his glasses on, chomping down on a cigar as he studied the racing form before each race.

I remember Dad telling a friend he had a bundle riding on a particular horse. It fascinated me to hear him talk about the big bets he was making. I was also fascinated by the colors of the jockey silks, and one day I told Dad that the jockey in pink and green would win the next race. When the race started, he stood up in the box, binoculars pressed to his eyes, still chomping away at his cigar. As always, he started to scream and talk to the horse he wanted to win. That one day, in that one race, by pure luck the horse I said would win came in first. He ran all around the Turf Club telling all of his friends, "My kid picks the horse by the jockey silks, says it's going to win—and it did! Whaddya think of that?"

There was one time at Del Mar I swear I thought my father would give up race horses and the track forever. We were having lunch at a seafood restaurant in La Jolla that looked out over the ocean so you could see the waves crash up against the rocks below. There were two elderly ladies sitting right behind us. Dad had a great fear of death and didn't even like to talk about it. I don't think he'd heard about it yet, but it was the same day Oliver Hardy died. Anyway, these two ladies were talking and one of them said to her friend, "Isn't it a shame? Lou Costello died today." Dad dropped his fork and as it clattered across his plate, he turned ashen grey. Then he slowly turned around to the ladies and said, "What!" You could've freeze-frozen the open-mouthed expressions on the faces of those two ladies. Dad tried to be funny about it, but he didn't finish his meal.

As Dad's tax problems closed in on him and we had to sell the Longridge home and later the ranch, he stopped racing horses or even keeping them. The cost was too much.

CHAPTER XVIII

Television

U NIVERSAL, showing less and less interest in Abbott & Costello films, produced only one picture starring the team in 1950. Dad was extremely disappointed in the studio's attitude and complained that Universal didn't give a damn about Abbott & Costello now that they'd bailed the studio out of near-bankruptcy. His griping fell on deaf ears, and naturally it went around the executive offices of not only Universal but every other studio in town that Lou Costello was difficult, Lou Costello was temperamental, and Lou Costello was a problem.

Abbott & Costello in the Foreign Legion reflected my father's concern about Universal's waning interest in continuing Abbott & Costello pictures. It was a stale offering of old routines that were only slightly recycled. The studio seemed to have developed a consensus that there was no need to improve the format or the skits. They were convinced the public would buy the name, just as they did any brand product. The studio was wrong. Audiences loved Abbott & Costello because they were *different*, and they expected to see new and different routines in their films (old routines, perhaps, but new to the motion picture viewers).

Under a revised contract with Universal, the team was now making about $800,000 a year. They had left Eddie Sherman quite a while ago and were represented for the time solely by the William Morris Agency. Under their previous contract, which Sherman had negotiated, they had been making upwards of $2 million a year, which included $200,000 a picture (based on two films a year) plus twenty percent of the profits and a bonus when a picture came in under budget. They had also been permitted to do pictures away from Universal.

Dad's ongoing contempt for Eddie Sherman, which had begun when Eddie asked for twenty-five percent and total control of the team, had been heightened upon the death of my grandfather. It eventually erupted when Dad ordered all payments to Mr. Sherman deferred until the matter of "overpayment" was resolved to my father's satisfaction. Sherman, in turn, sued both Bud and Dad. When the suit was finally settled Eddie Sherman won hands down. He would receive $400,000 over a period of four years for what he had not been paid over the previous three. Financially, however, the separation from Sherman had cut their income in half. So, once the legal hassle was resolved, Dad went to see Eddie (who was so startled he ran behind his desk, not knowing what mood Dad was in).

"Sit down, Eddie," Dad said, "I wanna talk to you." Sherman eyed him with suspicion but settled back in his leather chair.

"All right, Lou. What is it?"

"I want you back."

"How about Bud?"

"Yeah, Bud, too."

"Why the sudden change of heart?"

"Don't get the wrong idea, Eddie. This ain't no love affair. This is business. I figure if I gotta pay you all that money you're gonna earn it, so get to work."

It was as simple as that. Eddie Sherman once again became the personal manager of Abbott & Costello.

In order to take the sting out of his arrangement with Sherman, my father filed suit against Eddie Nassour, alleging that "defendants" made excessive, unreasonable and improper charges to the cost of *Africa Screams* and "delivered to their own use and benefit large sums due to the plaintiff (Lou Costello) and others entitled to a share of the profits of said motion picture." Dad contended the costs exceeded what the picture should've cost, to the amount of $250,000. Nassour, of course, blamed all the over-budget costs on my father and "his crazy friends." This dispute was also eventually settled, to the satisfaction of neither side.

Meanwhile, Dad was showing a restlessness and impatience

that even his most loyal friends were noticing, but disregarding. Most thought Dad was just "working out a personal problem." Whatever was bothering him seemed in no way to affect his relationship with his family—certainly not the one he had with us kids.

Not only did Dad bring Eddie Sherman back as their manager (with Bud's concurrence), but he and Bud acquired a new attorney by the name of Max Fink. Ironically, Max had represented Eddie Sherman in his suit against the team. Dad said, "Anybody who can beat me in a lawsuit belongs on my side."

Max continued to represent the team throughout their disputes over contracts with Universal, and he remembers:

> "I handled the legal work regarding *Jack and the Beanstalk* and *Abbott & Costello Meet Captain Kidd,* which were made at Warner Brothers on their 'away from the studio films' contract clause. All of this goes back many years. I recall that I negotiated Lou's deal on the fifty-two film shorts which made up the *Abbott & Costello Television Show* in the early fifties.
>
> "In my association with Lou (also Bud), I kept the relationship to business. Lou and I got along fine. There were no temper tantrums or anger. Maybe he had confrontations with other people, but not with me. As a client he was most easy to deal with."

For all the reasons given for the decline of Abbott & Costello pictures in the early fifties, probably nobody has a better explanation than director Charles Lamont:

> "I don't think it was bad scripts. Lou and Bud had final approval of them. What they didn't like was rewritten and what they wanted out was eliminated. I believe their popularity at the box office declined because their pictures were being mass produced, one right after another, and then rereleased along with their new ones. Universal was inundating the public with Abbott & Costello because their films were pulling the studio out of the red into the black, and during those war-torn years, when the audiences craved the team, the studio wanted to keep the cash coming in. I believe if Bud and Lou had limited themselves—say, to one film a year— they would've been just as popular. For example, you may like lobster, but if you eat it for thirty days a month, you'll eventually want to get away from it."

Lamont directed his first Abbott & Costello film in 1943 and did not direct one again for seven years. Then he went on to direct eight in a row. He explains why.

"I refused to do a second Abbott & Costello film after *Hit the Ice* was completed. I didn't want to be labeled an 'Abbott & Costello director.' I tried to explain that I loved working with Bud and Lou but wanted to do other things. Universal finally offered me a seven-year contract with a big salary. I forgot my ambitions and agreed to do comedy again. It looked like Abbott & Costello *was* my future."

Patricia Medina (Mrs. Joseph Cotten) co-starred with Dad and Bud when they did *Abbott & Costello in The Foreign Legion.*

"I was a young actress and impressionable. When producer Robert Arthur asked me to do the picture, I remember everyone saying to me, 'Oh—o—o—o, you don't know what's going to happen to you!' I asked what they meant. 'Wait till Costello pulls some of his gags on you. Watch the chair you're sitting in. It'll probably go up in smoke.' That was very unnerving. But nothing like that ever did happen. He was a gentleman at all times and the greatest comedian I had ever seen. You cannot be the kind of performer that Lou Costello was without being a true sophisticate. He was that. Most children are very sophisticated and Lou was definitely a sophisticated child."

Nowhere was that childishness more evident than in Dad's impulsive urges to just take off and go somewhere without telling anyone. During the early fifties, one day Dad and Uncle Pat were on their way home from the race track when Dad said, "Let's go to Honolulu, Pat."

"You gotta be crazy, Lou!" Uncle Pat said. "We've got nothing to wear."

Dad laughed. "What do ya really need, Pat? Get a Hawaiian shirt, pair of pants, and you're all set."

"What'll I tell Marty?"

"When we get to Honolulu, call her."

"That'll kill her."

"No it won't." And obviously it didn't. Mom and Pat's wife

Marty laughed like crazy at the two of them running off like that. It was some runaway—they stayed for nine days and my father never had a better time in his life.

Something was creeping into my father's personality that appeared only from time to time. My mother was acutely aware of it, but only occasionally did she express her feelings—after having had it up to the gills. At times when Dad came home from the studio, he'd go to the refrigerator, get himself a cold drink, and then walk back into the den and turn on the television, ignoring everyone in the house. Whenever my father did that, my mother became very angry. She was used to Dad coming home and spending time with her talking about the children and her day. Ophelia MacFashion was with us during this time and saw it going on.

> "When I would be calling dinner, it seemed by the time everyone got to the table, Lou was already finished and gone. He'd go out to the den, plop down in front of the television and watch old movies. With every commercial he'd hurry back into the kitchen to get something from the refrigerator and rush back to the TV. This would go on until one in the morning at times. Anne would follow him into the den and try to strike up a conversation. All Lou would reply was 'Yep.' One night she came into the kitchen, thoroughly disgusted, and said, 'You'd think Lou would do something else besides look at that goddamned television!' "

That was a part of my father that *no one* understood, because he was usually the total family man. In retrospect I think his behavior was motivated by having lost his son. For me to say something like that, the way he indulged my every whim, may sound somewhat strange, but he could be watching a kid playing baseball or some other sport on television and from a broad smile his face sometimes changed expression. It was almost as if it pained him deep down inside to see those little boys having such a good time—and my father loved children. I can only attribute that to his never getting over the loss of Butch. I think that accounts largely for his later flare-ups and displays of anger and temperament.

By the time Dad made *Abbott & Costello Meet the Invisible Man* and *Comin' Round the Mountain* in 1951, his personal hell was showing up in his relationship with Bud Abbott. Dad and Bud would argue in their dressing rooms and sometimes it got pretty loud. When they came out on the set to shoot a scene, there were times when Bud would have to give Dad a slap. Bystanders noticed that Dad was taking Bud's slaps more like blows. Nobody could understand why my father was so restrained. The anger would be raging in his eyes. One time Christie came up to Dad after a scene and said, "You know something, Lou, Bud's really whompin' ya."

Dad, biting his lip, said, "I know. But if I ever hit him back, that'll be the end of the relationship."

Dad's long relationship with John Grant was also on the wane. Dad, as well as other people, thought that Grant, who was now writing for Dean Martin & Jerry Lewis, was giving his best gags to them. He'd also written the movie *Sailor Beware* for Martin & Lewis, and Dad felt he had stolen the material from *Buck Privates*. Others agreed there was a close resemblance between the two pictures.

And yet, John Grant's expertise was never more evident than in *Comin' Round the Mountain*. During preproduction, and while the script was being written, John read every book and viewed every film he could find about rural life in America, including such well-remembered movies as *Sergeant York, Roseanna McCoy*, and *The Little Shepherd of the Ozarks*. With this research, he was now able to write true-to-life scenes reminiscent of American farm life and molded perfectly to the Abbott & Costello style. For instance, the turkey shoot scene was obviously from *Sergeant York* and the feud between the two clans came out of *Roseanna McCoy*. John constantly asked himself this question: How would Bud and Lou do it? So their routines were always tailored to their style of comedy. He felt the public would take nothing less.

Margaret Hamilton was cast in *Comin' Round the Mountain* but almost didn't do the picture with Dad.

"The only thing that bothered me, after hearing the story line and reading the script, was that I'd portrayed the witch in *The Wizard of Oz* with Judy Garland and just did not want to become typecast for those kind of parts. The studio convinced me that wasn't the case, so I accepted the role.

"Of course I went through the usual anxieties attendant to a Lou Costello picture. The first thing I heard was to be careful of the rest rooms, because Lou wired the toilets to give you a shock. Of course nothing like that actually happened at all. It was part of the legend being created about the man. What I remember most was his overabundance of energy, always tearing around the set like somebody with an itch that couldn't be scratched. He was a fun and dear man to work with."

Dad could get away with things in films that other comedians could not, because of his "little boy" approach. Red Skelton, for instance, who was an accomplished comic, had the "mean little kid" routine he did on radio. When he started doing television he couldn't get away with it, so he changed. He started doing things like putting his hat on upside down and telling little anecdotes about his son. There was a very tragic parallel between Red and my father in that they both lost sons they loved very much. After his son died from leukemia, Red stopped doing those anecdotes. Harpo Marx also successfully used the same naughty childlike quality in his character. He'd leer at some girl and then take the scissors and cut her skirt off—but it wasn't sexual, just funny.

In romantic scenes my father would become very excited and take on the demeanor of a nine-year-old boy. You got the feeling he was so innocent, he didn't know why he was excited. People loved that.

With television rapidly striding to a competitive position with motion pictures, it was reasonable to believe that Abbott & Costello would eventually appear in that medium, and they did. It was with a great deal of fanfare that Abbott & Costello debuted on the *Colgate Comedy Hour* on January 7, 1951. They were not the first, but the last hosts of this show. Testing the waters ahead of them, among others, were Eddie Cantor, Bob Hope, Durante, Donald O'Connor, and Martin & Lewis.

Although the motion picture audiences were familiar with Abbott & Costello material, television was another thing. Dad believed it was best to stick to their standard routines the first time out, to see how viewers reacted. So they did "Who's on First," "The Lemon Bit," "Mustard," "Crazy Horse," and "The Moving Candle."

The ratings were good, but critics claimed the team had done it all in one show and couldn't sustain a weekly series. The critics were wrong. The show continued, with Abbott & Costello as hosts, for three years—and always with the lion's share of the ratings. Even with their phenomenal television success, the critics found fault. After reading a particularly harsh review, Dad said, "I guess we're like Harry Truman. Nobody loves us but the people."

In addition to the *Colgate Comedy Hour*, production was begun on a weekly television series, the *Abbott & Costello Show*. The first episode was screened on Friday, December 5, 1952, at ten-thirty at night. The producers wanted to capture a young audience, the theory being that with no school on Saturday the children would be allowed to stay up to watch the show. Whoever picked that time slot had some smarts, because the show clicked immediately, especially with the under-fifteen set.

For all the dumb things he did in business, Dad was not totally without foresight. He owned the Abbott & Costello television show outright. So, in order for him to also become owner of all the material used in their movies, he included the old routines in the television series. There was nothing Universal could do about it. Abbott & Costello were still competing against themselves—but now, for a change, also for themselves, instead of for Universal. The NBC *Colgate Comedy Hour* was showing repeats on Sunday nights, so there was a tremendous amount of Abbott & Costello exposure in the early fifties.

Two cameras were used by director Jean Yarbrough, one was always kept on Dad to maintain some continuity because Jean never knew what he'd do next. The whole year's series was shot in a matter of two or three months, with each segment budgeted at $15,000. Dad brought in all of his old cronies and friends and put them to work on the show—people like Sid Fields; Joe Besser; Hillary Brooke; Gordon Jones; Joe Kirk (Dad's brother-in-law); Joan Shawlee, who had once been under contract to Dad (Dad had been responsible for Universal signing her as a young actress); and Bobby Barber, Dad's longtime sidekick. A chimp named Bingo also had a regular part on the show. Milt Bronson was always around, often as a foil in the audience—and there was always the guest star, one of Hollywood's fabulous character actors of the day.

Dad didn't always select big-name stars to work with him. As a matter of fact, he rarely did. Always the champion of the underdog or the kid on the way up, he defended the right of the new kid on the block to become a regular. Charlie Marion, who was a writer on the *Abbott & Costello Radio Show*, tells of Dad's empathy for the newcomer and of his generosity:

> "I got to know Bud and Lou when they were doing their radio show. At the time, I was young and inexperienced, but Lou didn't hesitate to give me a chance. He put me on as a writer for the *Abbott & Costello Show*. I'll never forget the story conferences they held in a big room at NBC Studios, with all the show's writers sitting around the table: Harry Crane, Leonard Stern, Martin Ragaway, and others.
>
> "Being new, I observed how the scripts were written. Someone would come up with a gag, and a secretary took it all down on her steno pad. I couldn't work that way, bouncing off gags around a table. As a result, I'd get very tongue-tied. Finally, one day Harry Crane looked at me just sitting there and saying nothing, and he said, 'What do we have over there, a deaf mute?' I was so shocked and embarrassed.
>
> "Lou, who sat in on the conferences with Bud, immediately turned to Harry and defended me. 'Lay off him. He'll get with it!' Later, after the writers had left the room, Lou came over to me and placed his arm around my shoulder. 'These jokesters here, well, they've been around a while,' he said. 'They just forget they were once new at this. You just stick with it and don't give up.' "

Charlie Marion met his wife Elena Verdugo while they were working with Bud and Dad on *The Little Giant*. When Charlie and Elena let Dad in on their plans to elope, my father was so excited for them he wanted to charter a plane and make it a biggie. Elena was to go home from the studio after the day's shooting, get her things, and then Dad would have a plane ready for the couple to take them wherever they wanted to go. He had called Louella Parsons and had a photographer waiting in the wings. Too many people found out about it, including the studio. Universal had a clause in Elena's contract prohibiting her from flying while the picture was being made, so the elopement fell through. They later married in a more conventional manner, but Dad was sure gung-ho.

Concurrently with the *Abbott & Costello Show*, Dad produced another twenty-six-part series, *I Am the Law*, starring

George Raft (Cosman Productions). MCA, which was later disbanded as an agency (after their purchase of Universal Studios, the government had forced them to get out of the agency business), distributed both shows.

I Am the Law was strictly an investment venture. George Raft said:

"Lou had been working closely with MCA and they were advising him how to go about producing the series. I believe Lou Wasserman, president of MCA, wanted to establish MCA as an important organization in television by selling the series to some beer company in Rochester, New York, or a wine company (which would enhance them) as sponsors. Syndication was wrong. They should've sold the series to a network. In those days if you weren't on the network, what good was the show? I think Lou had bad advice.

"I played a New York police lieutenant. To me, the only thing wrong with the show was the scripts. Lou had hired a director who employed radio writers, who wrote as if they were still in radio. Too much dialogue and not enough action. For example, in radio you'd have to say, 'I see the button and I'm going to press it,' but on screen, we see the button, so you just press it. But not those guys!

"One day I blew up. 'Dammit,' I said, 'the button is there! Any fool can see it. We don't have to describe it!' It got so I was having arguments every day up at Lou's offices with the writers. If I had known it was going to be that way when Lou first asked me, I would never have done the series. We wrapped the series and I went to Europe, where I had picture commitments.

"I gave Lou my power of attorney to set up distribution or whatever had to be done in my absence. When I returned, the show was syndicated and that's (in my opinion) what killed the series. I was sorry to see that happen to Lou. I finished up the series per my contract but that was it."

Joan Shawlee appeared in many of the Abbott & Costello television shows, usually as the straight woman for Dad. She had first worked with Dad in 1947, in *Buck Privates Come Home*.

"I was an eighteen-year-old dancer at the Copacabana in New York when Bud and Lou dropped in one night to see the show. When the waiter brought Lou's card backstage and said, 'Mr. Costello would like to talk to you,' I didn't believe him. What would a big star like Lou Costello want with a chorus girl? I was still terribly naive and living at home with my mother. After chatting a bit, Lou said they were preparing to do another film and looking for a female lead. Bud and Lou agreed they'd like to bring me to California and get me a studio contract. I said, 'I'd love to go, but you'll have to meet my mother.' Lou laughed, threw his hands up in the air and jokingly said to Bud, 'Out of ten thousand girls in New York, we had to find this one.'

"When I brought my mother out to meet them, I said, 'There's just one problem, Mr. Costello—I'd have to take my mother with me.' Lou assured me that was no problem, so he paid for our train fare, put me under contract—and immediately everybody in Hollywood started gossiping: 'She's Lou Costello's girlfriend.' I was never Lou's girlfriend.

"Lou had me over to their house a lot and I started to sense that Anne was getting a little upset with my being there so often. I was in a very awkward position and wasn't smart enough to know what to do about it. Anne did something about it for me. She said, 'Let's play gin rummy.' She *creamed* me! When we finished the game, she picked up the scores, smiled slyly, and said, 'Well, does that tell you anything?' "

It tells *me* that my mother was not asleep at the wheel. Although her jealous intuitions were unfounded, she was ready to fight all odds to keep her man.

CHAPTER XIX

McCarthyism and the Patriot

O N FEBRUARY 9, 1950 a new "ism" was born during a speech by Senator Joseph McCarthy of Wisconsin. Speaking at a local Republican Lincoln Day dinner at the old McClure Hotel in Wheeling, West Virginia, the Senator shook the very foundations of democracy when he held up a handful of "documents" that he claimed contained the names of 205 people "known to the Secretary of State as being members of the Communist Party and who nevertheless are still working and shaping the policy of the State Department." The seeds of suspicion were sown and a dark wave of fear that soon became known as McCarthyism crept over the country.

All my life my father was a hardline Republican. He found companionship and understanding in his producer, Robert Arthur, an extremely conservative Republican. As far back as the mid-forties Dad used to stop off at Arthur's office and complain about Communist-inspired labor strikes. He once told Bob, "You're the only one that I can talk to who shares my beliefs as a Republican."

Joe McCarthy was a demagogue, but to my father he was a man in shining armor, out to rid the country of Commies. Mr. Arthur says that "Lou would often talk to me at length about what was occurring. He was very much against Communism, as I was, and a supporter of Senator McCarthy. Lou also was a champion of those in our industry who were being framed as Communists and would loyally stand by them and fight for them. He was very pro-American and very much involved in his country."

Dad was thoroughly convinced that there was a Communist conspiracy to infiltrate the film industry. Bob Arthur still is: "Lou shared my feelings regarding the McCarthy era. It has since become a distorted issue in the industry about the Hollywood ten who were glamorized with this. To this day I am convinced there was a conspiracy. It made sense, because if there was anything that the Communists could get hold of, it was the motion picture business. It would be idiotic to think they wouldn't try. Lou felt very strongly about this and tried to do his part to protect the freedom of America."

Most people thought my father was a Democrat because he had long been such a great admirer of Franklin D. Roosevelt. But his admiration of Roosevelt was essentially based on Roosevelt's having been a wartime President who had enrolled my father in that national effort. Dad was an old-fashioned patriot, of a sort far more prevalent then than now. It was the kids that had him particularly concerned, because he believed they were wide open to philosophical and ideological propaganda, and that the Communists would stop at nothing to capture the minds of youth. That was why he made such an issue of the "Communist menace," which he believed to be very real.

Well-known entertainers were being blackballed and blacklisted by the movie industry, and people in Hollywood were scared to death by McCarthy's accusations and the hot winds of ultraconservatism that fanned them. Dad, among many other zealous conservatives, actually went so far as to carry petitions around to the studios, asking his fellow stars and anyone else working in the industry to sign, swearing they had no part in any Communist work or organization. Everyone was so frightened by what was going on that most of them didn't want to sign anything. Some of Dad's friends felt insulted to be asked, believing their politics to be nobody else's business—not even Lou Costello's. He had solicited Lucille Ball and she declined—but politely. One who didn't take it so politely was Dad's old friend and gag writer, John Grant. If you wanted to work for my father, then it was pretty much understood that you had to sign a non-Communist petition. Grant took exception to what he considered an ultimatum.

"Lou," he said, "after all these years do you have to question my loyalty?"

"If you really are a true-blue American, you won't mind saying so. Just sign the paper, John."

"I can't in clear conscience do that, Lou."

"If you want to continue working for me, you'll sign it."

"I never *worked* for you. I worked for the studios, if you want to put it on that basis."

"I don't give a damn who you worked for. Are you gonna sign that you're a red-blooded American or are you gonna let people wonder if you might be pink?"

"I guess I'm not going to be writing for Abbott & Costello anymore," John said, getting up and starting for the door in Dad's office.

"Does that mean you're quitting?"

"That means I guess I'm fired," Grant replied.

As the door shut behind him, Dad said, lowering his voice to a whisper, "Damn right it does." But he knew he'd gone too far. Dad never thought John was anything other than a good gag writer who loved his work, his wife, and his country, but each man had too much pride to restore the relationship. Dad missed John and later said to my mother, "Now why did John have to be so hardheaded?"

A Hearst newspaper reporter caught Dad at the Los Angeles airport, where he suffered a relapse of rheumatic fever prior to departing for a testimonial dinner in Phoenix for McCarthy. Dad could hardly speak but said he'd be happy to give him an interview when he felt better. Consequently, during his recovery he granted the interview. He was asked if he didn't feel his support of McCarthy was going to hurt him at the box office and, if that were true, how could he continue his advocacy of a man who more and more people were discovering was more dangerous than the Communist conspiracy he believed to exist.

"That reasoning doesn't make any sense to me," Dad replied. "Since when is it more important to have good box office appeal rather than to try and be a good American?"

Although Dwight D. Eisenhower and Senator McCarthy did not see eye to eye, Eisenhower did not publicly criticize McCarthy while campaigning for the 1952 presidential prize. Dad supported and worked for an Eisenhower victory and when the new President came to Los Angeles to speak at the Hollywood Bowl, Dad was invited—as was Bud Abbott. I have no idea why my mother didn't rush out to meet the new President of the United States, but she opted to stay home with us girls. Dad got on the phone and called his old friend May Mann, the Hollywood columnist, and asked her to accompany him and Bud.

Not everything was political in Dad's life at that time. To the contrary, his politics were peripheral to the busy schedule he kept. He also took out time for fun. Ann Corio, Mom and Dad's longtime friend from New York, had moved to California and purchased a beachfront home in Malibu. As a family we used to visit Ann on weekends for lasagna dinners or clam digs.

There was a limit in Malibu then of fifty clams per person at any given time. The Department of Fish and Game was rather strict in enforcing the limit, because the clam beds had to be preserved for future generations. Whenever Dad went clam digging, it was with a salt shaker in one pocket and a lemon in the other. He was absolutely wild about clams, fresh out of the shell, and would eat them as he dug them up. He had an expression: "One clam for me, and one for the bucket." He would eat as many as he would take back to the house. When he'd eaten his fill, the rest went into the bucket.

Once, while we were all walking back to Ann's home after digging for clams, a game warden approached us on the beach. Dad was way over his quota, but before the official could say anything, Dad yelled, "I have only a hundred fifty, warden, but as soon as I get two fifty, I'm leaving." You could hear my father up and down the beach. He kept the game warden so distracted with his jokes and antics that the poor man forgot to check his clam count.

Although Dad made only one film at Universal in 1952, he and Bud made two at Warner Brothers: *Jack and the Beanstalk* and *Abbott & Costello Meet Captain Kidd. Lost in Alaska* was their only offering from Universal. Uncle Pat wrote an adaptation of the original *Jack and the Beanstalk* story, from which Nat Curtis wrote the screenplay. Heavyweight boxer Buddy Baer played the giant to Dad's Jack. To enhance his stature as a giant, Baer was given boots with giant lifts to make him close to seven feet tall. There was one scene in which Buddy chases Dad down the long hallways of a castle. Wearing those heavy boots, Buddy literally ran out of one boot and continued the chase just the same. Everybody in the scene collapsed with laughter, but it was left just as it was shot. So if you see that picture on the late late movie, you'll understand if the giant seems to have a limp.

That picture was remembered by the studio more for three things that had nothing to do with grosses or net income: Patrick, the stage prop cow; the "talking harp"; and the golden egg that a chicken laid in the giant's castle. The cow found a home at our ranch; Patrick became a fixture in our upstairs sitting room; and the golden egg found a new nest in Dad's den.

Charles Laughton, the distinguished thespian, played Captain Kidd in Abbott & Costello's second Warner Brothers film and seemed to have the time of his life once his nervousness subsided. Dad, and then Laughton, had confided to Abe Haberman, the makeup man, that he was nervous about working with the other. Laughton further revealed that when he was down in the dumps, he'd "literally travel miles just to see an Abbott & Costello film. Doing that always seemed to pick me up and make me a little happier."

The studio brought in a stuntman, Sailor Vincent, to do all of Laughton's stunt work, but the actor began to enjoy doing it himself once the film got rolling. In one scene this magnificent actor of stage and screen was running around in long johns being beaten over the head with rubber prop shovels. It was like watching a little boy playing in the first winter's snow; he loved every moment of it.

While being made up one morning, Dad, who always liked to tell stories, told Abe about an incident that happened to him during the filming of *Buck Privates*. He said that he and Bud, still newcomers to the motion picture business, were feeling their way around. Someone yelled, "Set still!" (film jargon meaning that all actors have to be off the set so the set changes can be made). He and Bud walked back on the set and sat still. One of the crew walked up to them and said, "Come on. Off the set. I want the set still." Dad looked at Bud and then back at the guy and in total frustration said, "Well, we're settin' still! So get the hell on with your business!" He learned fast, though, and was soon bringing his usual courtesy and eagerness to the new medium.

When success comes, it's easy to get caught up in a self-indulgent world and forget where you came from. If you worked for the Costellos, you were never referred to as "hired help." You were part of the family and treated as such, not as employees. With all his extravagances, Dad never did that. He held high respect for his elders and much love and affection for his family.

Of course, he indulged his kids—who doesn't?

I was only five years old, but I'll never forget the splendor of Paddy's sweet sixteen, combination birthday and coming out party. Multicolored tents had been erected in the backyard around the pool, which was fragrant with dozens of fresh floating blossoms. A live band and a beautifully decorated birthday cake completed the picture.

But Dad disciplined us too. Paddy remembers the other side well:

"I'd been invited to an after-school party and since we wore uniforms at Marymount, I packed my dress clothes in a suitcase when I left for school that morning. Later that day someone in the family told my parents I'd left with a suitcase. To make matters worse, when I still hadn't come home from school by early evening, Mom and Dad had it all figured out I had eloped with one of the servicemen who stayed at our home. All the while I was having a good time at the party, my parents had been on the phone calling the Arizona, Nevada, and Mexican borders to see if I'd crossed the state line to get married. Eleven o'clock that night I wandered in from my party. Mom and Dad didn't say a word to me. They didn't have to. I knew I'd had it.

"My sweet sixteen party had already been organized; invitations had been sent out, and everybody had RSVP'd. Otherwise my parents might have cancelled it. I was hoping for a new car—I'd certainly hinted for one in very unsubtle terms—but I knew how upset my parents were with me and that a car would now be too much to expect.

"Well, the party went on and on and gifts were opened and I'd given up on the car. I was disappointed, but accepted it as my just punishment. About midnight Mom and Dad came over to me and Dad said, "Well, honey, your birthday has come and gone and you're starting on a new year." Then they walked me to the front window, where Dad pulled aside the drapes and gestured for me to look outside. Parked in the driveway was the most beautiful new car. I cannot remember ever being so excited.

"The following day the car went back to the dealer. That was my punishment—for not calling home and letting them know where I was."

Carole fondly remembers some of her experiences with Dad:

"Both Paddy and I were athletic in school and loved our horses. Dad enjoyed taking me to the track with him. I think he had me reading the racing form from the first day I was able to read. We'd sit in his box at the track and he'd look over at me reading the form and say, very boastfully and loud enough for those around him to hear, 'Look! The kid can read the racing form!'

"I remember how excited Dad was about Bold Bazooka winning the Starlet Stakes at Hollywood Park and edging his way to the Kentucky Derby. There was one race before the Derby—one that would certainly qualify our horse. It was the Garden Stakes in New Jersey. I was so excited. I said, 'I can see it now, Dad, the colors flying on the pole. Our colors at the Kentucky Derby.' I certainly shared his enthusiasm and excitement.

"I think he spent about $35,000 to have Bold Bazooka flown east, trainer and all. He rented the entire plane for the trip and had it specially padded for the flight. The trainer suffered a heart attack and died suddenly a week before the race, and it seemed only logical (when his son asked) that the trainer's son be allowed to take over. He had worked with his father all along preparing the horse, so Dad agreed he could go. Evidently, in the excitement, on the day of the race, the young man did not check over the horse's leg very carefully after the morning workout, because its shin was weak.

"None of us went to the race, not even Dad, and it wasn't televised. Dad got on the phone to one of his relatives in New Jersey and had them relay the news of the race as they heard it over the radio. We were all sitting around Dad as he pressed the phone to his ear and said, 'Jesus Christ! He's leading by five lengths and they can't get near him!' He was so excited, he literally chomped on his cigar while he listened for more news. After seconds of silence he screamed, 'He's out there! He's gonna do it!' Then his face fell, and I knew something had gone wrong. Tears came to my eyes. I'd never seen my father look so devastated.

"What happened was, the horse's shin bucked midway into the race and he limped the rest of the way home. He never raced again. We couldn't even use him for stud services, because he was just too uncontrollable—at one point he nearly ripped a man's thumb off—so Dad had him gelded.

"Dad always came over to Marymount to watch us play basketball and never hesitated to give us tips on how to play the game. We listened to what he had to say because he knew what he was talking about. I remember once he said, 'Now this is how you foul the other player whereby you don't get caught,' and explained the play to me. It worked.

"When I was in plays at school I don't think he ever missed coming to see me. He was always out there in the front row, looking very supportive and proud. I could see him sitting there in his chair, really nervous for me, and if I happened to glance out to the audience toward him he would smile and nod his head as if to say, 'Right on!'

"When I was in my early teens, living at Longridge, Dad asked me one year what I wanted for my birthday. I really had everything in the world that I wanted—my horse, my dogs—but I finally said, 'How about a bird aviary?' I think I had seen a picture of one in a magazine, and it looked like it might be fun to have a lot of birds. He made me feel like a princess who had just rubbed a magic ring. He had built in the garden, for me, a lovely gazebo-type bird aviary with screen netting enclosing the aviary and little perches inside. After it was built he took me down to a large pet store. Outside they had huge pens with all kinds of beautiful birds. I remember excitedly saying to the owner, 'I want twelve of these and six of these . . .' and on down the line. I ran from pen to pen calling out my order. I think I enjoyed the idea of having a bird aviary for all of a month and when I had to start cleaning it up, it wasn't so beautiful after all. The aviary remained with the birds and I remember eggs being laid and baby birds being born, but somebody else took over the cleaning chores."

By 1952 my father had set up three corporations: Television Corporation of America (TCA), which handled the royalties on the fifty-two television shows (which would later increase the income to his estate); Cosman Productions, which produced the George Raft series; and Exclusive Productions, which produced *Jack and the Beanstalk*.

The idea of TCA and the *Abbott & Costello Show* was that NBC, which was putting up the money for the production of the series and would get first rights to show, did not, however, have the exclusive rights. Dad could sell to whomever he got the best offer from, but the network had first rights of refusal. He did get offers from the other networks, but he had dollar signs in front of his eyes and decided to sell the television shorts independently, to be distributed by the Music Corporation of America (MCA), who took large distribution fees. As a result, it never did work out quite as well as if they had been sold outright, according to Ralph Handley, who would later be called in to straighten out my father's affairs following the IRS audit.

In the beginning the stockholders' relationship was as follows: ten percent for Pat Costello; ten percent for Marie (Cristillo) Kirk; ten percent for Helen Cristillo; seventy percent for Lou Costello and his immediate family. (When Dad died we girls inherited his share and an arrangement was worked out for us to buy out the shares of Pat, Marie, and my grandmother. Consequently we wound up with one hundred percent and became the sole stockholders of TCA, which we still are.)

My father was, to my knowledge, in no way a psychic, but he seemed to be preparing something for our future welfare. On October 30, 1952 both Bud and Dad signed a contract with Universal Pictures that was entitled Eleven Picture Participation Contract and covered the following films, in which the team had a participatory interest in the profits: *Buck Privates, One Night in the Tropics, In the Navy, Hold That Ghost, Keep 'Em Flying, Pardon My Sarong, It Ain't Hay, Who Done It, Hit the Ice, In Society,* and *Ride 'Em Cowboy.* The percentage breakdown, according to the contract, reflected the following ownership: ten percent for Edward Sherman; forty and one-half percent for the account of Bud Abbott; and forty-nine and one-half percent for the account of Lou Costello.

All of this is very important, because it plays a large part in events yet to come that would break my father's heart, his purse, and, I believe, his will to want to be funny.

CHAPTER XX

The IRS

IN 1953 THE FAMILY took another trip to Europe, aboard the *Queen Elizabeth*. There were the usual London fans and sold-out houses for my Dad and Bud, but frankly I was glad to get back home. So was my father, but he wouldn't have been had he known what was coming. Betty Abbott remembers how it all started—the beginning of the end for Abbott & Costello:

"There was a man named Fisher who turned Bud and Lou into the Internal Revenue Service. He had some connection with one of our attorneys and for whatever reason had information that not even Bud or Lou knew about and decided to do them in. He reported everything from card games right on down the line. He may have needed money and wanted to collect the percentages the government was paying on recovered taxes. Whatever his reason for doing it, I know it ruined Bud and Lou emotionally.

"Eventually Bud had to make lists of every item of clothing, right down to his shoes and socks. He had suits that cost from a hundred seventy-five to two hundred fifty dollars, which he needed for his livelihood. They disallowed everything in the audit. They even disallowed the chauffeur, who was essential since Bud could not drive because of his epilepsy. Eventually they disallowed our household help.

"I sat there with this man who was conducting the audit and it broke my heart to watch a foreigner who could barely speak English take everything we had. I remember he said to Bud, 'You paid thirty-five dollars for these shoes? From now on pay nineteen.' "

Unless you have been in a high salary bracket, it is impossible to know just how devastating the Internal Revenue Service can be. I can only compare it to a swarm of locusts swooping down on a summer wheat field. When they leave, you're stripped to bare bone. The lucky ones are those who have enough assets to liquidate and start over. Rarely does anyone get back to where he was.

Where some stars looked toward the future by investing in real estate or businesses, Dad was buying dry oil wells and backing flakey inventors. My older sisters used to tease him: "How's the oil well doing?" and he'd respond, "Don't worry, the wells will do fine, as soon as the snow clears." Problem was, the snow never cleared.

Dad never kept account of money. At parties, for instance, if he had one too many drinks (and it was rare that he drank), he'd go down a line passing out fifty-dollar bills. (Mom went right behind him collecting them back.)

The first person to really become aware that my father's finances were in an unhealthy state was Ralph Handley. He was working for a business management firm in Beverly Hills when Dad needed an accountant for one of his production companies. Handley relates their first meeting:

"I went over to Lou's office which, at the time, was at the old Hal Roach Studios, the same studio where the television shorts were filmed. When I arrived, everything was extremely chaotic concerning the accountant's work on Lou's investments and businesses. The accountant, a young man, was supposed to be taking care of everything properly, but obviously hadn't. I discovered that payroll taxes had not been filed on some of the corporations for over a year. Lou owed something like $18,000 in payroll taxes and penalties. I further discovered that money was missing from some of the accounts. When Lou was advised he immediately fired the accountant and would not even allow him to come on the lot. [It was not the first such experience between this accountant and my father.]

"After looking over the situation carefully, I found there were so many records missing and items unaccounted for that I asked Lou to bring the accountant back just to help me trace the jumbled accounts. There really was no way to unravel the mess without knowing how it got started and running a history of each account. Lou finally consented but was ready to call the police and have the man arrested and sent to jail. His wife came to Lou and begged him not to do that (again).

"I made a lot of demands on Lou, but he was very cooperative in every respect. He gave me full rein and asked his brother Pat (executive producer on the television shorts) and director Jean Yarbrough to supply me with any information I requested and they did.

"Once the accounting mess was cleared up, I moved my office from the studio over to Lou's office building on Sunset Strip. After going over his accounts I soon came to realize that Lou was not as well off financially as he thought he was or as he had been in his heyday with Bud. What had reduced his assets was the loose accounting by the people he had employed. Not only with the recent accountant, but with Al Blum before him. It was a simple case of nobody watching the store and too many fingers in the till.

"It was obvious to me from the start that the IRS would eventually do a complete audit, and they soon did. Deductions had been taken that were totally illegal and income had actually been omitted on the tax returns by whoever did his accounting and tax reports at the time. When the IRS did the audit, penalties were added on until the total bill amounted to something like $750,000 each for Bud and Lou."

Once the IRS moved in, it was apparent even to my father that the government intended to make an example of Abbott & Costello and throw a scare into other celebrities and the public in general. As Paul N. Strassels pointed out in his book, *All You Need To Know About the IRS*, the IRS likes lots of publicity when they do an audit, in order to bring taxpayers in line with their way of thinking. The bigger the audit, the larger the taxes and penalties due, the better. Public fright is a common ploy used by the IRS to discourage taxpayers from cutting corners or fudging on their returns.

Max Fink, Dad's lawyer, did not have a background in tax law. Arthur Manella of the law firm, Burger & Irell (now Irell & Manella), was called in by Mr. Fink to defend Dad against the IRS. Mr. Manella was a former special assistant to the Attorney General in the Department of Justice (Tax Division) in Washington, D.C.

A meeting was set up between Fink, Manella, and my father. Arthur Manella recalls his association with Dad:

"When we first met I didn't get the impression that Lou was greatly upset. I don't think he was aware of the nature of the problems facing him. Eventually, as I became more deeply enmeshed in his tangled tax inconsistencies, we began to have regular meetings. It's probably safe to say the government was going over the years from 1945 to 1953 with a fine-tooth comb. One asks the question: Isn't it unusual for the government to go back that many years? (Let's say it is unusual to accumulate things of that nature for that length of time.) What happened, I believe, is that Lou's accountants did not furnish the government with the information needed on his tax returns on an annual basis. The result was that the IRS felt none of the tax returns were complete, so they kept requesting 'an extension of time,' to insure that the statute of limitations did not run against them. Normally the IRS can go back three years, but because of the extensions, in Lou's case they were able to go back as much as seven years.

"Ralph Handley was extremely helpful to me in untangling Lou's finances. (He'd been working on that for a while before I came into the picture.) The tax problem for Lou was that we simply did not have books, records, or documentation to show what happened in those earlier years (the mid-forties and early fifties). When the government started to examine all those prior years, they found thousands of dollars claimed in deductions for travel, commissions, entertainment, and professional gifts, which all would have been legitimate deductions. But we had no documentation that these expenses had in fact occurred. Additionally, there were several occasions on which items of income had been completely omitted on the tax return."

Robert Arthur cites one example of my father's handling income in a way that most likely didn't get reported to the IRS:

"One day back in 1946 or 47, Leo Spitz called me to his office. There was a check for Lou in the amount of $100,000—an advance. I asked Leo if I could give it to Lou because he seemed to be in a financial bind. Leo looked up and simply stated, 'As long as you have to work with him, you might as well give it to him.' I personally delivered the money to Lou on the set. He took the check, looked at it, didn't say anything to me—just proceeded to cross over to a telephone on the soundstage. He dialed a number and when they answered he said, 'I'll take the yacht!'"

That check was probably delivered to the boat company, totally circumventing the usual route through accountants, etc.

When the IRS got down to the nitty-gritty and started digging up all that unreported income, they began to think in terms of "tax fraud," which would indicate there was a deliberate attempt to evade taxes by omitting income and by claiming deductions (without any documentation) that the government didn't believe actually occurred. If the IRS proved their case, they could've imposed a "fraud penalty" (a dollar penalty equal to fifty percent of the additional tax liability), or worse—a long jail sentence.

Manella continues:

"The government lawyers with whom I was dealing did not believe that a taxpayer could indeed inadvertently omit $100,000 of income. They did not believe that a taxpayer could find $150,000 worth of deductions and have absolutely no proof, unless the taxpayer intended to defraud the government. IRS lawyers were tough cookies who refused to believe that Lou knew nothing about his income tax returns, that it was all a matter of his signing what somebody else wrote down. Therefore, initially we were not very successful in dealing with them.

"I must say, I had doubts of my own—until I got to know Lou Costello. Then, in my heart, I knew Lou was innocent and totally unaware of what was going on with his finances. He was too patriotic to cheat his government. Perhaps that sounds corny, but that's the type of man Lou was.

"There was one item in particular they kept hammering at. It involved $100,000 that never appeared on Lou's tax return, which Universal Studios claimed had been paid to Lou. That was the one big item the IRS planned to nail Lou on. We did a lot of digging and I finally dredged up the fact that the $100,000 in question never actually reached Lou Costello, because the government, during the year in question, had a lien on Lou's earnings for taxes that he owed from prior years, so that money was paid directly to the Internal Revenue Service by Universal.

"I now had something to confront the IRS with and finally said to the government lawyer, 'Look, if you're trying to purposely hide income from Uncle Sam, you certainly aren't going to hide income paid directly to the United States Treasury! That's not the way you hide income.' He had to agree with me.

"We had succeeded in convincing the government that Lou wasn't trying to cheat or defraud the U.S. Government, that he wasn't a man who thought in such terms, and that his mind was on things other than dollars and cents and business in detail—that's why he hired 'experts.'

"Once over that hurdle, we were left with the major issue of deductions that could not be substantiated by valid proof. Not only were there no cancelled checks, receipts, vouchers, or records; to top it off, the person who had been responsible for preparing Lou's tax returns during most of those years had left the country and nobody knew where to find him.

"Tax cases are often settled out of court, because the government, for the most part, is settlement minded, especially when you are dealing with a legal *issue* rather than a legal principle. In Lou's case there was no legal issue involved in terms of concepts. It was the issue of, 'Had Lou Costello spent X dollars or Y dollars for entertainment, traveling, etc., or had he not?

"I too was anxious to settle, because at that time a court was entitled to make an 'estimate of expenses' when a taxpayer's books were inadequate. Although in making that estimate, the taxpayer would have all doubts against him resolved, I was aware that when the courts made such estimates, they were often very harsh against the taxpayer. I also knew the astronomical figures in this case would stun the average judge. Consequently I went for out-of-court settlement. Lou was in the ninety-percent income tax bracket, which meant that if he ended up owing the government a million dollars, he'd have to earn ten million in order to have one million left over! It would've been a virtual impossibility for him to recover from such a staggering assessment."

Dad was not helped by the Internal Revenue Investigator who turned up the following from an interview with Charles Barton:

"One time, as I was leaving the sound stage, a man approached me (I later found out he was an agent of the IRS) with a very direct question. He said, 'Mr. Barton, how many times have you been on Lou Costello's boat?' I said, 'About three times. Why?' He continued saying, 'Then it's not your office?' I looked at the man and said, 'My office? Hell, no!' I didn't know what Lou or his accountants had told the IRS. I later found out the government had been informed that I used the boat as my office when I was looking over scripts and/or working on them. When I saw Lou, I told him what had happened. I said, 'Lou, why didn't you tell me what you were saying to them? At least I could have tried to cover for you.' Lou shrugged his shoulders and said, 'I know, Charlie. I'm sorry. I really am.' Then he seemed to get angry—angry about the whole audit business. He waved his hand in dismissal and said, 'Aw, forget those guys, Charlie. To hell with them!' "

Arthur Manella had to explain the settlement procedure to Dad and give him the hard facts of the cost in dollars and cents.

"This, above all, is probably my most vivid memory of Lou Costello. After negotiations had been completed with the government, I phoned Lou and asked him to come to my office. In the settlement I negotiated, there were to be no fraud penalties and certain deductions were to be allowed for each of the years in question under the so-called Cohen Law (so named because of the government's tax battles with mobster Mickey Cohen).

"In any event, Lou came to my office having no idea what I was about to tell him. I wanted to relay the good news in person. When he walked into my office, concern was written all over his face. I let him sit down and then I said, 'Lou, everything is over. The issues have all been resolved.' I gave him the total amount he'd have to pay. [The original $750,000 had been reduced to $375,000.]

"At that point he absolutely broke down sobbing uncontrollably. It was a tremendous emotional release. He cried like a baby, his whole body shook as he cupped his face in his hands and let all of the tension that had built up over the months flow freely from his body in tears. Once he composed himself, I remember he embraced me and kept saying, 'Thank you! Thank you! Thank you!' I'll never forget the emotion of the moment. Rarely does a lawyer run into a situation where there is such heartfelt gratitude on the part of a client. It was a very touching moment for me."

That was not to be the end of the government hassling my father about taxes. Soon afterward, the government amended its original plea in order to include an additional $15,000 in taxable income, on which my father would have to pay back taxes. It looked as though Dad was headed for another round of litigation with the Internal Revenue Service. Manella couldn't understand the government's position so he got on the phone to the government lawyer, whom he knew well, and said, "Joe, what's this extra income you're talking about?"

The lawyer said, "I really can't tell you, Arthur."

"What do you mean, you can't tell me? We're about to go to trial on this issue and you're asserting an additional $15,000. You've got to tell me what the item is."

The government attorney hemmed and hawed but finally said, "Look, I'm not supposed to tell you this, because we're presenting our own case, but we have evidence that Lou failed to report an additional twenty grand in income."

"What income? I've checked the return and I don't see any additional income."

"From playing cards!"

Manella leaned back in his chair, took a deep breath, and said, "You've got to be out of your mind! Lou Costello may, on some particular day, have won $20,000 playing cards, but I can assure you that overall he's lost a hell of a lot more."

The gambling law is as follows: You cannot take a deduction for your gambling losses except to offset gambling winnings. For example, if you win $20,000 and you lose $35,000, you are allowed to wipe out the $20,000 in winnings, but you cannot take an additional $15,000 deduction.

The government's proof was a cancelled check written to Dad in the sum of $20,000. The person who wrote it said it had been given to Dad to pay off a gambling debt. As I've shown earlier, my father gambled in some pretty high-powered poker games and with some rather well-known Hollywood people. They had a gentleman's agreement that no one would report winnings or losses on their tax returns. This one guy violated the understanding. He lost one night, wrote out that check to Dad, and then proceeded to report the loss on his income tax return.

As Manella explained to Dad, it would've been extremely easy to prove that my father had far in excess of $20,000 in losses at the card table, but it meant that he'd have to go back and figure out all of his gambling winnings and losses, naming everybody he played cards with. Before long it would be one great big daisy chain for the IRS to untangle at the expense and embarrassment of everyone involved.

Dad listened to the full explanation and then said, "We both know I've lost thousands, Arthur, but there's no way I'd rat on my friends. No way! I'll pay the extra tax dues."

Manella followed Dad's wishes and the case was more or less settled "on the courthouse steps." The government dropped the entire matter.

Sometime later the IRS also got involved indirectly with Dad's race horse, *Bold Bazooka*, and the disastrous Garden Stakes race in New Jersey. Dad, desperately short of money for the horse's entrance fees and transportation costs to the East

Coast race, explained to Arthur Manella that the horse had the potential to make the Kentucky Derby, but if he didn't run in the Garden Stakes his chances would be nil. The government had confiscated a twenty-thousand-dollar purse Bold Bazooka had won in San Francisco. Arthur went to the federal attorneys and talked to them.

"I cannot remember my exact words, but I was essentially letting them know that the horse was a very big potential and could possibly help pay off the debt to the government. After some conversations with them, they agreed to turn over the money to Lou to get the horse to the New Jersey race.

"The day of the race I was with the IRS people and we were all sitting around a radio rooting for Lou's horse to win. We must've looked pretty hysterical. The horse, of course, had an accident and didn't complete the race. I thought the IRS people would kill me. After all, I had persuaded them to give the money back to Lou. The funny thing is, in actuality when the government turned that money over to Lou, they were in essence placing a twenty-thousand-dollar bet on a race horse."

Dad and Bud were interviewed, once the dust had settled, and Bud said, "I'm in a one hundred ten percent tax bracket—because of penalties on back taxes."

Dad commented: "I haven't been able to save a dime. I've already paid $40,000 this year and I'm $50,000 behind. If I fail to estimate correctly for any quarter, I get penalized. At this point I certainly can't afford to quit working and I certainly can't afford to die! It would wipe my family out."

There were some sadly humorous aftereffects of Dad's battle with the government over taxes. One involved the ranch on which he raised turkeys. In previous years he'd given away turkeys by the dozens to all his friends and to charity. Now he was forced to sell those turkeys to the same friends over the holidays—something he'd never have thought of doing when the money was coming in.

On the other hand, that last Christmas we spent on Longridge Avenue, Dad went over to Universal, climbed up on a ladder on the sound stage, and wrote out Christmas checks to all of the crew as if he had a million dollars in the account. Actually he was struggling. He wasn't insolvent by any means, but remember, a great deal of his money was tied up in trust for his family in the event of his death. He was always putting others before himself.

The Internal Revenue Service notwithstanding, Dad continued to gamble. Las Vegas was like a vast toyland for him and had been ever since he and Bud followed the Andrews Sisters into the Flamingo Hotel, which the girls had just played as the hotel's first act during its grand opening in 1946. The infamous Benny "Bugsy" Siegel ran the Flamingo and was almost driven crazy by my father, who walked all through the casino with a pile of hundred-dollar bills, tearing off the corners. Then he would walk up to the blackjack tables and lay down some of those corners. In a very loud and jovial voice he would announce, "Here's my bet!" The croupiers were afraid to say anything to Dad because of who *he* was, and at the same time they were scared to death of Siegel because of who *he* was. It bothered my father not one whit that Bugsy had a disdain for people who tore off the corners of big bills. Bugsy never said a word to Dad—probably because wherever Dad went, the crowds followed and also because Dad was spending more money at the tables than he was making in the showroom.

It was no different when Abbott & Costello returned to the Flamingo in 1953 to play the El Rancho Vegas in the main room. That time Dad had brought along his buddy, Bobby Barber. One night between shows, Bobby and his wife, Maxine, were walking through the casino and suddenly heard Dad's voice, loud and clear, saying, "Picture!" They found my father at a blackjack table, calling for the house photographer. Each time he'd win a hand he'd call the photographer to take a picture of him as proof that he'd won. Again the little boy in Dad needed to impress.

Nineteen fifty-three was also the year my parents were disappointed by my sister Paddy. She and her boyfriend, James Mobley (whose step-father, Stan Cardinet, was head of Cardinet Candies) eloped. One of Paddy's girlfriends from Marymount, Marilyn Grix, loaned her a wedding ring that had been her grandmother's so that she could get married. When Dad found out that Paddy had run off and gotten married, he got the whole story from my sister, asked for the ring, and personally delivered it back to Marilyn. It was nighttime when he knocked on her front door. When she opened it to see who was there, he shoved the ring in her face and angrily said, "Does this belong to you???"

Mom and Dad soon forgave Paddy, however, and gave her a splendid formal wedding at Saint Francis de Sales Church with a reception at our home afterward. The following spring Paddy and Jim presented Dad with his very first grandchild, Louis Costello Mobley, who was immediately nicknamed "Butch." Dad was jubilant because the baby was a boy. When the call came from the hospital, Dad took it and related the good news to the rest of the family—since we were all sitting around waiting to know. He and Mom immediately left for the hospital where they were allowed to look at the baby through the nursery window. When the nurse held up the baby for my parents to see and unwrapped the blanket to show them his tiny fingers and toes, Dad suddenly became very concerned and shouted through the window, "Don't drop that baby! Hold on to him tight!" Of course everyone there laughed in good humor. That nurse had handled more babies in a week than he'd seen in a lifetime. (Paddy had two more sons: Michael in 1956 and Christopher in 1957. Today all three boys have changed their last names to Cristillo and I'm sure Dad would be extremely proud of that.)

We spent our last Christmas in the Longridge house in 1953. I believe it was the most elaborate affair we ever had at the house, so much so that one would never suspect that my father had any financial difficulties. Presents, as usual, were stacked ceiling high and all the old friends, cronies, family, and "leeches" were there to dip into the well one more time. It would be an event long remembered by the Hollywood community for its lavishness—but more importantly for us, it was a time when our family was extremely united. Dad's health had suffered greatly from the IRS fiasco and he no longer enjoyed the financial clout he once had. We girls could see that Dad wasn't healthy, but we had no idea he was hurting in the pocketbook. He kept that from us. My father never spoiled our happiness with his hurt.

214

CHAPTER XXI

A New Home

IT BECAME INCREASINGLY EVIDENT to my parents that they would not be able to keep the Longridge Avenue home. Interest was adding up on the outstanding back taxes and Dad wasn't making as much money as he had in earlier days. *Abbott & Costello Go to Mars*, which he completed during the tax audit aftermath, was deemed to be the worst film the team ever made. Even the title was wrong—they went to Venus, not Mars. In 1954 he made only one film, *Abbott & Costello Meet Dr. Jekyll and Mr. Hyde*, which costarred Boris Karloff. It was not an outstanding picture from a critic's point of view but surprisingly (even to Dad and Boris Karloff) the film skyrocketed at the box office. It may have been the odd mixture of the sinister-looking Karloff and innocent-faced Lou Costello that propelled audiences into the theaters.

Nonetheless, Dad was making fewer and fewer films. He was having recurring attacks of rheumatic fever more frequently and for the first time in his life was actually worrying about money. It was becoming a matter of *when*, not *if*, he and Mom would have to sell the house that had been so much a part of his life and career.

De De Polo had introduced Dad to Michael Monteleone, who was president of the Sons of Italy and wanted my father to appear at a benefit for the Casino Memorial Orphanage in Italy, which Dad did. Whenever Mr. Monteleone visited our home to pose with my father for publicity photos, he would compliment my parents on its size and beauty. That was in 1952. The following year Mr. Monteleone was dealing with a real estate agent to help him sell an apartment building he owned in Hollywood.

"Would you consider a trade?" the agent had asked him.

"What's to trade?"

"A beautiful home in the San Fernando Valley. It's gorgeous and I think it might be just what you're looking for."

"Who owns it?"

"It belongs to Lou Costello but he has to sell because of tax problems. You probably read about it."

Mike jumped up from his chair, excited. "My God! I know that home and I know Lou." He recalls the situation. "If I had known Lou was considering selling his home I would've approached him on my own rather than go through a real estate broker."

Dad was asking $110,000 for the house, which was only a fraction of what he had spent to build and landscape it. Mr. Monteleone was anxious to make the deal, and it was made.

We already owned a second ranch by this time in the far northwest corner of Canoga Park, another community in the San Fernando Valley. The twenty-two–acre spread, which was also known as the L.C. Ranch (the earlier L.C. Ranch was sold and the stock moved to the new acreage) had cost $96,000. I don't think my parents would have sold our home if it hadn't been for the enormous sums needed for its upkeep as well as to maintain the ranch.

Mom was heartbroken over giving up the Longridge home. From the day she knew it was going she seemed to almost caress the door-facings as she moved from room to room. An almost blank expression of total misunderstanding filled her face as she so often said, "This home's been our life. We've loved it so much. What will I do now?"

The sale included all the furniture. De De assisted Mr. Monteleone when he inventoried the furnishings, with tears streaming down her face. Before the deal was completed and the escrow closed, Mr. Monteleone approached Dad and asked if he could take possession during the early part of December in order to move in with his children for Christmas.

Dad said, "Mike, I'll tell you what I'll do. Let *me* have it for Christmas and I'll let *you* have it for New Year's."

It was a Christmas to remember, and the first time Mr. Monteleone had witnessed a "Lou Costello Christmas":

"That December I took my daughters to see this great wonderment. I have never seen such traffic in my life as was going up Longridge Avenue! Lou was standing outside in the driveway passing out candies to the kids and their parents who came to ogle."

We had it all. Animated reindeer danced on the roof as a mechanical Santa Claus in the yard waved to one and all, and piped-in Christmas music caroled joyously throughout the neighborhood. Our beautiful white-flocked Christmas tree—so tall it brushed the ceiling—was set up in the living room so that all those passing by outside could admire it through the large front windows.

All of our family and friends had come to our house for one last celebration of traditional merriment and the lavish handing out of gifts. At the stroke of midnight on Christmas Eve, we all congregated in the theater, where the pool table was piled to the ceiling with brightly wrapped packages. And then, as he had each year before, Dad selected a gift, called out a name, and Carole, Paddy, and I passed them on. Larger gifts, such as horses or automobiles would be outside.

It wouldn't have been Christmas without the marvelous Syrian pastries and cookies that Mrs. Joe Elias baked and brought to the party.

What a grand finale it was, our tears of happiness blending with heartache and the sweet nostalgia of what would never be again.

I'm not sure if the Abbotts came that Christmas, but I'm sure they must have. My sisters tell me that the Abbott and Costello families had been somewhat closer in earlier years. Carole and Paddy always attended Bud's and Vicky's birthday parties, and the courtesy was returned. He was "Uncle Bud" to us as children, and his wife was "Aunt Betty."

We seemed to enjoy a more leisurely life at the ranch. I saw more of my dad, primarily because he wasn't working as much as he had in years before. He was slowly dissolving his relationship with Universal (Abbott & Costello made their last two films there in 1955: *Abbott & Costello Meet the Keystone Cops* and *Abbott & Costello Meet the Mummy*). Dad was quite ill with another rheumatic fever bout when *Mummy* was produced; still, he insisted on doing his own stunt work despite medical orders to the contrary. Bud's drinking had him bloated until he actually looked pudgier than my father. Considering some of their more recent films, however, it wasn't a bad picture to exit on. More importantly, it was a financial success.

It was a bad time for Mom, though. Rashes were breaking out all over her legs, just as they had whenever she brought us to the ranch for weekends, before we moved there to live. The doctor diagnosed her condition as nerves, because she didn't like the ranch. Her body, as well as her spirit, seemed to reject the place.

Some things remained the same. Bobby Barber was still a regular visitor and always seemed to be doing something with cement. I remember that he put in a cement walkway from the back of the main house to the pool area. He was very good with his hands and at making jokes and doing slapstick routines with Dad.

Another thing that never changed was my father's relationship with me. He took me everywhere. Mom would say, "She can't go right now, Lou. I need her for something."

Dad's reply was, "Naw, she doesn't have to do that." Then he'd take me by the hand and say, "Come on, Christy," and away we'd go. Maxine Barber always said my father needed to love someone young, needed to have someone young with him.

The ranch was very secluded. There was a main house, where our immediate family lived, with a swimming pool and two additional living units, separated by a laundry room. Mom's sister Irene and her family lived in one of those units; Paddy and Jim and their sons occupied the other. We all had horses. Paddy's was an Arabian named Stranger; Carole's was Mickey, a palomino; and the Shetland pony Scout belonged to me. Dad kept his race horses there as well.

Dad owned domestic livestock and we did slaughtering right on the ranch. The barn contained a deep-freeze locker where milk and sides of beef and pork were stored. In many respects we were an extremely self-sufficient farm family with an image far removed from that of the movie-star antics of my comedian father.

Mom, I believe, was more withdrawn. I know she drank more after we moved to the ranch, but none of us girls could understand why and no one ever made the effort to discuss it with us—certainly not my father. The guilt Mom felt about Butch, which she carried to her grave, and what she felt at having to give up her lovely home in Sherman Oaks to live in a setting totally alien to her nature combined to take a heavy toll on her emotions. She, in turn, often took her personal frustrations out on the people who worked for her. Ophelia MacFashion was one of those who sometimes felt the sting of my mother's bitterness:

"At times, for no apparent reason, Anne would just get mad at me. I knew she was frustrated and didn't like living at the ranch. She had to take it out on somebody and I didn't mind that it was me. I understood. She'd get angry and say, 'All right, Ophelia, just go home. I don't need you anymore, so go home.'

"I remember driving all the way home and I'd be so angry, because I knew she expected more of me than of anyone else. We were close. So close that it made me an easier target. I'd arrive home, tired and worn out, and after a little while I'd cool off and realize why she'd done it. My husband always said, 'Oh, don't pay Mrs. Costello no mind, Ophelia—just go back to work tomorrow.'

"So the next morning I'd show up for work and Anne would be so glad to see me. When it was time for me to go home in the evening (after she'd told me to go home the day before), she'd grab a big cardboard box and take me out to the freezer and start filling up the box with fresh meat. She'd say, 'Now go on down to Bob and tell him to give you some fresh eggs and milk.' She was an enormously generous woman. So, for the next three or four days, we'd get along real good. Then all hell would break loose again. I'd get to the ranch just as Anne was getting up. I'd hear her slippers on the flagstone hallway from their bedroom as she approached the kitchen, and I'd think, 'Oh, God! Here she comes.' She'd enter the kitchen in her robe and I'd say, as always, 'Good morning, Mrs. Costello.' If she was in a good mood, she'd respond in kind. If not, look out. Her usual routine was to sit down at the table and I'd pour her a cup of black coffee. She loved black coffee in the morning. I used to sit and watch her sip that coffee and she'd perk up right before my eyes. Usually she consumed three cups before she went back to her room and got dressed for the day. She converted me to drinking black coffee and I still drink it that way.

"There were times when Anne thought I was watching her or following her around and she'd get angry with me. Maybe it was because she sneaked to drink and was afraid somebody would catch her. I know she must've felt guilty about it. It worried me—it worried us all—but it wasn't my problem. After she'd finished her coffee in the morning, she'd return to her bedroom—and that's where she started drinking. She hid bottles everywhere. At times she'd give me money and say, 'Ophelia, take this and go to the store for me, will you? Get whatever you need for the children too. My treat.' Then, when she got mad at me, she'd change. 'Ophelia,' she'd say, 'you owe me for this (or) such and such.' Nevertheless, she was a wonderful lady and did wonderful things for me and my family.

"Even when they were still living in the Longridge house she was drinking. I knew her problems—and that's why I stayed on for such a long time with them. Lou sometimes had his doctor come to the house to talk to Anne about her drinking. It didn't help—only depressed her more to know that someone in the family knew about it and was concerned. The doctor wanted to know just how much she was consuming, so Lou told me to keep an eye on her. There were so many bottles hidden about the house, it was difficult to determine just how much she was going through.

"There was a comic aspect to it too. Anne would be suspicious of everybody after the doctor's visit, certain that somebody had finked on her. If she wanted a drink and I was in the bedroom with her, she'd find something for me to do in the kitchen or some other part of the house. If we were in the kitchen, the procedure would be reversed.

"Once the family moved permanently to the ranch in Canoga Park, Anne became more expert at hiding her bottles. I won't forget one election day when all the liquor stores and bars were closed during the voting hours. There was a little ranch market down the road from the house, and on this one particular election morning, she sent me down to that little market to buy some liquor. Everybody knew I worked for the Costellos, but I had my little note from Anne requesting a bottle of vodka. They quickly grabbed a bottle off the shelf and wrapped it for me. When I got back, no sooner did I walk into the kitchen than the phone rang. It was the owner of the market: 'My God,' he said, 'this is election day and we could get into a lot of trouble by selling liquor. One of the boys here sold it without realizing what day it was. Don't say anything to *anybody* about where you got it.' I assured him I wouldn't. By that time Anne had the bottle open and was pouring herself a drink.

"If Lou came home and asked me if she'd been drinking, I had three answers for three different occasions: If she'd been drinking heavily and it was obvious, I would stammer, lower my head, and mutter, 'Yes, Mr. Costello.' Now, if Anne and I had had one of our run-ins, I'd be inclined to reply rather candidly, 'Yes, she has.'

However, if he asked the question after we'd made up and everything was fine, I quite readily gave him a positive and cheery, 'Oh, no, Mr. Costello, she hasn't had a drop.'

"Lou's family contributed to Anne's drinking, I believe, because they always knew right away what was going on in the world of Lou Costello, whether it was business or personal. Anne was always the last to find out. She was treated like a child in many ways, given everything she wanted, charge accounts all over town—anything money could buy—but what she wanted most, money couldn't buy for her. She wanted to have her husband's love and have him show that he loved her. Lou didn't know how to do that. I know he loved Anne, but he never showed any emotions to prove it. He truly felt he was keeping her satisfied and happy, and Lou couldn't be changed. Anne knew there was nothing she could do about it, so depression set in and she drank."

One time Ophelia showed up for work in a brand-new fire-engine red Thunderbird. She parked it in the driveway and went about her duties in the house. After a while, when Dad came home from wherever he'd been, he popped into the kitchen and asked, "For Chrissake, whose Thunderbird is that in the driveway?"

"Oh, that's Ophelia's," Mom said.

Dad was stunned at first. "Ophelia's?" After recovering from his surprise, he stormed into the kitchen and shouted at Ophelia, "Where the hell did you get a Thunderbird?"

Ophelia laughed and said, "Well, Mr. Costello, I bought it. Don't you think it's pretty?"

He laughed and said, "Well, for Chrissake, I better come and work for *you!*"

Not too long afterward, Ophelia pulled into our driveway and found another new Thunderbird parked there. As she got out of the car, wondering where it came from, Dad came bouncing out of the house and said, "Hey, Ophelia, how do you like *my* Thunderbird?"

Mom was generous that way with everyone who worked for our family. I remember she had a dressmaker, Tilla de Thomas, from the time we moved to the ranch until Mom died. Tilla used to come to the ranch to do alterations and one time, for no apparent reason, Mom grew very serious as Tilla was taking some measurements and said, "Tilla, if everything came to an end right now, I'd just take Christy and go away." Afterward she found one of those big cardboard boxes and took Tilla out to the freezer where she loaded her up with steaks, ribs, and choice meat cuts, shaking her head as she filled the box. "Here, Tilla, take this home with you. There's no way in the world we can eat all of this meat."

When we moved to the ranch, De De relocated her offices from Longridge to the Lou Costello Building on Sunset Boulevard, and went to live in one of the apartments in the building Dad had received in the trade with Mike Monteleone. The Costello Building was already up for sale. Dad was trying to become as financially liquid as possible to pay off all the back taxes, because the interest on them was killing him so far as cash was concerned. Dad loved De De so much he just couldn't tell her personally that he was going to have to let her go when the building was sold. That fell to Uncle Pat, who took De De to lunch one day and explained the circumstances and that the building was being sold and she'd have to be terminated.

The vestiges of my father's fabulous years were being stripped away little by little. He never showed us girls in any way that he was anything other than what he'd always been. He was still the family man. If one of his daughters wanted to work in a picture, he arranged it. Carole was the one most interested in the business at the time (I wasn't really old enough to know what I wanted to do and Paddy didn't care that much) and she had bit parts in *Abbott & Costello Meet the Keystone Cops* and *Abbott & Costello Meet the Mummy*. For a while she even worked as a mail girl on the Universal lot, thanks to Dad's influence.

Carole, however, felt the sting of Dad's discipline just as Paddy had. My father had promised her a new convertible for her birthday—probably her sixteenth—and that was the day she chose to ditch school and escape with a girlfriend to the Bel-Air Country Club for lunch, practically next door to Marymount High School, where she was a student. They neglected to change from their uniforms and the Reverend Mother saw them leaving the campus. Carole explains:

"When I got home that day, it was obvious that the school had called Mom and Dad and reported that I'd left the grounds without permission. Dad was in the den when I walked in. He said, 'Did you have a nice day at school?' I think I replied, 'Oh, the same as always.'

222

"He looked at me and said, 'Really?' He reached over, picked up the phone and dialed a number. I stood watching him, sensing that something was wrong. He said into the telephone, 'Hello, this is Lou Costello. I want to cancel the red convertible I ordered.' He ran down the description, as I stood there, in great detail to the guy on the telephone. Then he said, 'Yes, that's the one—the one I ordered for my daughter Carole.'

"I went upstairs to my room absolutely furious with myself for what I'd done. I had to wait six months for a car, and then it was a *used* one. Dad knew how to put me in my place. It was another year before I got the new fire-engine red convertible—as a graduation present.

"As strict as our father was on the one hand, he didn't like to be put on the spot or feel foolish in front of people. And I took advantage of that more than once. I used to trade in cars on him. Within that same year Dad had given me the new convertible, I must've had two or three cars. One day I brought a car salesman up to the ranch, because I wanted him to talk to Dad about the MG I wanted. Dad didn't really want to buy it for me, but I embarrassed him so much he had to. I said, 'Oh, please Dad! Can't I have the MG?' I sounded like my entire life depended on it. The salesman looked at me and then at my father who, very sheepishly and, I'm sure, with great embarrassment, said yes."

One night Dad asked Carole to make a trip to the store for him, pretending he'd forgotten she was grounded; then he said, "Oh-oh, you're not supposed to leave the house. Well, I guess I'll have to go myself. Where are your keys?" We knew Dad was only looking for an excuse to drive my sister's new MG.

Carole looked up from a book and said, "Are you sure?" The car was very small and difficult to get in and out of, and Dad was going through one of his extra-pudgy periods.

"Sure I'm sure." He struggled, but managed to squeeze himself in behind the wheel, still chomping on his cigar.

When he got back from the store, Carole said, "I bet it's been a long time since you've driven a car with four forward gears."

Dad looked at Carole strangely and said, "How many?"

"Four, Dad."

He put the cigar back in his mouth and said, "I didn't use four."

Carole was afraid to think what he'd done to the gears. "Well, Dad, how many did you use?" she asked. Dad didn't say anything—just sneaked out of the room almost on tiptoes.

Another time Carole took Dad for a drive over Coldwater Canyon, a twisting, turning, treacherous road that winds like a loose string through the Santa Monica Mountains between the Valley and Beverly Hills. It was during a time when all the kids played a game whereby you wouldn't touch the brake going down the canyon. All you did was shift down. That's what she did the day she had Dad with her, and by the time they reached the other side of the mountain Dad's cigar was literally in shreds. Dad eased himself up in the seat, turned to his daughter and said, "Carole, if you ever drive again it will be a miracle!"

That's interesting because I don't think Dad ever owned a driver's license. He was a very bad driver—always tailgating something awful. Small wonder that he was chauffeured so often. He used to change lanes without looking back to see if there was another car in that lane, or even signalling. When a cop stopped him, the officer invariably said, "Oh, it's Lou Costello. How are ya, Lou?" A smile, an antic, an autographed photo and the citation was forgotten.

I attended Our Lady of the Valley school when we moved to Canoga Park. I wasn't very good at academics and had a tendency to be a little wild, which kept me constantly in dutch with the sisters. I wasn't mean, just mischievous. I did things like tossing one of the nun's bells over the hedge into the reservoir, cutting classes to hide in the chapel, and once I set off the fire alarm at school. Although today I sing with the big band of Bill Tole (Bill played Tommy Dorsey in the film, New York, New York), it wasn't until high school that I took even the slightest interest in music. Dad was a stickler for education, but he didn't push when it came to the arts. If we were interested in that direction, it was up to us to pursue it. But he insisted we study and learn academic fundamentals. I'm sure I wasn't his brightest hope in that area.

Dad allowed me, within limits, to be a brat. Still, there were times when he had a subtle firmness about him that even I couldn't penetrate. I remember one year in particular, when I was seven or eight years old, he took me trick or treating on Halloween. He dressed me up to look like him and we got into an argument because I didn't want a cigar. Nonetheless he placed the derby at a cocked angle on my head and shoved an unlit cigar into my mouth. I immediately spit it out and took my stand: "I won't put that smelly old cigar in my mouth, because it will burn my tongue." Dad took back the cigar, but every time someone opened a door after our knock, he quickly jammed it into my mouth just before the door was fully opened. It was his will against mine, and he won.

My father always did love kid things. Even my Aunt Marie once said that if Dad had lived to be eighty-five he still would've believed in Santa Claus. I remember one Christmas in particular, years after we had moved to the ranch, I let it slip to my father that I had told Paddy's oldest boy there was no Santa Claus. We were walking by the corral and he stopped dead in his tracks and looked at me as though he were going to break down sobbing any minute. Still, he never said a word—he just looked hurt. I wished he'd hit me or something—I would've appreciated that. He thoroughly crushed me by his silence.

I just can't get away from Christmas, because that's so much how I remember my father—a great big bundle of Christmas joy. He once took Joe Elias Christmas shopping. It was Christmas Eve afternoon and that night Dad was throwing his annual Christmas bash. Dad and Joe drove into Los Angeles, where they found a very crowded television and radio store. It was around five-thirty in the early evening and getting dark when they arrived. Dad sauntered into the store, Joe right behind, and approached a salesman. He casually asked the guy, "How many television sets do you have in the store?"

The clerk made an eyeball check and said, "Maybe two or three dozen. What type did you have in mind?"

Dad never batted an eyelash. He said, "Can you deliver all of them to my home—tonight?"

The salesman looked at my father as if to say, "I didn't understand the request."

Dad continued on, "I don't want any discount or nuthin'. Just total up the price for all the sets you have here."

Both the salesman and Joe Elias were in a state of shocked disbelief, but once convinced my father was not some kind of a nut, he began tallying up the cost—all the time assuring Dad that the store (which normally did not give same day delivery) would be happy to make an *immediate* delivery. The salesman routinely asked, "Check or charge?"

"Cash," Dad said, reaching down into his pocket and pulling out a roll of hundred dollar bills that totalled close to $30,000. You see, not only did my father enjoy giving, but he enjoyed, to some degree, the shock value of paying for large purchases with cash. (Many of those sets were for business associates and it was items like that, paid for with cash, that got him into a lot of trouble with the IRS—he never kept any of the receipts.)

Having sent the happy salesman home early by buying out the store, Dad was at home waiting when they were delivered. They were all tagged with gift cards for friends and family alike, and placed around the tree in time for the evening's festivities.

CHAPTER XXII

The Split

MILT BRONSON had been with my father in various capacities since 1943 and, by 1955, it seemed evident to him that Dad and Bud were on the fringes of a final breakup. When Milt was offered a good position in Las Vegas, he decided to take it. Dad, too, was aware that the team was close to splitting. Besides, he wanted to act in some dramatic roles. All of his life he'd been in comedy and all of his pictures had been made with Bud Abbott. The partnership was fraying around the edges; as a matter of fact it was tattered and the seams were weak.

When Milt had come to Dad and explained the offer he'd received from the hotel in Las Vegas, Dad said, "I think you should take it, Milt." He didn't try to talk him out of it, but it was a sad occasion for the two friends whose relationship went back to Dad's early burlesque days. Dad had brought Milt to California and he couldn't remember a day that they weren't together. They remained close friends until Dad's death and saw each other whenever Dad was in Las Vegas.

Michael Ansara was a newcomer to Hollywood, an actor from legitimate theater, when he did *Abbott & Costello Meet the Mummy* with Dad. He observed the strain between Dad and Bud:

> "They didn't seem to communicate between scenes. When the director called *cut*, Lou went in one direction and Bud in the other—without any conversation between them. I suspect a personality clash might've been the problem."

By 1955 Universal was being run by Milton Rackmil, and the number-one star at the studio was Jeff Chandler. Richard Dea-

227

con, who has become one of Hollywood's all-time great comic character actors, was also in that film. H.B. Warner suddenly got ill before production started, and Richard replaced him in the part of Semu, the leader of the cult who keeps the mummy alive in an underground temple. "Deke," as Richard is known throughout the film industry, was claustrophobic, and in one scene he was required to be buried alive. Dad overheard Richard discussing his phobia with one of the prop men, so he went up to Richard and said, "Deke, will it bother you if we just put a light amount of dirt over you and then immediately after the scene we'll take it right off of you?" Deacon assured him that would be all right.

Dad went to Charles Lamont, the director, and said, "Charlie, Richard's got claustrophobia, so let's do the scene and get him out of there in a hurry."

In those days a man would be laughed out of town for getting a perm or using a hair-blower. Even women didn't discuss face lifts. When Dad noticed that Deke placed his hand on his hip quite a bit, he asked the director to tell him not to do it. My father's attitude about that was a holdover from the days when gestures were considered signals: A hand on the hip was considered effeminate; hooking your fingers in your belt was okay; or, if you had your hand gloved and fisted on your hip, that was very male. It was a macho world and my father expected actors to conform.

Deke was requested to sign my father's anti-Communism pledge and it was Bobby Barber whom Dad sent to talk to Deke. Deke recalls what he said when Bobby approached him on the set:

"I knew Lou was thinking of America, which was fine, but I personally considered McCarthy one of the most evil things that ever happened. I refused to sign."

Bobby warned him that if it got back to Dad that he wouldn't sign, Deke would probably never work on the Universal lot again. Deke's refusal was never brought up again, however, and he continued working at Universal for many years thereafter. My father probably never knew about what had happened.

Meet the Mummy was the last Abbott & Costello film produced by Howard Christie, but it wasn't my father's last experience with him. After the split-up Howard produced the *Wagon Train* series for television and he arranged for Dad to appear in one of the segments.

Dad and Bud made their last film together in 1956. It was titled *Dance with Me Henry*, after a long-since-faded popular song, and it's greatest distinction is that it was their last film. I remember the day Dad took us all to the movie theater in Canoga Park to see it. Before the film began, with the house filled with kids, Dad was introduced by the manager not only as the world-renowned comedian but as the Honorary Mayor of Canoga Park, an honor he accepted with great pride. The kids were all excited and turned around to look toward the back of the theater, where we were all seated.

Dad got up and started walking down the aisle toward the stage. He started doing pratfalls and trips for the kids, and by the time he reached the stage, he had the audience howling. The louder the kids laughed, the more he became Lou Costello, the bumbling comic. I think that day, making those kids happy, had to be one of the great moments in my father's life.

Dad's career was accurately encapsulated on November 21, 1956, when he was the subject of Ralph Edwards' famous television biography series, *This Is Your Life*. The show was shot before a live audience at the NBC Studios in Burbank. Dad had been an excellent basketball player as a young man in Paterson, so Ralph Edwards said, "Well, Lou, we want to see if you can still do it! Here's a regulation backstop and basket—and here's a basketball. Let's see if you can score a basket in honor of the old Armory Five!"

Dad (in his fifties at the time) took the ball for a second and then said, "Well, here goes." He shot the basket with great ease.

It was a very nostalgic night on TV and it ended with tears. Seven children from the 10,000-member Lou Costello Jr. Youth Foundation came down the ramp to where Dad and Ralph Edwards were standing. One of them stepped forward with a gold watch in his hand and said, "Well . . . you've sure helped an awful lot of us kids, Mr. Costello, and we just want to say thanks to you. Here. We all chipped in and bought this for you." The boy handed Dad a gold watch and asked him to read the inscription on the back. Dad, with tears in his eyes, turned over the watch and read aloud the words, "Thanks for sharing your life with ours." Ralph Edwards remembers:

"If Lou showed any signs of nervousness in being on the show, it was probably because he had never played himself before. My wife Barbara recalls that what stood out in her mind the most was Lou's jolliness and his tremendous concern for others. It was as though he had a mission to make other people happy. That's what Barbara picked up that night and what I personally believe came through on the show."

Carole was graduated from Marymount High School that year and went on to the University of Oklahoma. Then, in December, 1956, Dad and Bud played their last engagement as a team in Las Vegas at the Sahara Hotel. Sid Kuller produced and wrote the show. It was a difficult time of year to play Las Vegas, and Stan Irwin, who was then vice president and director of entertainment at the Sahara, explains why:

"In those days we did shows in December, but later on Vegas learned that prior to Christmas, you just don't do it. Now more than half the Vegas hotels go into "show hiatus" right after Thanksgiving. Bud and Lou were there during the first part of December, which isn't a thrilling time to be any place in the night-club field. [That accounts for reports that the team didn't do well.] During the engagement, Lou was very sharp and alert onstage. Bud, however, was not as energetic. The straight man sets up the timing for the comic, and it threw Lou off that Bud wasn't delivering the right timing. I'm sure that added to the tension between them. Nonetheless, I cannot recall any time when Lou had to lead a drunk Bud Abbott off the stage [as was depicted in the television movie *Bud and Lou*].

"Although the crowds were sparse because of the holidays, the response was magnificent. They had a very successfull well-written show, and neither of them ever missed a performance."

(Stan Irwin later went on to do the voice of my father in the Hanna-Barbera Abbott & Costello cartoon series, a total of 156.)

The Sahara Hotel show was titled *Miltown Revisited*, a breezy combination of comedy and song—old and new—with Bud and Dad backed by sixteen young singers and dancers. Their salary was $30,000 a week, top dollar for the times. It was a fast-paced show opening on a scene in Central Park. The finale was their classic "Who's on First," which left the entire audience standing and cheering on opening night and every night thereafter.

Dad's doctor had ordered him not to do his usual pratfalls, banging into walls and falling down, plus all the slapstick punches and fake blows. But Dad ignored those instructions and went out onstage and did what he was known for. "How can I cheat the audience?" he said.

Both in 1956 and before they split in 1957, Dad and Bud appeared together a number of times on the *Steve Allen Show*. A news clip states:

> Film comedians Bud Abbott and Lou Costello were never nominated for an Academy Award, but they did something that no other entertainer has ever accomplished. They landed in baseball's most hallowed spot, The National Baseball Hall of Fame in Cooperstown, New York, thanks to their classic routine "Who's on First." A gold recording of "Who's on First" will be with Bud and Lou in New York when they formally present it to the Hall of Fame before a nationwide television audience on Steve Allen's show over NBC-TV today.

It was the twentieth anniversary of the routine, which they had performed more than fifteen thousand times.

There have been many stories as to why my father and Bud Abbott split up. It wasn't the sudden outburst that some have surmised or speculated. Their differences began over little things and finally grew to be so large they just couldn't handle being a team any longer. A few people who were around when it actually happened have this to say:

> *Columnist James Bacon:* "There was a part of Lou that wanted to go on to other things. He wanted to try doing dramatic roles and to see if he could go it alone. Bud's drinking was an important factor, however, and when it started to get out of hand, Lou came to me and said, 'I just can't cope with it anymore, Jim.' I think he was having a difficult enough time handling his wife's drinking at home, let alone having to face another with his working partner."

> *Charles Barton:* "Lou wanted the split. He wanted to be on his own and try his talent with dramatic roles."

Betty Abbott: "I wish I could honestly say what caused the split between Bud and Lou. Bud felt very bad about it. When Lou wasn't doing too hot, Bud was asked to join him, but Bud said, 'No. That offer has to come from Lou.' I do know that the tension had been coming for some time."

Sid Kuller (wrote, directed, and produced *Miltown Revisited*): "On opening night the first show was absolutely sensational! Bud and Lou got standing ovations, the kids were brilliant, and everything was just right on. We had a packed house. After the first show Bud went out into the casino and started to gamble. You know what happens when you sit there at a table. They start pushing the drinks on you. Came time for the midnight show—the show that all the NBC brass was attending—and Bud was absolutely out of it. He was drunk.

"They got out on the stage and it was the disaster of all times. Bud was such an embarrassment for poor Lou, was so totally out of it that there stood Lou with egg on his face! Bud didn't even know what the hell 'Who's on First' was! I remember that when Lou walked off the stage, after suffering through and trying to cope with Bud's drunkenness, he called Eddie Sherman and told said, 'I'm through. I'll never forgive him for what he did out there tonight. I've had it! He'll never do this to me again!'

"I was backstage with Eddie that night and I know Lou was livid, and rightly so. For Bud to expose himself like that on that stage with a packed house, plus the NBC brass, was unforgivable. The audience knew what was happening and I must say, it was the most terrible night of my life in show business.

"I always had the greatest respect for Lou Costello. He had a lot of resilience. I mean, look at what he had to cope with in his lifetime: losing a son, his wife's alcoholism, his health, the government coming down on him, then having to finally recognize and deal with Bud's alcoholism, and finally what happened on that stage in Vegas. That's a lot. Lou took a lot, but God bless him he always bounced back."

On July 14, 1957 they made their official announcement. The team of Abbott & Costello was history, but what a history! The long partnership, the early struggles, the stardom, the good times, and the big money—all officially laid to rest. They'd been together as a team for twenty-one years—a hell-of-a track record in any industry—and especially in show business. Comedy teams usually have a tough time in the world of instant-vision, yet

Abbott & Costello are still playing somewhere on television, every hour of the day year 'round. That speaks well of two men whose last motion picture was made twenty-five years ago. Abbott & Costello are truly a living legend.

It was inevitable that wherever Dad went and whatever he did, there would be someone who would ask him about Bud Abbott. In a *TV Guide* interview, right after the split, Dad said:

> "Bud was a dandy, a real sharp dresser. He was an easy-going kind of a guy. Me, I'm a worrier. I worried about Bud for twenty years. Would he be there for rehearsal? Would he make the airport on time? Did he know the material?"

When questioned by an Associated Press reporter as to why the team broke up, Dad responded:

> "It's funny, but I was seen as a single by millions of people on the *Steve Allen Show,* and you're the first one who's asked me why. I guess after twenty years, no one would believe that Abbott & Costello would split up."

CHAPTER XXIII

The Final Years

STEVE ALLEN had some observations on working with my father individually:

"Lou was a real pro who conserved all his energy until it was time to do the show. Then he would absolutely knock us all out with that burst of energy he had. It was an automatic union between all of us and Lou. He was the kind of guy who was so busy approaching you, you didn't have the chance to approach him first. We all loved him and working with him on the *Steve Allen Show.*

"During one of his appearances on my show I was trying to quit smoking. Lou, unaware of this, gave me a beautifully inscribed cigarette lighter. I was so proud of that gift, I couldn't *not* use it. As a result, I continued smoking for many years, using that lighter until it finally broke down. It was only after the lighter no longer functioned that I was able to give up smoking."

Dad brought a lot of Abbott & Costello to Steve Allen's show, including many of their old routines. He worked with the Allen regulars on those skits. Louis Nye and Tom Poston did the "Lemon Bit" with Dad. Jim Mulholland states in his book: "Lou participated in those sketches with renewed energy and enthusiasm. Possibly because he was now embarking upon a new career—without Abbott."

One of the first things Dad asked Louis Nye when he came on the show was whether he'd been in burlesque. Nye told him he hadn't. The "Lemon Bit" routine went so well with Nye and Poston that Dad went up to Louis again, after the show, and asked, "Was your father in burlesque?"

Nye said later, "Just having Lou ask me was a compliment." Nye goes on:

"Lou had that crackly voice, the face, and the animation—and with those qualities, the things he attempted to do would always pay off. He also had a lot of humility. When we'd be rehearsing a skit, he'd sometimes turn to me and say, 'Wanna try that again?' or 'What do you think?' Here was Lou Costello—a man who started in burlesque and certainly knew more about what worked and should feel right than we did—asking my opinion. He had great concern for the feelings of others."

In January of 1958 the *Steve Allen Show* was performed in Havana, Cuba. Although Dad spoke no Spanish, wherever he went crowds followed him through the streets chanting: "Lou Coteo! Hey! Ee's Lou Coteo." All of Dad's films had been dubbed in Spanish and shown throughout Spanish-speaking countries around the world. Consequently, the fans assumed that he was fluent in their language. Of course, he nodded as though he understood every word, while signing autographs and passing out Lou Costello buttons, key chains, and other mementos for the fans.

Dad missed Bud, of that there can be no doubt. But he was a professional who understood that an actor must work to survive emotionally. Alone, he gained the opportunity to be creative with entertainers he'd never worked with, and he loved it.

Dad was having more fun and was completely relaxed in his work, although Mom's drinking and unhappiness troubled him. That was the one burr under his saddle. Everything else in his life seemed to be improving. The rheumatic fever relapses were a part of his being and he accepted them, adjusting his schedule to fit them in, more or less.

One afternoon Sid Kuller came out to the ranch and saw a different Lou Costello.

"He walked down the walkway to meet me and was in tears. My first thought was that he was sick and I asked if he needed a doctor. He shook his head and put his hand up to stop me. He said, 'Come with me and I'll show you what's wrong, Sid.'

"Lou took me around the back to where there were fruit trees and grape vines. He bent down and began to extract vodka bottles from the bushes, where his wife had hidden them. I saw another side of Lou that day, because he wasn't the funny little comic that we all saw him as, but a perplexed and hurt man. I'm sure he knew why she drank—the baby's death in 1943—but just didn't know what to do to stop her. I was seeing a Lou Costello I had never before seen in any of our meetings."

No matter what my father may have told others or how much he suffered from my mother's indiscretions with the bottle, he was very gentle with her when she drank. Once, when she was beyond understanding and had collapsed to the floor, my father ever so gently picked her up, took her to the bedroom, and tucked her in as he would a little child, without one word of recrimination.

Dad's last motion picture was *The Thirty-Foot Bride of Candy Rock* (1958) at Columbia Pictures. It was a bomb and fortunately it wasn't released until after Dad's death. I don't think he could've handled having his first movie without Bud Abbott be a failure. I remember going with Mom, Carole, and some other people to see it at a theater in the Valley, where it was being sneak-previewed. Afterward, when we were outside, Mom said, "This would've killed Lou if he'd seen it." *The New York Times* was much kinder: "Lou Costello's last legacy to his fans is something to leave them laughing . . . in *The Thirty-Foot Bride of Candy Rock,* he signs off in high spirits as a man on the threshold of a blissful everafter."

Nobody noticed that my father might be in ill health. Uncle Pat did all of Dad's running in the chase scenes, but that wasn't unusual. (Paddy's husband Jim had a bit appearance in the film in the role of a soldier who taps the helmet of another soldier manning a bazooka. His one line was, "Fire!")

Dad, though, was much less boisterous on the set than he had been in the Abbott & Costello pictures. He wasn't part of a team now—just another actor in a picture. This time he went off alone between takes, finding himself a quiet corner so he could study lines. It was the first time in his movie career that he actually studied dialogue for a film. There was now something about the man that seemed almost melancholy.

Lewis Rachmil, who produced the picture, sensed the difference in Dad's approach.

"Lou appeared at first as if he might be just a bit overwhelmed in not having Abbott as his foil. Many times during the first few days of shooting he'd come up to me and ask, 'How do I do this?' We were filming by a process method [Dorothy Provine was the bride and her scenes were shot and blown up to give her the appearance of a thirty-foot bride, while Dad's were then superimposed over Dorothy's] and Lou was working in front of a blank screen. Lou would ask, 'Well, how high is she? Where is she supposed to be?' As a result, Lou became increasingly nervous. He came to me one day and said, 'Lewis, I've never acted alone before,' and that's exactly what he had to do in many of his scenes with Dorothy.

"I stayed on the set during much of the filming and watched Lou. He could get so wound up, but then could also sink into tremendous lows. He seemed to lack that confidence he'd always shown before. He missed Bud."

Dad, for the first time in his career, would go to lunch and be late returning, holding up the production. Rachmil decided that everyone would eat on the set so Dad wouldn't wander away. Dad picked up what was happening immediately and began to complain. "I'm a prisoner," he said. Lewis assured him it was merely that he wanted everybody to eat together.

Rachmil also felt that Dad subconsciously fought learning lines, which became a mental block for him. He was always very apologetic, however, when he blew a line and would ask, "Would you let me do it again?" Another factor was his relationship with Dorothy Provine. She had just come off a film at Warner Brothers and seemed to feel that working in this picture was really a little below her abilities. Her name never became a household word.

Whenever Dad was upset, he ate. During the making of this picture, he developed a never-ending compulsion for food, insulating himself against his fears and uncertainty. He also surrounded himself with his cronies. When his old friends—like Bobby Barber—weren't on the set with him, encouraging him and playing pranks, he'd fall into lethargic moods.

He made his dramatic debut in television's *General Electric Theater*. It was a segment entitled "Blaze of Glory," co-starring Jonathan Harris. As Harris recalls, Dad developed an immediate fascination with what he thought was his British accent:

"Lou was very fascinated with the precision of my speech and was stunned to discover that I had been born in New York City. Before he realized that I was from New York, he used to remark, 'You British actors talk funny.' My stock response was, 'British actors don't talk funny. Only British actors from the Bronx talk funny.' It became a running joke with us and we both collapsed in laughter every time we went through it.

"Lou sometimes would wander away from the script and get carried away with some of the comedic points. When I would chastise him for not giving me the proper cues, he used to say, 'You got the general idea and you rode with it. I might put you in my act.

"In one scene I had to use a rose, which was a prop rose. Lou watched me in a scene and said, 'You smell that rose like it was real.' I replied, 'I have to pretend that it's a real rose.' The following day he gave me a beautiful red rose that was real. 'Now you don't have to pretend,' he said."

Howard Christie was now producing *Wagon Train* for television and a story came up which he felt was just right for Dad. He had seen the *General Electric Theater* episode and felt Dad had the ability to do a beautiful job in a straight acting role. The story was "The Tobias Jones Story," in which Dad played the role of a drunk. Howard very capably describes the situation:

"Lou was very nervous and said, 'I'm just wondering if I can really do it, Howard.' I said, 'Of course you can. I had this part written for you and I know you can do it.' From the moment Lou walked on that sound stage at Universal to do 'Tobias Jones,' there was never any sign of nervousness. He threw every ounce of himself into that part and did a brilliant job as the hopeless drunk, a character named Tobias Jones, accused of murdering a man on a wagon train. He was magnificent."

Dad was more comfortable working at Universal in familiar surroundings with his old producer Howard Christie and the friends he knew so well. That made the difference in his performance.

In an interview with *TV Guide*, Dad explained his feelings about "Tobias Jones": "It's easy to me. No falls, no pushing around, no seltzer in the face. But I had a real tough time with this guy inside of me at first. This guy inside me kept saying, 'What a perfect spot for a tumble, kiddo! Go ahead, and then eight to one you forget the next line.'"

Harry Von Zell, Dad's old friend who had been the announcer on the *Fred Allen Show,* was the official writer for Dad's segment of *Wagon Train.* He describes a scene which shows just how dramatic my father could get:

"There was one scene between Lou and the little girl (Beverly Washburn) that runs maybe ten minutes. She's trying to reason with Tobias, reaching into this man to try and bring him out of his funk. Prior to the scene being shot, the makeup lady came over with her tear-producing glycerine to make him able to cry in the scene. I went over to her and said, 'Why don't we rehearse Lou first without the glycerine? He might be uncomfortable thinking you have to give him something to produce the tear effect.' She agreed.

"When it came time to shoot, Lou was crying crocodile tears. That little girl reached him so much and so impressively, he was actually crying real tears. After the show aired, Lou gave Beverly Washburn all the credit. He insisted it was the little girl who brought out that dramatic quality in him. I don't think it ever occurred to him for one minute that he already had that quality inside him."

Dad still ad-libbed, a habit of almost forty years. He did a scene with Ward Bond, the star of the series, in which he makes a long speech. He's already been accused of murder and he's looking into the camera (talking to Bond) and saying, "You know I could never have done that. It can't be me . . . I'd never do that." Evidently, somewhere along the way he forgot his lines, because he hesitated and then continued. "How could you suspect me? I'd never do that, I could never murder anyone . . . How are ya, Ward?" Of course the entire set collapsed in fits of laughter. His voice had a tear in it, his face carried a sad expression, and he was just so serious when he dropped the bombshell line. That was Lou Costello at his dramatic un-dramatic best.

Because of the great notices he received for his performance he was approached by a producer to star him in a dramatic play on Broadway—but that never took place. Dad's last acting role was now behind him.

Also in 1958, the ranch was sold. The back taxes and mounting expenses made it not just impractical but impossible to keep. There were really just the three of us now—Dad, Mom, and me. Carole was away at college and Paddy was married and had her own family. Dad never really accepted the fact that his girls were grown up and out on their own. I think, with my older sisters away, he clung a bit more tenaciously to me in the hope that I'd always stay a kid so he'd have somebody to play with.

When the ranch was sold, the three of us moved into a two-bedroom apartment on Ethel Avenue in Sherman Oaks. In a few brief years we had gone from a twenty-four room mansion to one of those conglomerations of cubicles in the San Fernando Valley. But that was never intended to be permanent. Dad had already purchased a lot on Longridge Terrace and a new home was in the process of being built for us. Mom, was happy to get away from the ranch as she had never liked the place.

It seemed as if my father's life was coming full circle, back to burlesque, but nobody imagined how quickly the circle would be completed. During the summer of 1958, Dad was asked to appear at the Dunes Hotel in Las Vegas in the *Minsky's Follies of 1958* stage show. He was repeating what he'd done thirty years earlier on Broadway, with a modern twist. It was strictly burlesque and featured Dad in many of his old Abbott & Costello skits, such as "Crazy House" and "Lemon Bit." Sid Fields, who had played the landlord in the Abbott & Costello television series, played opposite Dad in the Bud Abbott role.

Scheduled to run six weeks, the show broke all house records and the owners of the hotel hoped to extend the show for another six weeks. They even offered Dad a new white Thunderbird as a bonus if he'd consent to stay on. At this juncture, he didn't lie to himself about his health. The six weeks had taken a lot out of him and he reluctantly declined the offer, feeling that he could come back again and that by now he had made his point—he could work comedy without Bud Abbott. The grateful hotel gave him the car anyway, because he'd been such a pleasure for everyone to work with.

It was my father's last stage appearance and what a marvelous way to bow out—a sold-out house rising in unison to their feet, applauding and shouting and clamoring for just one more encore. Because he'd been offered only $10,000 a week to do the show instead of $30,000, Eddie Sherman had advised against playing the engagement. "People will laugh at you, Lou, not with you," he counseled. "You don't want to look like a broken-down comic, down on his luck and looking for a handout." How totally wrong Sherman was. My father always said, "Eddie Sherman has the heart of a banker and the artistic soul of an illiterate."

Marty Ragaway went backstage to see Dad at the Dunes and they sat down and really talked. Ragaway saw a different man than the one he'd written radio shows for:

"I had always thought Lou had a tendency to be somewhat superficial with everyone around him when he and Bud were working together. Yet, when we sat down in his dressing room and talked that night after the show, he seemed to understand all that had happened in his life—his errors, faults . . . things like that. He seemed to be psychoanalyzing himself. Had he lived longer, I believe he would've been a sensational dramatic actor. He wanted so much to be successful at that. One of the last things he said to me was, 'Look Marty, this is a whole new experience for me. I love it and yet I'm scared to death.' "

Shortly after we moved into the apartment, Mom suffered a minor heart attack and was hospitalized. She had started to develop asthma and Dad was really frightened that something would happen to her. It was close to Halloween and she'd already done most of her Christmas shopping. I think she just wore herself out running around in the crowds. Much to all our great relief, she was in the hospital only a short time.

Dad was getting progressively more ill. He spent a great deal of time in bed, as he said, "resting." Carole, not really enjoying college, gave it up and came back home to live with us, where she shared a room with me—which was a great delight, because I was now getting old enough to appreciate an older sister who'd been away to college. But she wasn't happy at home. She had other ideas. What she really wanted to do was go to New York and study with Stella Adler, the famous drama teacher. Dad disagreed, even though she was almost twenty. I believe he was really worrying whether she had any really stable plans, because in almost the same breath she talked of the Royal Academy in London and the Sorbonne in Paris. Dad frowned and said, "I think you're too young to go bounding around the world by yourself."

"Well, can I at least try it in New York?" she asked.

Aunt Marie, remembering the confrontation between my father and his parents when he wanted to "go to Hollywood and become a movie star," sided with Carole. "Lou," she said, "if she wants to go, then let her go."

Uncle Pat was against it. "How can you go to New York and leave your family?"

Dad listened to everybody and then turned to his brother and said, "I have to let her go, Pat. If she wants acting that bad, then she should go and see if she can do it." He knew it was a rough, hard road and it was with sad and somewhat confused feelings that he gave Carole his blessing. He knew it to be a business full of pain, sometimes depressing—often a back-stabbing business— and he was frightened for his daughter.

The morning Carole left, Dad, clad in his bathrobe, was sitting in a chair next to the front door. It was quite early and as she opened the door to leave, he looked up and she could see that he had spent the night crying. He really did hate to let her go.

Six months later, when she sang on the *Jack Paar Show,* Dad was ecstatic when he talked to her on the phone. "You really handled yourself like a pro out there." He especially liked the idea that she wasn't introduced as Lou Costello's daughter (something I've fought against throughout my professional career). He even praised the way she looked. Before she left for New York he had complained to Mom, "Jesus Christ, Anne, teach this girl how to dress, will ya?"

Not too long before Dad's death, he took me up to the top of Longridge Terrace, where our new home was being built. It was a clear, beautiful night. It was gorgeous. Only the framework of the house was up. From where we stood we could see the entire San Fernando Valley. Dad stood where the sliding glass doors would later be, rocking back and forth on his heels as was his tendency. He seemed to be reflecting. After a while he turned to me where I was standing beside him and very softly said, "You know, someday, Christy, I'm gonna be up here among the stars." It was the last time he ever saw the place and I'm happy he shared that moment with me. The home wasn't completed until after his death.

It was the last week in February of 1959; I was eleven. I'd

come home from school and was hunkered down over a type-writer behind a big chair typing up the family newsletter that I published once a week and sold for a dime to family members. I took a break and went into the kitchen, where Mom was starting to prepare the evening meal. It must've been around five o'clock. I got a bottle of soda from the refrigerator and started back to resume my typing. As I passed my parents' bedroom I saw my father standing between the two bedposts, holding on, and he was dripping wet, as if he had just got out of the shower and hadn't dried off. It was an odd sight and I wandered into the bedroom, looking strangely at my father. He looked at me and sort of hung his head. He whispered, "Christy, go get your mother."

That was followed by a flurry of activity. Mom called Dr. Immerman. Dad was put to bed by my mother and somebody—Mom or the doctor—called the ambulance. I remember it took a long time, and it was around seven o'clock before the ambulance arrived. By that time I was back at my little German typewriter that Dad had looked all over town to find for me at Christmas. Though I didn't take Dad's illness very seriously at the time, I'd noticed a difference in him when he was making the film at Columbia. He'd come home from the studio and I'd want to play, but he'd be so tired he just wanted to rest. I noticed the slow-up in his activities, probably more than anybody else, because I spent so much time with him.

There was a basketball game on the television set in the living room, but nobody was paying any attention to it. As they wheeled my father out of the house, he motioned to me and then to the television, and in a barely audible voice said, "Let me know what the score is, Christy."

It was the last time I ever saw my father alive and those were his last words to me.

It fell to my mother to inform the family that he was in Doctors Hospital in Beverly Hills. Bobby Barber and Eddie Sherman were the only friends she told. Bobby, of course, went to the hospital every day, trying to cheer Dad up. Mom talked to Carole long distance and said, "Before you read it in the papers, I want you to know that Daddy's in the hospital, but he's all right, honey. He's okay."

That didn't sound all right to Carole, who caught a plane out of New York that night and arrived in Los Angeles in the early morning hours. Mom was concerned that Dad would become very upset if Carole just suddenly popped in. Mom and Aunt Marie agreed that there had to be some other reason for her being in California, so they concocted the story that she'd come out to the Coast for a screen test. Carole prepared her story for Dad, but she wasn't ready for the shocker that faced her when she entered his hospital room. He was hooked up to all kinds of tubes, with needles taped to his arm, and looked terrible. When Dad saw my sister, an expression of concern crossed his face. "Carole?" he said. "What are you doing in L.A.?"

She smiled, took his hand, and tried to sound convincing when she said, "I'm out here to do a screen test for Columbia."

He sort of chuckled, his face brightening, and said, "Hot damn! Look at that. She leaves town, goes to New York, and she gets a screen test back in L.A. Just like what happened to me." He seemed especially proud and happy.

Bobby Barber had also been to see my father and he was shocked because he could see how the fluids were building up in Dad's body. He was quite bloated and had a bad color. But Bobby, as always, joked. He took my father's hand and, gently squeezing it, said, "Hey Lou! Ya gotta get outta here 'cause I can't keep pullin' off these gags by myself."

My sisters went to the hospital to see Dad, and I was the only one left out. I felt that was very unfair. I was eleven years old and as close to my father as any of them. But each time I asked to go, someone put me off with, "You don't want to see your father the way he is, with all those tubes up his nose. It's not a very pleasant sight."

"I don't care," I argued. "I just want to see Daddy and talk to him. If he sees me he's gonna feel better. I just know it." But my pleas fell on deaf ears. To this day I think it is a disgrace that children aren't allowed to share family problems and grief. Children are people, too.

Mom went to the hospital every morning, went again in the evening, picking up Aunt Marie on the way. On March 3 Eddie Sherman was at the hospital with my father. My sister Carole was enroute to the hospital, and Mom was at home with me, getting ready to go back to the hospital. I remember it was afternoon, about the same time of day when he left for the hospital, and Mom had put on a beautiful red dress. She seemed so happy. I just knew that Dad must be feeling better. Earlier she had phoned Aunt Marie and asked her to be ready when she came by for her.

The phone rang and I answered it. It was Dr. Immerman and he wanted to talk to my mother. I said, "I'll get her." As Mom came to the telephone, she looked so beautiful and was adjusting an earring. She took the phone and listened, saying nothing, but her face totally drained of color. She finally replaced it in the cradle and went to her bedroom without a word to me. The door closed behind her and then the air was shattered with a blood-curdling scream. "Oh my God," she cried, "my baby's dead." I knew my father was gone.

Carole was two blocks from the hospital when the music on the car radio was interrupted with an announcement that my father had died. She pulled the car over to the side of the road and kept repeating to herself that it couldn't be true, that it was a mistake. Carole recalls that she started to cry and the mascara ran down her face. "All I could think of," she said, "was that Daddy hated for me to look messy. He expected us to look well groomed. So I combed my hair and fixed my makeup before going on to the hospital."

My mother had given Eddie Sherman specific instructions when it looked like Dad was having a bad go of it. "Eddie," she said, "if anything should happen to Lou, please don't say anything to anyone until we've had a chance to let his children and family know first. It would kill his mother to get that kind of news unexpectedly." He promised her that he wouldn't think of doing such a thing in the first place.

When Carole arrived at the hospital, the nurses and doctors in the hallway tried to stop her from going into Dad's room, but she pushed past them and went on in. She was crying. The curtain was drawn around the bed and a sheet had been pulled up over Dad's face. Eddie Sherman was there, sitting at the side of Dad's bed. He was on the phone with Louella Parsons. "Yes, Louella," he was saying, "died a few minutes ago. The last thing he ate? Oh yes, a strawberry soda. Strawberry, that's right." Carole describes that incredible scene:

"I couldn't believe what he was doing. I slowly walked into the room and said, 'Eddie, please don't do that now. Please put the phone down and leave.' He brushed me away and began to relate my father's last words. I again asked him not to do it. I might've been a hospital orderly there to change a bedpan for all he cared. Anger and hurt consumed me. I grabbed the telephone cord and yanked it right out of the wall and slung it across the room. I was getting hysterical and kept screaming, 'Not now! Not now!'

"Eddie was a little man and I towered over him. I grabbed him by the coat lapels and pushed him out of the room. I don't remember much after that until I looked up from the chair where I was sitting beside Dad's bed and saw a doctor with a hypodermic needle and Eddie Sherman at his elbow. I stood up as they came closer to me and again screamed, 'Not now! Not . . . now! Please leave me alone!' I think I knocked the syringe right out of the doctor's hand and said, 'You really are incredibly stupid for grown-ups!' "

I called Aunt Marie, because my mother was screaming hysterically and I was frightened for her. I said, "Aunt Marie, my Dad just died," and I hung up. She was at our house within minutes to be with Mom. People began to assemble at our house, so with the knowledge that Mom had someone with her, Aunt Marie went back home. She didn't want Grandma to hear it from a stranger. She arrived at her home and walked into the living room, where she found my grandmother watching Abbott & Costello shorts on television. She was wringing her hands and had obviously already heard about Dad from a program interruption. Grandma turned to Aunt Marie and said, "You're not going to tell me that my Lou is dead."

Aunt Marie looked at her son Joseph, whose big eyes grew to three times their size and who was pale as a ghost.

"Mother," she said, "as long as I live I hope I never have to tell you another thing like this again."

My sister Paddy was at first blessed in her grief in that she had a husband and her three sons to give her comfort and consolation. You must remember we were a very close family and no matter what happened, the love was always there. Paddy was special to Dad, just as we all were individually. We were a sad and heartbroken family and within six months, Paddy's marriage ended and she was left not only without a father, but no husband and three boys to raise.

Bud Abbott had never been told of my dad's hospitalization. He too was quite ill at the time and it was feared the shock would be too much for him. He later told my grandmother, "Mom, I don't know why they didn't tell me. Maybe if I had known I could've gone up there and helped Lou. My heart is broken. I've lost the best pal anyone ever could have."

Ann Corio was in New York when Dad died but flew out to California immediately to be with Mom and help rid our apartment of the freeloaders who moved in like a swarm of locusts for one last feast. Carole wasn't so subtle. Eddie Sherman's actions in the room where my father died had exposed to her a seedy side of Hollywood that Dad had so much tried to protect us from. She was a shocked, heartbroken, angry young lady. Again, she remembers her feelings and how she ₅ave vent to them:

"I was just an incredibly angry child and wanted to lash out at anyone who even appeared to be a leech or hanger-on. At the apartment house following the funeral, people were all over the place. Mom was seated in one of those big Queen Anne chairs and just looked so tiny and so very lost. Mary Lester came over to handle the food for the friends and family who would soon be assembling.

"However, the first to come were total strangers to me. They walked in the door laughing and joking around and eating the food and drinking booze, just as they had in the old days of Longridge Avenue. Mom just sat midst all the commotion and confusion with her hands folded in her lap, really quite out of it. I very quietly asked everybody to leave and they just stood around and started to laugh as if to say, 'Who's this kid telling *us* to get out?' I did better than that. I told them exactly what I thought of them. 'You're all leeches who've hung on to my dad's coattails for years. You've eaten our food, sat at his bar, and drunk his liquor at Longridge, but now it's over. Get out!' They slowly started to file out the door."

My father's funeral was an all-star affair, as was the rosary the night before. I was the only one of his children who wanted to see him in the casket. My sisters wanted to "remember him as he was," but I felt cheated. I hadn't seen him at the hospital, so Mom and I knelt before the casket at the funeral home. I'm glad I did that and I don't feel there was anything wrong with it. Dammit, he was my father!

There were approximately five hundred people crowded into

the old Saint Francis de Sales Church for Dad's funeral and hundreds more outside—fans who packed the sidewalks to pay their last respects. Among those attending were fellow comedians and superstars, including Danny Thomas, Red Skelton, Joe E. Brown, George Jessel, Jerry Colonna, Ronald Reagan, Leo Carrillo, Alan Mowbray, and many more.

The pallbearers, led by Bud Abbott—who, contrary to some reports, was not drunk, but overcome with grief—included Eddie Sherman, Howard Christie, Norman Abbott, Ralph Handley, Dr. Immerman, Morris Davis, and Dad's most beloved friend, Bobby Barber.

Dad was laid to rest with Butch in the mausoleum of Calvary Cemetery in East Los Angeles, not too far from his beloved Lou Costello Jr. Youth Center. Mexicans, Puerto Ricans, blacks, and whites lined the roadway to the tomb in a display of international homage to a funny little man who made so many millions happy with his stumbling, bumbling comedics. It was a marvelous tribute to the man who never grew up, the boy in the overgrown body who never wanted to do anything more than play with the other kids. My father had a great rapport with the world.

Bobby Barber expressed it all at the church following the funeral. One of the pallbearers, he went over to help my grandmother into the limousine after the casket was placed in the hearse. He assisted in seeing that the rest of the family were all in their cars. Caught up in the confusion and chaos, somebody forgot to tell one of the drivers that Bobby was to ride in one of the family cars. As the entourage pulled away from the church, Bobby started running after one of the limousines, tears streaming down his face. The driver finally saw him and stopped the car. As Bobby got in he said, trying to smile through his tears, "Even in death, Lou's playing tricks on me."

Epilog

THE SUMMER AFTER Dad's death Mom and I moved into the new house on Longridge Terrace. She was very lonely and her drinking had increased since my father's death. I know she loved her children, but my father was really her life. She and Carole were constantly at odds with each other, and the beautiful bedroom that was Carole's remained empty.

Mom almost begged De De to move in with us. She said, "Carole doesn't want to live with us. You know how much we clash. I love her, but we just can't live together. If you'll move up here, De De, you can live your own life and it won't cost you a cent. You don't have to feel like you'd have to be a companion for me. Please, please move up here." De De did think it over, but she knew of Mom's sorrow and loneliness—and the drinking—and decided to decline.

Mom would start to drink and get overly stimulated and not be able to sleep and then she'd want to sit up and talk till all hours of the night. De De was working a day job and wouldn't be able to handle not getting her rest. My grandmother seemed to enjoy making Mom's life more miserable than it already was. After we moved into our new home, she said to Mom one day, "Anne, you shouldn't have moved into that house. Not without Lou."

The hangers-on were all gone and the few friends that seemed to care about Mom diminished. I know Ralph Handley tried to be helpful to her but Uncle Pat was executor of the estate and that seemed to put a barrier between Mom and Ralph. Also, once again Mom was left out in the cold as to what was going on in her own life. Uncle Pat controlled everything and she was the last to know about anything happening with Dad's estate. There had always been a sort of tacit understanding between Mom and Uncle Pat. When Dad died, all the pretenses fell apart. Aunt Marie was the one person on Dad's side of the family who'd always been my mother's true friend and she was loyal to the end. I will love her forever for all the kindness she always showed my mother and her understanding of Mom's problems.

Mom was a wreck. She talked constantly of wanting Dad back. Friends tried to share her grief and ease the pain, but I think she truly wanted to die and set out to will her own death so she could be with Dad. She often got on the phone with Paddy very late at night and talked of dying, of not wanting to live anymore. She was simply too far gone to stand on her own two feet. She'd become dependent on my father—and on vodka. Without Dad, the drink wasn't enough to sustain her.

I remember that Mom had already done a lot of Christmas shopping and everybody was wondering what it was going to be like without Dad. There was a certain unspoken sadness at our house, but I still had my mother and that was the most important thing in the world to me. Carole moved into the new house with us for a while, but everytime Mom drank heavily she seemed to take out all her frustrations on Carole and they'd clash terribly. Still, they loved each other so desperately. Their disagreements hadn't started after Dad died—they'd been fighting ever since Carole was a child.

Their last big run-in happened after Carole moved back out and just before Mom died. Carole had come up to borrow a movie projector and Mom was in some other world. I doubt she even knew who she was talking to, but she refused to let Carole take the projector. She kept screaming, until Carole finally left.

The night before she died, my mother went completely out of her mind. She seemed to be hallucinating and when her sister, my Aunt Mayme, came up, she literally kicked her out of the house. She simply did not know what she was doing.

When I woke up the next morning, I went to call my sister Paddy and Mom was on the phone—speaking to herself. I left the room, dismayed. I went back later and found her lying on the floor and, not knowing exactly what to do first, I called Paddy who thought maybe Mom had fainted, which she'd done before. I called out "Mom" and shook her several times and when she didn't wake up, I called Paddy again. In a matter of minutes that seemed to a twelve-year-old like hours, I knew my mother was dead. I was now a twelve-year-old orphan.

The fire department was soon there with the rescue unit. My sisters arrived—and oh, God, how deeply it hit Carole. That night at the mortuary she spent some time alone with Mom and kept repeating over and over and over, "Oh no, I don't hate you, Momma. I love you. I—love—you!"

When Dad died, Mom was in no condition to make any kind of arrangements, so Paddy and Carole did what was necessary. When it came time to make funeral arrangements for Mom, it once again fell to my sisters. Carole, especially, felt it was an unfair burden to be placed on their shoulders:

> "It seemed to me that the adults in the family could have been able to handle things. For some reason they couldn't, or didn't. I mean, here were two kids twenty-three and twenty years of age who did it for Dad because poor Mom was a grief-stricken wreck, and the other family members were unable to. Here we were doing it again for Mom."

Later on, when the estate was being prepared for probate, someone in the family raised the question of my mother's casket costing as much as Dad's. Carole was infuriated by the remark. I didn't understand the significance of that until later on.

When Mom's will was read, we were all assembled in the living room on Longridge Terrace. My sisters and I didn't understand half the stuff the lawyer was saying and Carole, at one point, questioned something he said. She said, "I don't understand what you mean by that."

It was sort of funny, because he suddenly threw the will halfway across the room and shouted, "Are you accusing me of being a thief?"

Carole looked at him quite calmly and said, "I wasn't, but I'm sure going to think about it now." I understood her frustration. It seemed that everyone wanted to give us girls a hard time after Mom was gone. We were totally orphaned and although Uncle Pat had control of my inheritance and was my guardian, it was Paddy who moved up to the Longridge Terrace house with her three boys to be with me. About six months later, she was involved in an automobile accident and was in bed for weeks recuperating. While she was still in a cast, Uncle Pat had a for-sale sign placed in front of the house, and it was sold. He claimed it was necessary because of estate costs.

Orphans though we may have been and all that, we were Mom and Dad's children and they endowed us with a tenacity of purpose to overcome all the obstacles that were thrown at us. There were times when Paddy, Carole, and I did not feel like members of the Costello family.

In 1961, when I was getting ready to graduate from the eighth grade at St. Victor's in West Hollywood, Carole went with me to Studio City to buy a graduation dress. The dress I fell in love with cost $80. We were both very excited about it and Carole asked the saleslady to put it on the charge. She said, "We'll have to call Mr. and Mrs. Costello to verify it," meaning Uncle Pat and his wife Marty. When Carole called them, Uncle Pat said the dress was too expensive and refused to okay the purchase. Carole was absolutely livid. She said, "How dare you! This is *his* daughter's graduation. We were never denied anything as kids, so don't you tell me she can't have this dress!" I was so proud of her. Nonetheless, she finally had to borrow money out of her trust fund to pay for the dress.

What some members of our family didn't seem to understand was, our parents' deaths didn't weaken our relationships with each other. It strengthened them, because we were now three against the world if that's what it took—and sometimes it did.

We've had our problems and there's always another crisis around the corner, but the three of us have survived—because Lou and Anne Costello were our parents.

Filmography of Lou Costello

One Night in the Tropics (Universal: 1940)
    Producer: Leonard Spigelgass
    Director: A. Edward Sutherland

Buck Privates (Universal: 1941)
    Producer: Alex Gottlieb
    Director: Arthur Lubin

In the Navy (Universal: 1941)
    Producer: Alex Gottlieb
    Director: Arthur Lubin

Hold That Ghost (Universal: 1941)
    Producer: Alex Gottlieb
    Director: Arthur Lubin

Keep 'Em Flying (Universal: 1941)
    Producer: Glenn Tryon
    Director: Arthur Lubin

Ride 'Em Cowboy (Universal: 1942)
    Producer: Alex Gottlieb
    Director: Arthur Lubin

Rio Rita (Metro-Goldwyn-Mayer: 1942)
    Producer: Pandro S. Berman
    Director: S. Sylvan Simon

Pardon my Sarong (Universal: 1942)
    Producer: Alex Gottlieb
    Director: Erle C. Kenton

Who Done It? (Universal: 1942)
    Producer: Alex Gottlieb
    Director: Erle C. Kenton

It Ain't Hay (Universal: 1943)
    Producer: Alex Gottlieb
    Director: Erle C. Kenton

Hit the Ice (Universal: 1943)
    Producer: Alex Gottlieb
    Director: Charles Lamont

In Society (Universal: 1944)
    Producer: Edmund L. Hartmann
    Director: Jean Yarbrough

Lost in a Harem (Metro-Goldwyn-Mayer: 1944)
    Producer: George Haight
    Director: Charles Riesner

Here Come the Co-eds (Universal: 1945)
    Producer: John Grant
    Director: Jean Yarbrough

The Naughty Nineties (Universal: 1945)
    Producer: Edmund L. Hartmann and John Grant
    Director: Jean Yarbrough

Abbott & Costello in Hollywood (Metro-Goldwyn-Mayer: 1945)
    Producer: Martin A. Gosch
    Director: S. Sylvan Simon

Little Giant (Universal: 1946)
    Producer: Joe Gershenson
    Director: William A. Seiter

The Time of Their Lives (Universal: 1946)
    Producer: Val Burton
    Director: Charles Barton

Buck Privates Come Home (Universal: 1947)
    Producer: Robert Arthur
    Director: Charles Barton

The Wistful Widow of Wagon Gap (Universal: 1947)
    Producer: Robert Arthur
    Director: Charles Barton

The Noose Hangs High (Eagle-Lion: 1948)
    Producer: Charles Barton
    Director: Charles Barton

Abbott & Costello Meet Frankenstein (Universal: 1948)
    Producer: Robert Arthur
    Director: Charles Barton

Mexican Hayride (Universal: 1948)
    Producer: Robert Arthur
    Director: Charles Barton

Abbott & Costello Meet the Killer, Boris Karloff (Universal: 1949)
    Producer: Robert Arthur
    Director: Charles Barton

Africa Screams (United Artists: 1949)
    Producer: Edward Nassour (A Huntington Hartford Production)
    Director: Charles Barton

Abbott & Costello in the Foreign Legion (Universal: 1950)
    Producer: Robert Arthur
    Director: Charles Lamont

Abbott & Costello Meet the Invisible Man (Universal: 1951)
    Producer: Howard Christie
    Director: Charles Lamont

Comin' Round the Mountain (Universal: 1951)
    Producer: Howard Christie
    Director: Charles Lamont

Jack and the Beanstalk (Warner Brothers: 1952)
    Producer: Alex Gottlieb
    Director: Jean Yarbrough

Abbott & Costello Meet Captain Kidd (Warner Brothers: 1952)
    Producer: Alex Gottlieb
    Director: Charles Lamont

Lost in Alaska (Universal: 1952)
    Producer: Howard Christie
    Director: Jean Yarbrough

Abbott & Costello Go to Mars (Universal: 1953)
    Producer: Howard Christie
    Director: Charles Lamont

Abbott & Costello Meet Dr. Jekyll and Mr. Hyde (Universal: 1954)
    Producer: Howard Christie
    Director: Charles Lamont

Abbott & Costello Meet the Keystone Cops (Universal: 1955)
    Producer: Howard Christie
    Director: Charles Lamont

Abbott & Costello Meet the Mummy (Universal: 1955)
    Producer: Howard Christie
    Director: Charles Lamont

* *Dance With Me Henry* (United Artists: 1956)
    Producer: Bob Goldstein
    Director: Charles Barton

The Thirty-Foot Bride of Candy Rock (Columbia: 1958)
    Producer: Lewis J. Rachmil
    Director: Sidney Miller

The World of Abbott & Costello (Universal: 1965)
    Producer: Max J. Rosenberg and Milton Subotsky
    Director: (Comprised solely of film clips from Abbott & Costello films at
    Universal)

Short Subjects:

Picture People (RKO: 1941): Features Hollywood celebrities

Screen Snapshots (Columbia: 1941): Features Hollywood celebrities entertain-
    ing soldiers at military bases during World War II

Meet the People (Republic: 1941): One-reeler covering Los Angeles newspaper
    benefit

* The last picture made with Bud Abbott.

News of the Day (Metro-Goldwyn-Mayer: 1952): With Charles Laughton promoting the sale of U.S. Savings Bonds

Note: Lou appeared with Bud Abbott in one short at Universal prior to their first film promoting Franklin Delano Roosevelt's "daylight savings time."

Radio:

The Kate Smith Hour (ninety-nine weeks)

The Abbott & Costello Show (ABC: 1941–46; NBC: 1946–49)

The Abbott & Costello Show (ABC Saturday mornings—three years)

Television:

The Abbott & Costello Show—CBS (Debuted December 1952): Ran two seasons

Following the Abbott & Costello split, Lou appeared on the television shows listed below:

The Steve Allen Show (Comedy)
Wagon Train (Dramatic role—highly critiqued)
General Electric Theatre (Dramatic role)